6/99

INTERPRETING HAMLET

MATERIALS FOR ANALYSIS

Interpreting Hamlet

SELECTED AND EDITED BY

RUSSELL E. LEAVENWORTH

The Voice out of the Whirlwind: The Book of Job

SELECTED AND EDITED BY

RALPH E. HONE

Little Rock, U.S.A.

SELECTED AND EDITED BY

WILSON RECORD AND *JANE CASSELS RECORD*

Interpreting Hamlet

MATERIALS FOR ANALYSIS

Selected and Edited by

RUSSELL E. LEAVENWORTH

FRESNO STATE COLLEGE

Howard Chandler, Publisher
660 MARKET STREET
SAN FRANCISCO 4, CALIFORNIA

CONTENTS

vi *Contents*

pg246

Introduction

HAMLET has probably excited more argument than any other single human production. This collection furnishes a few critical benchmarks for plotting some of these arguments. It includes the source of the play in a seventeenth-century translation, an illustration of textual problems, and a number of essays and fragments which provide interpretations of the play from both the acting and the critical traditions. The items are arranged in a roughly chronological order.

The first extended record of the Hamlet legend is found in the *Historia Danica* of the twelfth-century writer Saxo Grammaticus. His narrative of Amleth's revenge was revived in a considerably inflated French translation of Francis de Belleforest and included in his *Histoires Tragiques,* 1564–1570. It was upon this book that Shakespeare (or Thomas Kyd, or . . . ?) drew for the hypothetical original version of *Hamlet.* One may find some fascinating subjects for analysis by comparing this source with the play in its later form. How much does any one scene of the play owe to its source in matters of characterization, scene development, imagery? And how important to the play are any one of the many things which the playwright added to the source? A number of critical interpretations of *Hamlet* draw some of their arguments from the source. In this collection, Stoll and Jones both make assertions about the play on the basis of the source, although their conclusions are poles apart. There is, of course, a void of information that leaves room for considerable speculation concerning the genesis of the play; and a major question remains as to what extent the source offers clues to the playwright's intentions in *Hamlet.*

The three textual versions of the "To be, or not to be" soliloquy exhibit some of the kinds of problems editors of *Hamlet* attempt to solve. *Hamlet* exists in three "substantive" texts, versions which offer readings different from each other. The First Quarto of 1603 is a "bad" quarto, and it represents the text so peculiarly that no theory of its provenience fully accounts for it. The most satisfactory explanation suggests that its text was pieced together by an actor with a fragmentary memory who played the part of Marcellus in a shortened version of the play specially designed for production in the provinces by a limited traveling company. But there are other hypotheses equally ingenious. The Second Quarto of 1604–1605 is a "good" quarto. It is almost twice the length of that in the First Quarto, and it sounds with the true Shakespearean ring in almost every line. The third text is that of the First Folio of 1623. It lacks some 200 lines found in the Second Quarto, and it provides about 80 new lines. In addition, there are many verbal differences between the two texts. Modern editors usually prefer the Second Quarto readings, but add to its version the new lines from the First Folio—a procedure which results in a text that was certainly never acted in Shakespeare's time.

The relationships between these three texts, and the relationships they bear to the lost Shakespeare manuscripts and playhouse promptbooks, are subjects of lively current arguments among bibliographical experts. Students with logical minds and a flair for technology might find the editorial problems irresistible. The mere process of editing the soliloquy and defending the principles involved is a neat project for a longish paper. Or determining the guiding principles of the editor of a typical modern text makes a nicely complex investigation, especially if questions of spelling and punctuation are raised. For while modernized spelling and pointing are justifiable in editions for the general public, the technical editor is committed to the ideal of reproducing the closest possible approximation to Shakespeare's final manuscript. The obstacles in the way of reaching this ideal with *Hamlet* are appalling.

In the meantime, no one seems to have been waiting for the perfect text of *Hamlet*. It has been the stage's most successful play for more than 350 years. It is seldom acted in its entirety, anyway. *Hamlet* is a very long play. Every actor in the leading role has had an individual interpretation which made some scenes less relevant than others, and so the "superfluous" lines and scenes were cut out. The stage history of *Hamlet* records some remarkable amputations that its text has endured without complete disability. A study of the portions of the play which certain actors have cut might yield some interesting results.

The few items offered in this collection on the stage history span the production of *Hamlet* from its first performances to the present. Students interested in the technical aspects of staging *Hamlet* might compare the simplicity of production advocated by Reynolds as possible in the Globe playhouse with the complications touched upon by Gielgud, complications which arise when the play is adapted to the proscenium stage. Several of the scenes require a good deal of thought for their production on any stage. In addition to the several discussions of *Hamlet's* staging in this volume, an extensive bibliography could be compiled of argument on how the play scene (III, ii) should be staged. Problems of scenery and costuming also offer attractive possibilities for investigation, and for this purpose Gielgud's essay provides an excellent point of departure. It goes without saying that no one should engage in discussion of production problems without first having in mind the interpretation of the play which his production aims to support.

It is often remarked that no one noticed that Hamlet was delaying his revenge until Goethe and other late eighteenth-century romantic critics began exploring the prince's psyche. The researches of Conklin, partly represented in this collection, attempt to trace how this line of criticism affected and was affected by the acting interpretations of the time. By the nineteenth century the question of whether Hamlet was actually mad or only pretending to be was a major issue. By then, records of actors' interpretations were more plentiful than for any previous era. But the student attempting to determine how any one actor portrayed Hamlet should supplement the reviews of performances with information from letters, memoirs, descriptions of promptbooks, and whatever other data are available. Reviewers are often more intent on evaluating a performance than on describing what it meant. Reviews by men like Hazlitt and Shaw, included here, are therefore especially valuable for being written by critics with firm and explicit views of their own on what *Hamlet* should mean, and they directly examine the actors' interpretations.

The kind of sense that actors make of the play would seem to have a special validity, since *Hamlet* is a play that is acted, not a closet play. Yet by far the larger body of criticism has been by readers of *Hamlet* and for readers of *Hamlet*. Some critics have claimed that the play yields its meaning only upon careful and thoughtful reading, compared to which a stage performance is inevitably crude and obscure. Certainly some subtleties discovered by "literary" critics in this volume would be extremely hard to translate into voice, gesture, and action. It must be conceded that, as literature, *Hamlet* has cheerfully borne the weight of all the various philosophical and psychological doctrines heaped upon it. Kantians, Hegelians, Marxists, Roman Catholics, Freudians, Jungians, and existentialists have found reflected in this play the most central symbols of their ideologies. And so have the philosophically uncommitted, who perhaps take comfort in Hamlet's remark, "There is nothing either good or bad but thinking makes it so."

The critical essays in this collection represent a sampling of the kinds of approaches which have been made to *Hamlet*. Bradley, Eliot, Knight, Stoll, Jones, and Fergusson propound quite divergent but extremely influential points of view. The student attempting, therefore, to organize a coherent interpretation of *Hamlet* would presumably not find all of these interpreters equally convincing. Rewarding papers on interpretive questions might best take a fairly small point made by one critic which is contradicted by another, or is contradictable by the student himself, and resolve the issue on the basis of which view receives the most substantial support from the text of the play. A single term of a critic, such as Bradley's "Melancholy" or Eliot's "objective correlative," might bear a short paper's examination. Or a quite different kind of paper might draw from one of the critics an interpretation of the play, and then in detail explain how one scene important to that interpretation could be staged and acted in order to make the meaning clear to an audience.

Some fascinating character problems exist in the personalities of Claudius, Gertrude, Ophelia, and others. Several critics make these minor (!) characters important to their analyses of *Hamlet*, and reviewers are always quick to notice if the actor of one of them is out of key with the rest of the performers. If any students find the study of a minor character more appealing than that of Hamlet, they will find ample material in this volume to stimulate speculation. Yet the phrase "Hamlet without the Prince" has become a proverbial expression for emptiness. He is on stage for practically the whole play, compelling attention every minute. All attempts to pluck the meaning out of the play depend, ultimately, on the interpretation of Hamlet's character. Here, as Hamlet tells everyone, is "the heart of the mystery."

The Hystorie of Hamblet, Prince of Denmarke,

BY

FRANCIS DE BELLEFOREST

It is almost universally agreed that Francis de Belleforest's Histoires Tragiques *(1559) provided the story for the playwright
who first put* Hamlet *on the stage prior to 1590. This story was
translated by an unknown hand and printed for Thomas Pavier's
bookshop in 1608. The translation, of course, could not have
influenced the play; probably the play's popularity occasioned the
translation. The following extract is quoted from* A New Variorum Edition of Shakespeare, *Vol. IV,* Hamlet, *Part 2 (Philadelphia, 1877), pp. 91-109.*

CHAP. I.

*How Horvendile and Fengon were made Governours of the Province of
Ditmarse, and how Horvendile marryed Geruth, the daughter to Roderick,
chief K. of Denmark, by whom he had Hamblet: and how after his marriage his brother Fengon slewe him trayterously, and marryed his brothers
wife, and what followed.*

YOU MUST understand, that long time before the kingdome of Denmark
received the faith of Jesus Christ, and imbraced the doctrin of the
Christians, that the common people in those dayes were
barbarous and uncivill, and their princes cruell, without faith   The Danes
or loyaltie, seeking nothing but murther, and deposing (or   in times past
at the least) offending each other, either in honours, goods,   uncivill.
or lives; not caring to ransome such as they took prisoners, but rather sacri-

ficing them to the cruell vengeance naturally imprinted in their hearts: in such sort, that if ther were sometime a good prince or king among them, who beeing adorned with the most perfect gifts of nature, would adict himselfe to vertue, and use courtesie, although the people held him in admiration (as vertue is admirable to the most wicked) yet the envie of his neighbors was so great, that they never ceased untill that vertuous man were dispatched out of the world. King Rodericke, as then raigning in Denmarke, after hee had appeased the troubles in the countrey, and driven the Sweathlanders and Slaveans from thence, he divided the kingdom into divers provinces, placing governours therein; who after (as the like happened in France) bare the names of Dukes, Marqueses, and Earls, giving the government of Jutie (at this present called Ditmarsse) lying upon the conntray of the Cimbrians, in the straight or narrow part of land that sheweth like a point or cape of ground upon the sea, which neithward bordereth upon the countrey of Norway, two valiant and warlike lords Horvendile and Fengon, sonnes to Gervendile, who likewise had beene governour of that province. Now the greatest honor that men of noble birth could at that time win and obtaine, was in exercising the art of piracie upon the seas, assayling their neighbours, and the countries bordering upon them; and how much the more they used to rob, pill, and spoyle other provinces, and ilands far adjacent, so much the more their honours and reputation increased and augmented: wherin Horvendile obtained the highest place in his time, beeing the most renouned pirate that in those dayes scoured the seas and havens of the north parts: whose great fame so mooved the heart of Collere, king of Norway, that he was much grieved to heare that Horvendile surmounting him in feates of armes, thereby obscuring the glorie by him alreadie obtained upon the seas: (honor more than covetousnesse of richer (in those dayes) being the reason that provoked those barbarian princes to overthrow and vanquish one the other, not caring to be slaine by the handes of a victorious person). This valiant and hardy king having challenged Horvendile to fight with him body to body, the combate was by him accepted, with conditions, that hee which should be vanquished should loose all the riches he had in his ship, and that the vanquisher should cause the body of the vanquished (that should bee slaine in the combate) to be honourably buried, death being the prise and reward of him that should loose the battaile: and to conclude, Collere, king of Norway (although a valiant, hardy, and couragious prince) was in the end vanquished and slaine by Horvendile, who presently caused a

The cruel-tie of the Danes.

Rodericke king of Denmarke.

Jutie at this time, called then Ditmarsse.

Horvendile a king and a pirate.

Collere king of Norway.

Horvendile slew Collere.

tombe to be erected, and therein (with all honorable obsequies fit for a prince) buried the body of king Collere, according to their auncient manner and superstitions in these dayes, and the conditions of the combate, bereaving the kings shippes of all their riches; and having slaine the kings sister, a very brave and valiant warriour, and over runne all the coast of Norway, and the Northern Ilands, returned home againe layden with much treasure, sending the most parte thereof to his soveraigne, king Rodericke, thereby to procure his good liking, and so to be accounted one of the greatest favourites about his majestie.

The king, allured by those presents, and esteeming himselfe happy to have so valiant a subject, sought by a great favour and coutesie to make him become bounden unto him perpetually, giving him Geruth his daughter to his wife, of whom he knew Horvendile to bee already much inamored. And the more to honor him, determined himselfe in person to conduct her into Jutie, where the marriage was celebrated according to the ancient manner: and to be briefe, of this marriage proceeded Hamblet, of whom I intend to speake, and for his cause have chosen to renew this present hystorie. *Hamlet sonne to Horvendile.*

Fengon, brother to this prince Horvendile, who [not] onely fretting and despighting in his heart at the great honor and reputation wonne by his brother in warlike affaires, but solicited and provoked by a foolish jealousie to see him honored with royall aliance, and fearing thereby to bee deposed from his part of the government, or rather desiring to be onely governour, thereby to obscure the memorie of the victories and conquests of his brother Horvendile, determined (whatsoever happened) to kill him; which hee effected in such sort, that no man once so much as suspected him, every man esteeming that from such and so firme a knot of alliance and consanguinitie there could proceed no other issue then the full effects of vertue and courtesie: but (as I sayd before) the desire of bearing soveraigne rule and authoritie respecteth neither blood nor amitie, nor caring for vertue, as being wholly without respect of lawes, or majestie devine; for it is not possible that hee which invadeth the countrey and taketh away the riches of an other man without cause or reason, should know or feare God. Was not this a craftie and subtile counsellor? but he might have thought that the mother, knowing her husbands case, would not cast her sonne into the danger of death. But Fengon, having secretly assembled certain men, and perceiving himself strong enough to execute his interprise, Horvendile his brother being at a banquet with his friends, sodainely set upon him, where he slewe him as traiterously, as cunningly he purged himselfe of so detestable a murther to his subjects; *Fengon, his conspiracie against his brother.* *Fengon killeth his brother.*

8 *Belleforest*

for that before he had any violent or bloody handes, or once committed parricide upon his brother, hee had incestuously abused his wife, whose honour hee ought as well to have sought and procured as traiterously he pursued and effected his destruction. And it is most certaine, that the man that abandoneth himselfe to any notorious and wicked action, whereby he becommeth a great sinner, he careth not to commit much more haynous and abhominable offences, and covered his boldnesse and wicked practise with so great subtiltie and policie, and under a vaile of meere simplicitie, that beeing favoured for the honest love that he bare to his sister in lawe, for whose sake, hee affirmed, he had in that sort murthered his brother, that his sinne found excuse among the common people, and of the nobilitie was esteemed for justice: for that Geruth, being as courteous a princesse as any then living in the north parts, and one that had never once so much as offended any of her subjects, either commons or courtyers, this adulterer and infamous murtherer, slaundered his dead brother, that hee would have slaine his wife, and that hee by chance finding him upon the point ready to do it, in defence of the lady had slaine him, bearing off the blows, which as then he strooke at the innocent princesse, without any other cause of malice whatsoever. Wherein hee wanted not false witnesses to approove his act, which deposed in like sort, as the wicked calumniator himselfe protested, being the same persons that had born him company, and were participants of his reason; so that instead of pursuing him as a parricide and an incestuous person, al the courtyers admired and flattered him in his good fortune, making more account of false witnesses and detestable wicked reporters, and more honouring the calumniators, then they esteemed of those that seeking to call the matter in question, and admiring the vertues of the murthered prince, would have punished the massacrers and bereavers of his life. Which was the cause that Fengnon, boldned and incouraged by such impunitie, durst venture to couple himself in marriage with her whom hee used as his concubine during good Horvendiles life, in that sort spotting his name with a double vice, and charging his conscience with abhominable guilt, and two-fold impietie, as incestuous adulterie and parricide murther: and that the unfortunate and wicked woman, that had received the honour to bee the wife of one of the valiantest and wiseth princes in the north, imbased her selfe in such vile sort, as to falsifie her faith unto him, and which is worse, to marrie him, that had bin the tyranous murtherer of her lawfull husband; which made divers men thinke that she had beene the causer of the murther, thereby to live in her adultery

Marginal notes: Slanderers more honoured in court then vertuous persons. / The incestuous marriage of Fengon with his brothers wife.

without controle. But where shall a man find a more wicked and bold woman, then a great parsonage once having loosed the bands of honor and honestie? This princesse, who at the first, for her rare vertues and courtesses was honored of al men and beloved of her husband, as soone as she once gave eare to the tyrant Fengon, forgot both the ranke she helde among the greatest names, and the dutie of an honest wife on her behalfe. But I will not stand to gaze and mervaile at women, for that there are many which seeke to blase and set them foorth, in which their writings they spare not to blame them all for the faults of some one, or few women. But I say, that either nature ought to have bereaved man of that opinion to accompany with women, or els to endow them with such spirits, as that they may easily support the crosses they endure, without complaining so often and so strangely, seeing it is their owne beastlinesse that overthrowes them. For if it be so, that a woman is so imperfect a creature as they make her to be, and that they know this beast to bee so hard to bee tamed as they affirme, why then are they so foolish to preserve them, and so dull and brutish as to trust their deceitfull and wanton imbraceings. But let us leave her in this extreamitie of laciviousnesse, and proceed to shewe you in what sort the yong prince Hamblet behaved himselfe, to escape the tyranny of his uncle.

If a man be deceived by a woman, it is his owne beastlinesse.

CHAP. II.

How Hamblet counterfeited the mad man, to escape the tyrannie of his uncle, and how he was tempted by a woman (through his uncles procurement) who thereby thought to undermine the Prince, and by that meanes to finde out whether he counterfeited madnesse or not: and how Hamblet would by no meanes bee brought to consent unto her, and what followed.

GERUTH having (as I sayd before) so much forgotten herself, the prince Hamblet perceiving himself to bee in danger of his life, as beeing abandoned of his owne mother, and forsaken of all men, and assuring himselfe that Fengon would not detract the time to send him the same way his father Horvendile was gone, to beguile the tyrant in his subtilties (that esteemed him to bee of such a minde that if he once attained to mans estate he wold not long delay the time to revenge the death of his father) counterfeiting the mad man with such craft and subtill practises, that hee made shewe as if hee had utterly lost his wittes: and under that vayle hee covered his pretence, and defended his life from the treasons and practises of the tyrant his uncle. And all though hee had beene at the schoole of the Romane Prince, who, because hee counterfeited himselfe to bee a foole, was called Brutus, yet hee imitated his fashions, and his wisedom. For every day beeing in the queenes palace, (who as then was more carefull to please her whoremaster, then ready to revenge the cruell death of her husband, or to restore her sonne to his inheritance), hee rent and tore his clothes, wallowing and lying in the durt and mire, his face all filthy and blacke, running through the streets like a man distraught, not speaking one worde, but such as seemed to proceede of madnesse and meere frenzie; all his actions and jestures beeing no other than the right countenances of a man wholly deprived of all reason and understanding, in such sort, that as then hee seemed fitte for nothing but to make sport to the pages and ruffling courtiers that attended in the court of his uncle and father-in-law. But the yong prince noted them well enough, minding one day to bee revenged in such manner, that the memorie thereof should remaine perpetually to the world.

Beholde, I pray you, a great point of a wise and brave spirite in a yong prince, by so great a shewe of imperfection in his person for advancement, and his owne imbasing and despising, to worke the meanes and to prepare the way for himselfe to bee one of the happiest kings in his age. In like sort, never any man was reputed by any of his actions more wise

Brutus esteemed wise, for counterfeiting the foole. Read Titus Livius and Halicarnassus.

and prudent then Brutus, dissembling a great alteration in his minde, for that the occasion of such his devise of foolishnesse proceeded onely of a good and mature counsell and deliberation, not onely to preserve his goods, and shunne the rage of the proude tyrant, but also to open a large way to procure the banishment and utter ruine of wicked Tarquinius, and to infranchise the people (which were before oppressed) from the yoake of a great and miserable servitude. And so, not onely Brutus, but this man and worthy prince, to whom wee may also

David counterfeited the mad man before king Aches.

adde king David, that counterfeited the madde man among the petie kings of Palestina to preserve his life from the subtill practises of those kings. I shew this example unto such, as beeing offended with any great personage, have not sufficient means to prevaile in their intents, or revenge the injurie by them receaved. But when I speake of revenging any injury received upon a great

Rom, viii. 21.

personage or superior, it must be understood by such an one as is not our soveraigne, against whome wee maie by no meanes resiste, nor once practise anie treason nor conspiracie against his life: and hee that will followe this course must speake and do all things whatsoever that are pleasing and acceptable to him whom hee meaneth to deceive, practise his actions, and esteeme him above all men, cleane contrarye to his owne intent and meaning; for that is rightly to playe and counterfeite the foole, when a man is constrained to dissemble and kisse his hand, whome in hearte hee could wishe an hundred foote depth under the earth, so hee mighte never see him more, if it were not a thing wholly to bee disliked in a christian, who by no meanes ought to have a bitter gall, or desires infected with revenge. Hamblet, in this sorte counterfeiting the madde man, many times did divers actions of great and deepe consideration, and often made such and so fitte answeres, that a wise man would soone have judged from what spirite so fine an invention mighte proceede; for that standing by the fire and sharpning sticks like poynards and prickes, one in smiling manner asked him wherefore he made those little staves so sharpe at the points? I prepare (saith he) piersing dartes and sharpe arrowes to revenge my fathers death. Fooles, as I said before, esteemed those his words as nothing; but men of quicke spirits, and such as hadde a deeper reache began to suspect somewhat, esteeming that under that kinde of folly there lay hidden a greate and rare subtilty, such as one day might bee prejudiciall to their prince, saying, that under colour of such rudness he shadowed a crafty pollicy, and by his devised simplicitye, he concealed a sharp and pregnant spirit: for which cause they counselled the king to try and know, if it were possible, how to discover the intent and meaning of the yong prince; and they could find no better nor more fit invention to intrap him, then to set some faire and beawtifull woman in a secret place, that with flattering speeches and all the craftiest meanes she could use, should purposely seek to allure his mind to have his pleasure of her: for the nature of all young men, (especially such as are brought up wantonlie) is so transported with the desires of the flesh, and entreth so greedily into the pleasures therof, that it is almost impossible to cover the foul affection, neither yet to dissemble or hyde the same by art or industry, much lesse to shunne it. What cunning or subtilty so ever they use to cloak theire pretence, seeing occasion offered, and that in secret, especially in the most inticing sinne that rayneth in man, they cannot chuse (being constrayned by voluptuousnesse) but fall to naturall effect and working. To this end certaine courtiers were appointed to leade Hamblet into a solitary place within the woods, whether they brought the woman, inciting him to take their pleasures together, and

A subtill answere of Prince Hamlet.

Nature corrupted in man

Subtilities used to discover Hamblets madnes.

12 *Belleforest*

to imbrace one another, but the subtill practises used in these our daies,

Corrupters of yong gentlemen in princes courts and great houses.

not to try if men of great account bee extract out of their wits, but rather to deprive them of strength, vertue and wisedome, by meanes of such devilish practitioners, and intefernall spirits, their domestical servants, and ministers of corruption. And surely the poore prince at this assault had him in great danger, if a gentleman (that in Horvendiles time had been nourished with him) had not showne himselfe more affectioned to the bringing up he had received with Hamblet, then desirous to please the tirant, who by all meanes sought to intangle the sonne in the same nets wherein the father had ended his dayes. This gentleman bare the courtyers (appointed as aforesaide of this treason) company, more desiring to give the prince instruction what he should do, then to intrap him, making full account that the least showe of perfect sence and wisedome that Hamblet should make would be sufficient to cause him to loose his life: and therefore by certain signes, he gave Hamblet intelligence in what danger hee was like to fall, if by any meanes hee seemed to obaye, or once like the wanton toyes and vicious provocations of the gentlewoman sent thither by his uncle. Which much abashed the prince, as then wholy beeing in affection to the lady, but by her he was likewise informed of the treason, as being one that from her infancy loved and favoured him, and would have been exceeding sorrowfull for his misfortune, and much more to leave his companie without injoying the pleasure of his body, whome shee loved more than herselfe. The prince in this sort having both deceived the courtiers, and the ladyes expectation, that affirmed and swore that hee never once offered to have his pleasure of the woman, although in subtilty hee affirmed the contrary, every man there upon assured themselves that without all doubt he was distraught of his sences, that his braynes were as then wholly void of force, and incapable of reasonable apprehension, so that as then Fengons practise took no effect: but for al that he left not off, still seeking by al meanes to finde out Hamblet's subtilty, as in the next chapter you shall perceive.

CHAP. III.

How Fengon, uncle to Hamblet, a second time to intrap him in his politick madness, caused one of his counsellors to be secretly hidden in the queenes chamber, behind the arras, to heare what speeches passed between Hamblet and the Queen; and how Hamblet killed him, and escaped that danger, and what followed.

AMONG THE FRIENDS of Fengon, there was one that above al the rest doubted of Hamblets practices in counterfeiting the madman, who for that cause said, that it was impossible that so craftie a gallant as Hamblet, that counterfeited the foole, should be discovered with so common and unskilfull practises, which might easily bee perceived, and that to finde out his politique pretence it were necessary to invent some subtill and crafty meanes, more attractive, whereby the gallant might not have the leysure to use his accustomed dissimulation; which to effect he said he knewe a fit waie, and a most convenient meane to effect the kings desire, and thereby to intrap Hamblet in his subtilties, and cause him of his owne accord to fall into the net prepared for him, and thereby evidently shewe his secret meaning. His devise was thus, that King Fengon should make as though he were to goe some long voyage concerning affaires of great importance, and that in the meane time Hamblet should be shut up alone in a chamber with his mother, wherein some other should secretly be hidden behind the hangings, unknowne either to him or his mother, there to stand and heere their speeches, and the complots by them to bee taken concerning the accomplishment of the dissembling fooles pretence; assuring the king that if there were any point of wisedome and perfect sence in the gallants spirit, that without all doubte he would easily discover it to his mother, as being devoid of all feare that she would utter or make knowne his secret intent, beeing the woman that had borne him in her bodie, and nourished him so carefully; and withall offered himselfe to be the man that should stand to harken and beare witnesse of Hamblets speeches with his mother, that hee might not be esteemed a counsellor in such a case wherein he refused to be the executioner for the behoofe and service of his prince. This invention pleased the king exceeding well, esteeming it as the onelie and soveraigne remedie to heale the prince of his lunacie; and to that ende making a long voyage, issued out of his

(margin note: Another subtilty used to deceive Hamblet.)

pallace, and road to hunt in the forrest. Mean time the counsellor entred

Hamblets
subtilty.

secretly into the queenes chamber, and there hid himselfe behind the arras, not long before the queene and Hamblet came thither, who beeing craftie and pollitique, as soone as hee was within the chamber, doubting some treason, and fearing if he should speake severely and wisely to his mother touching his secret practises he should be understood, and by that meanes intercepted, used his ordinary manner of dissimulation, and began to come like a cocke beating with his armes, (in such manner as cockes use to strike with their wings)

A cruell re-
venge taken
by Hamblet
upon him that
would have
betraid him.

upon the hangings of the chamber: whereby, feeling something stirring under them, he cried, A rat, a rat!* and presently drawing his sworde thrust it into the hangings, which done, pulled the counsellour (halfe dead) out by the heeles, made an end of killing him, and beeing slaine, cut his bodie in pieces, which he caused to be boyled, and then cast it into an open vaulte or privie, that so it mighte serve for foode to the hogges. By which meanes having discovered the ambushe, and given the inventer thereof his just rewarde, hee came againe to his mother, who in the meane time wepte and tormented her selfe to see all her hopes frustrate, for that what fault soever she had committed, yet was shee sore grieved to see her onely child made a meere mockery, every man

Queene
Geruthes re-
pentance.

reproaching her with his folly, one point whereof she had as then seene before her eyes, which was no small pricke to her conscience, esteeming that the gods sent her that punishment for joyning incestuously in marriage with the tyrrannous murtherer of her husband, who like wise ceased not to invent all the means he could to bring his nephew to his ende, accusing his owne naturall indiscretion, as beeing the ordinary guide of those that so much desire the pleasures of the bodie, who shutting up the waie to all reason, respect not what maie ensue of their lightnes and great inconstancy, and how a pleasure of small moment is sufficient to give them cause of repentance during their lives, and make them curse the daye and time that ever any such apprehensions entred into theire mindes, or that they closed their eies to reject the honestie requisite in ladies of her qualitie, and to despise the holy institution of those dames that had gone before her, both in nobilitie and vertue, calling to mind the great prayses and commendations

---

* The English translator at this point is influenced by the play. Saxo's counsellor hides in the straw of the queen's bed, and Belleforest's counsellor hides under a quilt. The wall hangings and the exclamation "A rat, a rat!" come from the play.

given by the danes to Rinde, daughter to king Rothere, the chastest lady in her time, and withall so shamefast that she would never consent to marriage with any prince or knight whatsoever; surpassing in vertue all the ladyes of her time, as shee herselfe surmounted them in beawtie, good behaviour, and comelines. And while in this sort she sate tormenting herselfe, Hamlet entred into the chamber, who having once againe searched every corner of the same, distrusting his mother as well as the rest, and perceiving himselfe to bee alone, began in sober and discreet manner to speak unto her, saying,

Rinde a princes of an admirable chastitie.

What treason is this, O most infamous woman! of all that ever prostrated themselves to the will of an abhominable whore monger, who, under the vail of a dissembling creature, covereth the most wicked and detestable crime that man could ever imagine, or was committed. Now may I be assured to trust you, that like a vile wanton adultresse, altogether impudent and given over to her pleasure, runnes spreading forth her armes joyfully to imbrace the trayterous villanous tyrant that murthered my father, and most incestuously receivest the villain into the lawfull bed of your loyall spouse, imprudently entertaining him in steede of the deare father of your miserable and discomforted soone, if the gods grant him not the grace speedilie to escape from a captivity so unworthie the degree he holdeth, and the race and noble familie of his ancestors. Is this the part of a queene, and daughter to a king? to live like a brute beast (and like a mare that yieldeth her bodie to the horse that hath beaten hir companion awaye), to followe the pleasure of an abhominable king that hath murthered a farre more honester and better man then himself in massacring Horvendile, the honor and glory of the Danes, who are now esteemed of no force nor valour at all, since the shining splendure of knighthood was brought to an end by the most wickedest and cruellest villaine living upon earth. I, for my part, will never account him for my kinsman, nor once knowe him for mine uncle, nor you my deer mother, for not having respect to the blud that ought to have united us so straightly together, and who neither with your honor nor without suspicion of consent to the death of your husband could ever have agreed to have marryed with his cruell enemie. O, queene Geruthe, it is the part of a bitch to couple with many, and desire acquaintance of divers mastiffes: it is licentiousnes only that hath made you deface out of your minde the memory of the valor and vertues of the good king your husband and my father: it was an unbrideled desire that guided the daughter of Roderick to imbrace the tyrant Fengon, and not to remember Horvendile (unworthy of so strange intertainment), neither that he killed his brother traiterously, and that shee being his fathers wife betrayed him, although he so well favoured and loved her, that for her sake he utterly bereaved Norway of her riches and valiant souldiers to augment the treasures of Roderick, and make Geruthe wife to the hardyest prince in Europe: it is not the parte of a woman, much lesse of a princesse, in whome all modesty, curtesse, compassion, and love ought to abound, thus to leave her deare child to fortune in the bloody and murtherous hands of a villain and traytor. Bruite beasts do not so, for lyons, tygers, ounces and leopards fight for the safety and defence of their whelpes; and birds that have beakes, claws, and wings, resist such as would ravish them of their yong ones; but you, to the contrary, expose and deliver mee to death, whereas ye should defend me. Is not this as much as if you should betray me, when you knowing the perversenes of the tyrant and his intents, ful of deadly counsell as touching the race and image of his brother, have not once sought, nor desired to finde the meanes to save your child (and only son) by sending him into Swethland, Norway, or England, rather than to leave him as a pray to youre infamous adulterer? bee not offended, I praye you, Madame, if transported with dolour and griefe, I speake so boldely unto you, and that I respect you lesse then dutie requireth; for you, having forgotten mee, and wholy rejected the memorye of the deceased K. my father, must not bee abashed if I also surpasse the bounds and limits of due consideration. Beholde into what distresse I am now fallen, and to what mischiefe my fortune, and your over great lightnesse, and want of wisedome have induced mee, that I am constrained to playe the madde man to save my life, in steed of using and practising armes, following adventures, and seeking all meanes to make my selfe knowne to bee the true and undoubted heire of the valiant and vertuous king Horvendile. It was not without cause, and juste occasion, that my gestures, countenances, and words, seeme all to proceed from a madman, and that I desire to have all men esteeme mee wholly deprived of sence and reasonable understanding, bycause I am well assured, that he that hath made no conscience to kill his owne brother, (accustomed to murthers, and allured with desire of governement without controll in his treasons), will not spare, to save himselfe with the like crueltie, in the blood and flesh of the loyns of his brother by him massacred: and, therefore, it is better for me to fayne madnesse, than to use my right sences as nature hath bestowed them upon me: the bright shining clearnes therof I am forced to hide under this shadow of dissimulation, as the sun doth hir beames under some great cloud, when the wether in sommer time overcasteth. The face of a mad man serveth to cover my gallant countenance, and the gestures of a fool are fit for me, to the end that guiding my self wisely therein, I may preserve my life for the Danes, and the memory of my late deceased father; for the desire of revenging his death is so engraven in my heart, that if I dye not shortly, I hope to take such and so great vengeance, that these countryes shall for ever speake thereof. Neverthelesse, I must stay the time, meanes, and occasion, lest by making over great hast, I be now the cause of mine owne sodaine ruine and overthrow, and by that meanes end before I beginne to effect my hearts desire. Hee that hath to doe with a wicked, disloyall, cruell, and discourteous man must use craft and politike inventions, such as a fine witte can best imagine, not to discover his interprise; for seeing that by force I cannot effect my desire, reason alloweth me by dissimulation, subtiltie, and secret practises to proceed therein. To conclude, weepe not (madame) to see my folly, but rather sigh and lament your owne offence, torment-ing your conscience in regard of the infamie that hath so defiled the ancient renowne and glorie that (in times past) honoured queene Geruth; for wee are not to sorrowe and grieve at other mens vices, but for our owne misdeedes, and great folloyes. Desiring you, for the surplus of my proceedings, above all things (as you love your owne life and welfare) that neither the king nor any other may by any meanes know mine intent; and let me alone with the rest, for I hope in the ende to bring my purpose to effect.

We must use subtiltie to a disloyall person.

Wee must weepe for our owne faults and not for other mens.

Although the queene perceived herselfe neerely touched, and that Hamlet mooved her to the quicke, where she felt herself interested, never-thelesse shee forgot all disdaine and wrath, which thereby she might as then have had, hearing her selfe so sharply chiden and reprooved, for the joy she then conceaved, to behold the gallant spirit of her sonne, and to thinke what she might hope, and the easier expect of his so great policie and wisdome. But on the one side she durst not lift up her eyes to beholde him, remembering her offence, and on the other side she would gladly have imbraced her son, in regard of the wise admonitions by him given unto her, which as then quenched the flames of unbridled desire that before had mooved her to affect K. Fengon, to ingraff in her heart the vertuous actions of her lawful spouse, whom inwardly she much lamented, when she beheld the lively image and portraiture of his vertue and great wisdome in her childe, representing his fathers haughtie and valiant heart: and so, overcome and vanquished with this honest passion, and weeping most bitterly, having long time fixed her eyes upon Hamlet, as beeing ravished into some great and deepe contemplation, and as it were wholy amazed, at the last imbracing him in her armes (with the like love that a vertuous mother may or can use to kisse and entertaine her owne childe), shee spake unto him in this manner.

I know well (my sonne) that I have done thee great wrong in marrying with Fengon, the cruell tyrant and murtherer of thy father, and my loyall spouse: but when thou shalt consider the small meanes of resistance, and the treason of the palace, with the little cause of confidence we are to expect or hope for of the courtiers, all wrought to his will, as also the power hee made ready, if I should have refused to like of him, thou wouldest rather excuse then accuse me of lasciviousnes or inconstancy, much lesse offer me that wrong to suspect that ever thy mother Geruthe once consented to the death and murther of her husband: swearing unto thee (by the majestie of the Gods) that if it had layne in my power to have resisted the tyrant, although it had beene with the losse of my blood, yea and my life, I would surely have saved the life of my lord and husband, with as good a will and desire as, since that time, I have often beene a meanes to hinder and impeach the shortning of thy life, which being taken away, I will no lomger live here upon earth. For seeing that thy sences are whole and sound, I am in hope to see an easie meanes invented for the revenging of thy fathers death. Neverthelesse, mine owne sweet soone, if thou hast pittie of thy selfe, or care of the memorie of thy father (although thou wilt do nothing for her that deserveth not the name of a mother in this respect), I pray thee, carie thine affayres wisely: bee not hastie, nor over furious in thy interprises, neither yet advance thy selfe more than reason shall moove thee to effect thy purpose. Thou seest there is not almost any man wherein thou mayest put thy trust, nor any woman to whom I dare utter the least part of my secrets, that would not presently report it to thine adversarie, who, although in outward shew he dissembleth to love thee, the better to injoy his pleasures of me, yet hee distrusteth and feareth mee for thy sake, and is not so simple as to be easily perswaded that thou art a foole or mad; so that if thou chance to doe any thing that seemeth to proceed of wisedome or policie (how secretly soever it be done) he will presently be informed thereof, and I am greatly afraide that the devils have shewed him what hath past at this present between us, (fortune so much pursueth and contrarieth our ease and welfare) or that this murther that now thou hast committed be not the cause of both our destructions, which I by no meanes will seeme to know, but will keepe secret both thy wisedome and hardy interprise; beseeching the Gods (my good soone) that they, guiding thy heart, directing thy counsels, and prospering thy interprise, I may see thee possesse and injoy that which is thy right, and weare the crowne of Denmarke, by the tyrant taken from thee; that I may rejoyce in thy prosperitie, and therewith content my self, seeing with what courage and boldnesse thou shalt take vengeance upon the murtherer of thy father, as also upon all those that have assisted and favoured him in his murtherous and bloody enterprise. Madame (sayd Hamlet) I will put my trust in you, and from henceforth meane not to meddle further with your affayres, beseeching you (as you love your owne flesh and blood) that you will from hence foorth no more esteeme of the adulterer, mine enemie whom I wil surely kill, or cause to be put to death, in despite of all the devils in hel: and have he never so manie flattering courtezans to defend him, yet will I bring him to his death, and they themselves also shall beare him company therein, as they have bin his perverse counsellors in the action of killing my father, and his companions in his treason, massacre and cruell enterprise. And reason requireth that, even as trayterously they then caused their prince to bee put to death, that with the like (nay well, much more) justice they should pay the interest of their fellonious actions.

You know (Madame) how Hother your grandfather, and father to the good king Roderick, having vanquished Guimon, caused him to be burnt, for that the cruell vilain had done the like to his lord Gevare, whom he betrayed in the night time. And who knoweth not that traytors and perjured persons deserve no faith nor loyaltie to be observed towardes them, and that conditions made with murtherers ought to bee esteemed as cobwebs, and accounted as if they were things never promised nor agreed upon: but if I lay handes upon Fengon, it will neither be fellonie nor treason, hee being neither my king nor my lord, but I shall justly punish him as my subject, that hath disloyaly behaved himselfe against his lord and soveraigne prince. And seeing that glory is the rewarde of the vertuous, and the honour and praise of those that do service to their naturall prince, why should not blame and dishonour accompany traytors, and ignominious death al those that dare be so bold as to lay violent hands upon sacred kings, that are friends and companions of the gods, as representing their majestie and persons. To conclude, glorie is the crown of vertue, and the price of constancie; and seeing that it never accompanieth with infelicitie, but shunneth cowardize and spirits of base and trayterous conditions, it must necessarily followe, that either a glorious death will be mine ende, or with my sword in hand, (laden with

[margin: Hother, father to Rodericke. Guimon burnt his lord Gevare.]

[margin: We must observe neither faithfulnesse or fidelitie to traytors or parricides.]

tryumph and victorie) I shall bereave them of their lives that made mine unfortunate, and darkened the beames of that vertue which I possessed from the blood and famous memory of my predecessors. For why should men desire to live, when shame and infamie are the executioners that torment their consciences, and villany is the cause that withholdeth the heart from valiant interprises, and diverteth the minde from honest desire of glorie and commendation, which indureth for ever? I know it is foolishly done to gather fruit before it is ripe, and to seeke to enjoy a benefit, not knowing whither it belong to us of right; but I hope to effect it so well, and have so great confidence in my fortune (that hitherto hath guided the action of my life) that I shall not dye without revenging my selfe upon mine enemie, and that himselfe shall be the instrument of his owne decay, and to execute that which of my selfe I durst not have enterprised.

After this, Fengon (as if hee had beene out some long journey) came to the court againe, and asked for him that had received the charge to play the intilligencer, to entrap Hamlet in his dissembled wisedome, was abashed to heare neither newes nor tydings of him, and for that cause asked Hamlet what was become of him, naming the man. The prince that never used lying, and who in all the answers that ever he made (during his counterfeit madnesse) never strayed from the trueth (as a generous minde is a mortal enemie to untruth) answered and sayd, that the counsellor he sought for was gone downe through the privie, where being choaked by the filthynesse of the place, the hogs meeting him had filled their bellyes.

CHAP. IIII.

How Fengon the third time devised to send Hamblet to the king of England, with secret letters to have him put to death: and how Hamblet, when his companions slept, read the letters, and instead of them counterfeited others, willing the king of England to put the two messengers to death, and to marry his daughter to Hamblet, which was effected; and how Hamblet escaped out of England.

A MAN would have judged any thing, rather then that Hamblet had committed that murther, nevertheless Fengon could not content himselfe, but still his minde gave him that the foole would play him some tricke of liegerdemaine, and willingly would have killed him, but he feared king Rodericke, his grandfather, and further durst not offend the queene, mother to the foole, whom she loved and much cherished, shewing great griefe and heavinesse to see him so transported out of his wits. And in that conceit, seeking to bee rid of him, determined to finde the meanes to doe it by the ayde of a stranger, making the king of England minister of his massacreing resolution, choosing rather that his friende should defile his renowne with so great a wickednesse, then himselfe to fall into perpetuall infamie by an exploit of so great crueltie, to whom hee purposed to send him, and by letters desire him to put him to death.

Hamblet, understanding that he should be sent into England, presently doubted the occasion of his voyage, and for that cause speaking to the queene, desired her not to make any shew of sorrow or griefe for his departure, but rather counterfeit a gladnesse, as being rid of his presence; whom, although she loved, yet she dayly grieved to see him in so pittifull estate, deprived of all sence and reason: desiring her further, that she should hang the hall with tapestrie, and make it fast with nayles upon the walles, and keepe the brands for him which hee had sharpened at the points, then, when as he said he made arrowes to revenge the death of his father: lastly, he counselled her, that the yeere after his departure being accomplished, she should celebrate his funerals; assuring her that at the same instant she should see him returne with great contentment and pleasure unto her for that his voyage. Now, to beare him company were assigned two of Fengons faithful ministers, bearing letters ingraved in wood, that contained Hamlets death, in such sort as he had advertised the king of England. But the subtile Danish prince (beeing at sea) whilst his companions slept, having read the letters, and knowne his uncles great treason, with the wicked and villainous mindes of the two courtyers that led him to the slaughter, raced out the letters that concerned his death, and in stead thereof graved others, *Hamblets craft to save his life.* with commission to the king of England to hang his two companions; and not content to turne the death they had devised against him upon their owne neckes, wrote further, that king Fengon willed him to give his daughter to Hamlet in marriage. And so arriving in England, the messengers presented themselves to the king, giving him Fengons letters; who having read the contents, sayd nothing as then, but stayed convenient time to effect Fengons desire, meane time using the Danes familiarly, doing them that honour to sit at his table (for that kings as then were not so curiously, nor solemnely served as in these our dayes,) for in these dayes meane kings, and lords of small revenewe are as difficult and hard to bee seene, as in times past the monarches of Persia used to bee: or as it is reported of the great king of Aethyopia, who will not permit any man to see his face, which ordinarily hee covereth with a vaile. And as the messengers sate at the table with the king, subtile Hamlet was so far from being merry with them, that he would not taste one bit of meate, bread, nor cup of beare whatsoever, as then set upon the table, not without great wondering of the company, abashed to see a yong man and a stranger not to esteeme of the delicate meates and pleasant drinkes served at the banquet, rejecting them as things filthy, evill of tast, and worse prepared. The king, who for that time dissembled what he thought, caused his ghests to be conveyed into their chamber, willing one of his secret servantes to hide himselfe therein, and so to certifie him what speeches past among the Danes at their going to bed.

Now they were no sooner entred into the chamber, and those that were appointed to attend upon them gone out, but Hamlets companions asked him, why he refused to eate and drinke of that which hee found upon the table, not honouring the banquet of so great a king, that entertained them in friendly sort, with such honour and courtesie as it deserved? saying further, that hee did not well, but dishonoured him that sent him, as if he sent men into England that feared to bee poysoned by so great a king. The prince, that had done nothing without reason and prudent consideration, answered them, and sayd: What, think you, that I will eat bread dipt in humane blood, and defile my throate with the rust of yron, and use that meat that stinketh and savoureth of mans flesh, already putrified and corrupted, and that senteth like the savour of a dead carryon, long since cast into a valt? and how woulde you have mee to respect the king, that hath the countenance of a slave; and the queene, who in stead of great majestie, hath done three things more like a woman of base parentage, and fitter for a waiting gentlewoman then beseeming a lady of her qualitie and estate. And having sayd so, used many injurious and sharpe speeches as well against the king and queene, as others that had assisted at that banquet for the intertainment of the Danish ambassadors; and therein Hamblet said trueth, as hereafter you shall heare, for that in those dayes, the north parts of the worlde, living as then under Sathans lawes, were full of inchanters, so that there was not any yong gentleman whatsoever that knew not something therein sufficient to serve his turne, if need required: as yet in those dayes in Gothland and Biarmy, there are many that knew not what the Christian religion permitteth, as by reading the histories of Norway and Gothland, you maie easilie perceive: and so Hamlet, while his father lived, had bin instructed in that devilish art, whereby the wicked spirite abuseth mankind, and advertiseth him (as he can) of things past.

It toucheth not the matter herein to discover the parts of devination in man, and whether this prince, by reason of his over great melancholy, had received those impressions, devining that, which never any but himselfe had before declared, like the philosophers, who discoursing of divers deep points of philosophie, attribute the force of those divinations to such as are saturnists by complection, who oftentimes speake of things which, their fury ceasing, they then alreadye can hardly understand who are the pronouncers; and for that cause Plato saith, many deviners and many poets, after the force and vigour of their fier beginneth to lessen, do hardly understand what they have written, although intreating of such things, while the spirite of devination continueth upon them, they doe in such sorte discourse thereof that the authors and inventors of the arts themselves by them alledged, commend their discourses and subtill disputations. Likewise I mean not to relate that which divers men beleeve, that a reasonable soul becometh the habitation of a meaner sort of devels, by whom men learn the secrets of things natural; and much lesse do I account of the supposed governors of the world fained by magitians, by whose means they brag to effect mervailous things. It would seeme miraculous that Hamlet shold divine in that sort, which after prooved so true (if as I said before) the devel had not knowledg of things past, but to grant it he knoweth things to come I hope you shall never find me in so grose an error. You will compare and make equall derivation, and conjecture with those that are made by the spirit of God, and pronounced by the holy prophets, that tasted of that marvelous science, to whome onely was declared the secrets and wondrous workes of the Almighty. Yet there are some imposturious companions that impute so much devinitie to the devell, the father of lyes, that they attribute unto him the truth of the knowledge of thinges that shall happen unto men, alledging the conference of Saul with the witch, although one example out of the Holy Scriptures, specially set downe for the condemnation of wicked man, is not of force to give a sufficient law to all the world; for they themselves confesse that they can devine, not according to the universal cause of things, but by signes borrowed from such like causes, which are all waies alike, and by those conjectures they can give judgement of thinges to come, but all this beeing grounded upon a weake support, (which is a simple conjecture) and having so slender a foundation, as some foolish or late experience the fictions being voluntarie. It should be a great folly in a man of good judgement, specially one that imbraceth the preaching of the gospell, and seeketh after no other but the trueth thereof, to repose upon any of these likelihoods or writings full of deceipt.

As touching magical operations, I will grant them somewhat therein, finding divers histories that write thereof, and that the Bible maketh mention, and forbiddeth the use thereof: yea, the lawes of the gentiles and ordinances of emperors have bin made against it in such sort, that Mahomet, the great hereticke and friend of the devell, by whose subtiltyes hee abused most part of the east countries, hath ordained great punishments for such as use and practise those unlawfull and damnable artes, which, for this time leaving of, let us returne to Hamblet, brought up in these abuses, according to the manner of his country, whose companions hearing his answere reproached him of folly, saying that hee could by no meanes show a greater point of indiscretion, then in despising that which is lawfull, and rejecting that which all men receaved as a necessary thing, and that hee had not grossely so forgotten himselfe as in that sorte to accuse such and so excellent a man as the king of England, and to slander the queene, being then as famous and wise a princes as any at that day raigning in the ilands thereabouts, to cause him to be punished according to his deserts; but he, continuing in his dissimulation, mocked him, saying that hee had not done any thing that was not good and most true. On the other side, the king being advertised thereof by him that stood to heare the discourse, judged presently that Hamlet, speaking so ambiguously, was either a perfect foole, or else one of the wisest princes in his time, answering so sodainly, and so much to the purpose upon the demaund by his companions made touching his behavior; and the better to find the trueth, caused the babler to be sent for, of whome inquiring in what place the corn grew whereof he made bread for his table, and whether in that ground there were not some signes or newes of a battaile fought, whereby humaine blood had therein been shed? the babler answered that not far from thence there lay a field ful of dead mens bones, in times past slaine in a battaile, as by the greate heapes of wounded sculles mighte well appeare, and for that the ground in that parte was become fertiler then other grounds, by reason of the fatte and humours of the dead bodies, that every yeer the farmers used there to have in the best wheat they could finde to serve his majesties house. The king perceiving it to be true, according to the yong princes wordes, asked where the hogs had bin fed that were killed to be served at his table? and answere was made him, that those hogs getting out of the said fielde wherein they were kepte, had found the bodie of a thiefe that had beene hanged for his demerits, and had eaten thereof:

whereat the king of England beeing abashed, would needs know with what water the beer he used to drinke of had been brued? which having knowne, he caused the river to bee digged somewhat deeper, and therin found great store of swords and rustie armours, that gave an ill savour to the drinke. It were good I should heere dilate somewhat of Merlins prophesies, which are said to be spoken of him before he was fully one yeere old; but if you consider wel what hath al reddy been spoken, it is no hard matter to divine of things past, although the minister of Sathan therein played his part, giving sodaine and prompt answeres to this yong prince, for that herein are nothing but natural things, such as were wel known to be true, and therefore not needfull to dreame of thinges to come. This knowne, the king, greatly moved with a certaine curiositie to knowe why the Danish prince saide that he had the countenance of a slave, suspecting thereby that he reproached the basenes of his blood, and that he wold affirme that never any prince had bin his sire, wherin to satisfie himselfe he went to his mother, and leading her into a secret chamber, which he shut as soone as they were entred, desired her of her honour to shewe him of whome he was ingendred in this world. The good lady, wel assured that never any man had bin acquainted with her love touching any other man then her husband, sware that the king her husband onely was the man that had enjoyed the pleasures of her body; but the king her sonne, alreadie with the truth of the Danish princes answers, threatned his mother to make her tell by force, if otherwise she would not confesse it, who for feare of death acknowledged that she had prostrated her body to a slave, and made him father to the king of England; whereat the king was abashed, and wholy ashamed. I give them leave to judge who esteeming themselves honester than theire neighbours, and supposing that there can be nothing amisse in their houses, make more enquirie then is requisite to know the which they would rather not have known. Neverthelesse dissembling what he thought, and biting upon the bridle, rather then he would deprive himselfe by publishing the lasciviousnes of his mother, thought better to leave a great sin unpunished, then thereby to make him selfe contemptible to his subjects, who peradventure would have rejected him, as not desiring to have a bastard to raigne over so great a kingdome.

But as he was sorry to hear his mothers confession, on the otherside he tooke great pleasure in the subtilty and quick spirit of the yong prince, and for that cause went unto him to aske him, why he had reproved three things in his queene convenient for a slave, and savouring more of basenes then of royaltie, and far unfit for the majesty of a great prince? The king, not content to have receaved a great displeasure by knowing him selfe to be a bastard, and to have heard with what injuries he charged her whom hee loved best in all the world, would not content himself untill he also understood that which displeased him, as much as his owne proper disgrace, which was that his queen was the daughter of a chambermaid, and with all noted certaine foolish countenances she made, which not onely shewed of what parentage she came, but also that hir humors savored of the basenes and low degree of hir parents, whose mother, he assured the king, was as then yet holden in servitude. The king admiring the young prince, and behoulding in him some matter of greater respect then in the common sort of men, gave him his daughter in marriage, according to the counterfet letters by him devised, and the next day caused the two servants of Fengon to be executed, to satisfie, as he thought, the king's desire. But Hamlet, although the sport plesed him wel, and that the king of England could not have done him a greater favour, made as though he had been much offended, threatning the king to be revenged, but the king, to appease him, gave him a great sum of gold, which Hamlet caused to be molten, and put into two staves, made hollow for the same purpose, to serve his tourne there with as neede should require; for of all other the kings treasures he took nothing with him into Denmark but onely those two staves, and as soone as the yeere began to bee at an end, having somewhat before obtained licence of the king his father in law to depart, went for Denmarke; then, with all the speed hee could to returne againe into England to marry his daughter, and so set sayle for Denmarke.

CHAP. V.

How Hamblet, having escaped out of England, arrived in Denmarke the same day that the Danes were celebrating his funerals, supposing him to be dead in England; and how he revenged his fathers death upon his uncle and the rest of the courtiers; and what followed.

HAMBLET in that sort sayling into Denmark, being arrived in the contry, entered into the pallace of his uncle the same day that they were celebrating his funeralls, and going into the hall, procured no small astonishment and wonder to them all, no man thinking other but that hee had beene deade: among the which many of them rejoyced not a little for the pleasure which they knew Fengon would conceave for so pleasant a losse, and some were sadde, as remembering the honourable king Horvendile, whose victories they could by no meanes forget, much lesse deface out of theire memories that which apperteined unto him, who as then greatly rejoyced to see a false report spread of Hamlets death, and that the tyrant had not as yet obtained his will of the heire of Jutie, but rather hoped God would restore him to his sences againe for the good and welfare of that province. Their amazement at the last beeing tourned into laughter, all that as then were assistant at the funerall banquet of him whome they esteemèd dead, mocked each at other, for having beene so simply deceived, and wondering at the prince, that in his so long a voyage he had not recovered any of his sences, asked what was become of them that had borne him company into Greate Brittaine? to whome he made answere (shewing them the two hollow staves, wherein he had put his molten golde, that the King of England had given him to appease his fury, concerning the murther of his two companions), and said, Here they are both. Whereat many that already knew his humours, presently conjectured that hee had plaide some tricke of legerdemane, and to deliver himselfe out of danger, had throwne them into the pitte prepared for him: so that fearing to follow after them and light upon some evil adventure, they went presently out of the court. And it was well for them that they didde so, considering the tragedy acted by him the same daie, beeing accounted his funerall, but in trueth theire last daies, that as then rejoyced for their overthrow; for when every man busied himselfe to make good cheare, and Hamlets arivall provoked them more to drinke and carouse, the prince himselfe at that time played the butler and a gentleman attending on the tables, not suffering the pots nor goblets to bee empty, whereby hee gave the noble men such store of liquor, that all of them being ful laden with wine and gorged with meate, were constrained to lay themselves downe in the same place where they had supt, so much their sences were dulled, and overcome with the fire of over *Drunkenes a vice over common in the north partes of the world.* great drinking (a vice common and familiar among the Almaines, and other nations inhabiting the north parts of the world) which when Hamlet perceiving, and finding so good opportunitie to effect his purpose and bee revenged of his enemies, and by the means to abandon the actions, gestures, and apparel of a mad man, occasion so fitly finding his turn, and as it were effecting it selfe, failed not to take hold thereof, and seeing those drunken bodies, filled with wine, lying like hogs upon the ground, some sleeping, others vomiting the over great abundance of wine which without measure they had swallowed up, made the hangings about the hall to fall downe and cover them all over; which he nailed to the ground, being boorded, and at the ends thereof he stuck the brands, whereof I spake before, by him sharpned, which served for prickes, binding and tying the hangings in such sort, that what force soever they used to loose themselves, it was unpossible to get from under them: and presently he set fire in the foure corners of the hal, in such sort, that all that were as then therein not one escaped away, but were forced to purge their sins by fire, and dry up the great abundance of liquor by them received into their bodies, all of them dying in the inevitable and mercilesse flames of the whot and burning fire: which the prince perceiving, became wise, and knowing that his uncle, before the end of the banquet, had withdrawn himselfe into his chamber, which stood apart from the place where the fire burnt, went thither, and entring into the chamber, layd hand upon the sword of his fathers murtherer, leaving his own in the place, which while he was at the banket some of the courtiers had nailed fast into the scaberd, and going to Fengon said: I wonder, disloyal king, how thou canst sleep heer at thine ease, and al thy pallace is burnt, the fire thereof having burnt the greatest part of thy courtiers and ministers of thy cruelty, and detestable tirannies; and which is more, I cannot imagin how thou sholdst wel assure thy self and thy estate, as now to take thy ease, seeing Hamlet so neer thee armed with the shafts by him prepared long since, and at this present is redy to revenge the traiterous injury by thee done to his lord and father.

A strange revenge taken by Hamlet.

A mocke but yet sharp and stinging, given by Hamlet to his uncle.

Fengon, as then knowing the truth of his nephews subtile practise, and hering him speak with stayed mind, and which is more, perceived a sword naked in his hand, which he already lifted up to deprive him of his life, leaped quickly out of the bed, taking holde of Hamlets sworde, that was nayled into the scaberd, which as hee sought to pull out. Hamlet gave him such a blowe upon the chine of the necke, that hee cut his head cleane from his shoulders, and as he fell to the ground sayd, This just and violent death is a just reward for such as thou art: now go thy wayes, and when thou commest in hell, see thou forget not to tell thy brother (whom thou trayterously slewest), that it was his sonne that sent thee thither with the message, to the ende that beeing comforted thereby, his soule may rest among the blessed spirits, and quit mee of the obligation that bound me to pursue his vengeance upon mine owne blood, that seeing it was by thee that I lost the chiefe thing that tyed me to this alliance and consanguinitie. A man (to say the trueth) hardie, couragious, and worthy of eternal commendation, who arming himself with a crafty, dissembling, and strange shew of beeing distract out of his wits, under that pretence deceived the wise, pollitike, and craftie, thereby not onely preserving his life from the treasons and wicked practises of the tyrant, but (which is more) by an new and unexpected kinde of punishment, revenged his fathers, death, many yeeres after the act committed: in no such sort that directing his courses with such prudence, and effecting his purposes with so great boldnes and constancie, he left a judgement to be decyded among men of wisdom, which was more commendable in him, his constancy or magnanimitie, or his wisdom in ordring his affaires, according to the premeditable determination he had conceaved.

Commendation of Hamlet for killing the tyrant.

If vengeance ever seemed to have any shew of justice, it is then, when pietie and affection constraineth us to remember our fathers unjustly murdered, as the things wherby we are dispensed withal, and which seeke the means not to leave treason and murther unpunished: seeing David a holy and just king, and of nature simple, courteous, and debonaire, yet when he dyed he charged his soone Salomon (that succeeded him in his throane) not to suffer certaine men that had done him injurie to escape unpunished. Not that this holy king (as then ready to dye, and to give account before God of all his actions) was careful or desirous of revenge, but to leave this example unto us, that where the prince or countrey is interested, the desire of revenge cannot by any meanes (how small soever) beare the title of condemnation, but is rather commendable and worthy of praise: for otherwise the good kings of Juda, nor others had not pursued them to death, that had offended their predecessors, if God himself had not inspired and ingraven that desire within their hearts. Hereof the Athenian lawes beare witnesse, whose custome was to erect images in remembrance of those men that, revenging the injuries of the commonwealth, boldly massacred tyrants and such as troubled the peace and welfare of the citizens.

How just vengeance ought to be considered.

Davids intent in commanding Salomon to revenge him of some of his enemies.

Hamblet, having in this manner revenged himselfe, durst not presently declare his action to the people, but to the contrary determined to worke by policie, so to give them intelligence, what he had done, and the reason that drewe him thereunto: so that beeing accompanied with such of his fathers friends that then were rising, he stayed to see what the people would doe when they shoulde heare of that sodaine and fearefull action. The next morning the townes bordering there aboutes, desiring to know from whence the flames of fire proceeded the night before they had seene, came thither, and perceiving the kings pallace burnt to ashes, and many bodyes (most part consumed) lying among the ruines of the house, all of them were much abashed, nothing being left of the palace but the foundation. But they were much more amased to beholde the body of the king all bloody, and his head cut off lying hard by him, whereat some began to threaten revenge, yet not knowing against whom; others beholding so lamentable a spectacle, armed themselves, the rest rejoycing, yet not daring to make any shewe thereof; some detesting the crueltie, others lamenting the death of their Prince, but the greatest part calling Horvendiles murther to remembrance, acknowledging a just judgement from above, that had throwne downe the pride of the tyrant. And in this sort, the diversities of opinions among that multitude of people being many, yet every man ignorant what would be the issue of that tragedie, none stirred from thence, neither yet attempted to move any tumult, every man fearing his owne skinne, and distrusting his neighbour, esteeming each other to bee consenting to the massacre.

[*The Hystorie of Hamblet* continues for three more chapters, but their events contributed nothing to the play. After justifying his actions in a long speech to the people, Hamblet is elected king. Then he travels to England, marries two wives, and returns. Somewhat later a treacherous uncle, in conspiracy with the second wife, murders Hamblet and marries the confederate.]

BIBLIOGRAPHY ENTRY FOR RESEARCH PAPERS:

Belleforest, Francis de. *The Hystorie of Hamblet, Prince of Denmarke.* London, 1608. Reprinted in *A New Variorum Edition of Shakespeare.* Philadelphia, 1877. Excerpt in *Interpreting Hamlet,* ed. Russell E. Leavenworth, San Francisco, 1960.

FIRST FOOTNOTE:

* Francis de Belleforest, *The Hystorie of Hamblet, Prince of Denmarke* (London, 1608), reprinted in *A New Variorum Edition of Shakespeare* (Philadelphia, 1877), excerpts in *Interpreting Hamlet,* ed. Russell E. Leavenworth (San Francisco, 1960), pp. 5-30.

SUBSEQUENT FOOTNOTES:

* Belleforest, *op. cit.,* IH, p. ██.
* Belleforest, *Hystorie of Hamblet,* IH, p. ██.
* Belleforest, *IH,* p. ██.

In place of "*IH,*" "ed. Leavenworth" may be used in these subsequent-footnote forms.

"To be, or not to be, . . ."

THREE TEXTUAL VERSIONS

These facsimiles from three versions of Hamlet *are from books in the collection of the Henry E. Huntington Library and Art Gallery, San Marino, California, and are reproduced by their permission. For some remarks about the First Quarto, the Second Quarto, and the First Folio, see the Introduction to this book, p. 2. For documentation forms, see page 37.*

FROM THE FIRST QUARTO, 1603.
PORTIONS OF SIGNATURES D_4v AND E_1r.

King. see where hee comes poring vppon a booke.
                    Enter Hamlet.
  Cor. Madame, will it pleafe your grace
To leaue vs here?
  Que. With all my hart.   *exit.*
  Cor. And here *Ofelia*, reade you on this booke,
And walke aloofe, the King fhal be vnfeene.
  Ham. To be, or not to be, I there's the point,
To Die, to fleepe, is that all? I all:
No, to fleepe, to dreame, I mary there it goes,
For in that dreame of death, when wee awake,
And borne before an euerlafting Iudge,
From whence no paffenger euer retur'nd,
The vndifcouered country, at whofe fight
The happy fmile, and the accurfed damn'd.
But for this, the ioyfull hope of this,
Whol'd beare the fcornes and flattery of the world,
Scorned by the right rich, the rich curffed of the poore?
                                            The

Prince of Denmarke

The widow being oppreſſed, the orphan wrong d,
The taſte of hunger, or a tirants raigne,
And thouſand more calamities beſides,
To grunt and ſweate vnder this weary life,
When that he may his full *Quietus* make,
With a bare bodkin, who would this indure,
But for a hope of ſomething after death?
Which puſles the braine, and doth confound the ſence,
Which makes vs rather beare thoſe euilles we haue,
Than flie to others that we know not of.
I that, O this conſcience makes cowardes of vs all,
Lady in thy orizons, be all my ſinnes remembred.

   Ofel. My Lord, I haue ſought opportunitie, which now
I haue, to redeliuer to your worthy handes, a ſmall remembrance, ſuch tokens which I haue receiued of you.

   Ham. Are you faire?

   Ofel. My Lord.

   Ham. Are you honeſt?

   Ofel. What meanes my Lord?

   Ham. That if you be faire and honeſt,
Your beauty ſhould admit no diſcourſe to your honeſty.

   Ofel. My Lord, can beauty haue better priuiledge than
with honeſty?

   Ham. Yea mary may it; for Beauty may transforme
Honeſty, from what ſhe was into a bawd:
Then Honeſty can transforme Beauty:
This was ſometimes a Paradoxe,
But now the time giues it ſcope.
I neuer gaue you nothing.

   Ofel. My Lord, you know right well you did,
And with them ſuch earneſt vowes of loue,
As would haue moou'd the ſtonieſt breaſt aliue,
But now too true I finde,
Rich giftes waxe poore, when giuers grow vnkinde.

   Ham. I neuer loued you.

   Ofel. You made me beleeue you did.

               E   *Ham.*

That show of such an exercise may cullour
Your lowlines; we are oft too blame in this,
Tis too much proou'd, that with deuotions visage
And pious action, we doe sugar ore
The deuill himselfe.

   King. O tis too true,
How smart a lash that speech doth giue my conscience.
The harlots cheeke beautied with plastring art,
Is not more ougly to the thing that helps it,
Then is my deede to my most painted word :
O heauy burthen.

Enter Hamlet.

   Pol. I heare him comming, with-draw my Lord.
   Ham. To be, or not to be, that is the question,
Whether tis nobler in the minde to suffer
The slings and arrowes of outragious fortune,
Or to take Armes against a sea of troubles,
And by opposing, end them, to die to sleepe
No more, and by a sleepe, to say we end
The hart-ake, and the thousand naturall shocks
That flesh is heire to; tis a consumation
Deuoutly to be wisht to die to sleepe,
To sleepe, perchance to dreame, I there's the rub,
For in that sleepe of death what dreames may come
When we haue shuffled off this mortall coyle
Must giue vs pause, there's the respect
That makes calamitie of so long life :
For who would beare the whips and scornes of time,
Th'oppressors wrong, the proude mans contumely,
The pangs of despiz'd loue, the lawes delay,
The insolence of office, and the spurnes
That patient merrit of th'vnworthy takes,
When he himselfe might his quietas make
With a bare bodkin; who would fardels beare,
To grunt and sweat vnder a wearie life,
But that the dread of something after death,
The vndiscouer'd country, from whose borne

G 2

The Tragedie of Hamlet

No trauiler returnes, puzzels the will,
And makes vs rather beare those ills we haue,
Then flie to others that we know not of.
Thus conscience dooes make cowards,
And thus the natiue hiew of resolution
Is sickled ore with the pale cast of thought,
And enterprises of great pitch and moment,
With this regard theyr currents turne awry,
And loose the name of action. Soft you now,
The faire *Ophelia*, Nimph in thy orizons
Be all my sinnes remembred.

   Oph. Good my Lord,
How dooes your honour for this many a day?

   Ham. I humbly thanke you well.

   Oph. My Lord, I haue remembrances of yours
That I haue longed long to redeliuer,
I pray you now receiue them.

   Ham. No, not I, I neuer gaue you ought.

   Oph. My honor'd Lord, you know right well you did,
And with them words of so sweet breath compos'd
As made these things more rich, their perfume lost,
Take these againe, for to the noble mind
Rich gifts wax poore when giuers prooue vnkind,
There my Lord.

   Ham. Ha, ha, are you honest.

   Oph. My Lord.

   Ham. Are you faire?

   Oph. What meanes your Lordship?

   Ham. That if you be honest & faire, you should admit
no discourse to your beautie.

   Oph. Could beauty my Lord haue better comerse
Then with honestie?

   Ham. I truly, for the power of beautie will sooner transforme honestie from what it is to a bawde, then the force of honestie can translate beautie into his likenes, this was sometime a paradox, but now the
time giues it proofe, I did loue you once.

   Oph. Indeed my Lord you made me belieue so.

   Ham. You should not haue beleeu'd me, for vertue cannot so
enocutat our old stock, but we shall relish of it, I loued you not.

And there did feeme in him a kinde of ioy
To heare of it: They are about the Court,
And (as I thinke) they haue already order
This night to play before him.

   Pol. 'Tis moſt true:
And he beſeech'd me to intreate your Maieſties
To heare, and ſee the matter.

   King. With all my heart, and it doth much content me
To heare him ſo inclin'd. Good Gentlemen,
Giue him a further edge, and driue his purpoſe on
To theſe delights.

   Roſin. We ſhall my Lord.   *Exeunt.*

   King. Sweet *Gertrude* leaue vs too,
For we haue cloſely ſent for *Hamlet* hither,
That he, as 'twere by accident, may there
Affront *Ophelia.* Her Father, and my ſelfe (lawful eſpials)
Will ſo beſtow our ſelues, that ſeeing vnſeene
We may of their encounter frankely iudge,
And gather by him, as he is behaued,
If t be th'affliction of his loue, or no,
That thus he ſuffers for.

   Qu. I ſhall obey you,
And for your part *Ophelia*, I do wiſh
That your good Beauties be the happy cauſe
Of *Hamlets* wildeneſſe : ſo ſhall I hope your Vertues
Will bring him to his wonted way againe,
To both your Honors.

   Ophe. Madam, I wiſh it may.

   Pol. *Ophelia*, walke you heere. Gracious ſo pleaſe ye
We will beſtow our ſelues : Reade on this booke,
That ſhew of ſuch an exerciſe may colour
Your lonelineſſe. We are oft too blame in this,
'Tis too much prou'd, that with Deuotions viſage,
And pious Action, we do ſurge o're
The diuell himſelfe.

   King. Oh'tis true:
How ſmart a laſh that ſpeech doth giue my Conſcience ?
The Harlots Cheeke beautied with plaiſt'ring Art
Is not more vgly to the thing that helpes it,
Then is my deede, to my moſt painted word.
Oh heauie burthen !

   Pol. I heare him comming, let's withdraw my Lord.
        Exeunt.

       Enter Hamlet.

   Ham. To be, or not to be, that is the Queſtion :
Whether 'tis Nobler in the minde to ſuffer
The Slings and Arrowes of outragious Fortune,
Or to take Armes againſt a Sea of troubles,
And by oppoſing end them : to dye, to ſleepe
No more ; and by a ſleepe, to ſay we end
The Heart-ake, and the thouſand Naturall ſhockes

That Flesh is heyre too? 'Tis a consummation
Deuoutly to be wish'd. To dye to sleepe,
To sleepe, perchance to Dreame; I, there's the rub,
For in that sleepe of death, what dreames may come,
When we haue shuffiel'd off this mortall coile,
Must giue vs pawse. There's the respect
That makes Calamity of so long life :
For who would beare the Whips and Scornes of time,
The Oppressors wrong, the poore mans Contumely,
The pangs of dispriz'd Loue, the Lawes delay,
The insolence of Office, and the Spurnes
That patient merit of the vnworthy takes,
When he himselfe might his *Quietus* make
With a bare Bodkin? Who would these Fardles beare
To grunt and sweat vnder a weary life,
But that the dread of something after death,
The vndiscouered Countrey, from whose Borne
No Traueller returnes, Puzels the will,
And makes vs rather beare those illes we haue,
Then flye to others that we know not of.
Thus Conscience does make Cowards of vs all,
And thus the Natiue hew of Resolution
Is sicklied o're, with the pale cast of Thought,
And enterprizes of great pith and moment,
With this regard their Currants turne away,
And loose the name of Action. Soft you now,
The faire *Ophelia*? Nimph, in thy Orizons
Be all my sinnes remembred.
    Ophe. Good my Lord,
How does your Honor for this many a day?
    Ham. I humbly thanke you : well, well, well.
    Ophe. My Lord, I haue Remembrances of yours,
That i haue longed long to re-deliuer.
I pray you now, receiue them.
    Ham. No, no, I neuer gaue you ought.
    Ophe. My honor'd Lord, I know right well you did,
And with them words of so sweet breath compos'd,
As made the things more rich, then perfume left :
Take these againe, for to the Noble minde
Rich gifts wax poore, when giuers proue vnkinde.
There my Lord.
    Ham. Ha, ha : Are you honest?
    Ophe. My Lord.
    Ham. Are you faire ?
    Ophe. What meanes your Lordship ?
    Ham. That if you be honest and faire, your Honesty
sho uld admit no discourse to your Beautie.
    Ophe. Could Beautie my Lord, haue better Comerce
then your Honestie ?
    Ham. I trulie : for the power of Beautie, will sooner
transforme Honestie from what it is, to a Bawd, then the
force of Honestie can translate Beautie into his likenesse.
This was sometime a Paradox, but now the time giues it
proofe. I did loue you once.
    Ophe. Indeed my Lord, you made me beleeue so.

DOCUMENTATION OF SHAKESPEARE MATERIALS

Identifying a Shakespeare source often requires a more explicit description than would be necessary for most books. One reason is that early printings of the plays have marked differences from one copy to another even in the same edition, making it necessary to specify the copy used; thus in the specimens below, the owner library's catalog number is given.

In a research work on Shakespeare it is often needless or even pedantic to give full details of authorship; *Hamlet* mentioned in a footnote is the Shakespeare play unless the contrary is stated. The edition of a cited play is likely to be the significant matter for the documentation. Thus footnotes are kept brief in a field of research that demands many footnotes. But even brief footnotes must tell the whole truth—if you are referring to a First Folio version of *Hamlet,* both competence and honesty demand that you say whether you saw the actual First Folio volume or a facsimile in another book. Note the method of observing this rule in these specimens:

BIBLIOGRAPHY ENTRIES FOR RESEARCH PAPERS:

Shakespeare, William. *The Tragedy of Hamlet, Prince of Denmarke.* London, 1603 (The First Quarto). Excerpt facsimile from Huntington Library example (69304) in *Interpreting Hamlet,* ed. Russell E. Leavenworth. San Francisco, 1960.

Shakespeare, William. *The Tragedie of Hamlet, Prince of Denmarke.* London, 1604-1605 (The Second Quarto). Excerpt facsimile from Huntington Library example (69305) in *Interpreting Hamlet,* ed. Russell E. Leavenworth. San Francisco, 1960.

Shakespeare, William. *Mr. William Shakespeare's Comedies, Histories, & Tragedies. Published according to the True Originall Copies.* London, 1623 (The First Folio). Excerpt facsimile from Huntington Library example (56422) in *Interpreting Hamlet,* ed. Russell E. Leavenworth. San Francisco, 1960.

FIRST FOOTNOTES:

* *Hamlet,* First Quarto, facsimile from Huntington Library example (63904) in *Interpreting Hamlet,* ed. Russell E. Leavenworth (San Francisco, 1960), pp. 31-32.

* *Hamlet,* Second Quarto, facsimile from Huntington Library example (69305) in *Interpreting Hamlet,* ed. Russell E. Leavenworth (San Francisco, 1960), pp. 33-34.

* *Hamlet,* First Folio, facsimile from Huntington Library example (56422) in *Interpreting Hamlet,* ed. Russell E. Leavenworth (San Francisco, 1960), pp. 35-36.

SUBSEQUENT FOOTNOTES:

* *Hamlet,* 1st quarto, *IH,* p. ▉▉.
* *Hamlet,* 2nd quarto, *IH,* p. ▉▉.
* *Hamlet,* 1st folio, *IH,* p. ▉▉.

G. C. LICHTENBERG

ON

David Garrick as Hamlet

Georg Christoph Lichtenberg (1742–1799) was a professor of physics at Göttingen University whose fame as a satirist and man of letters overshadowed his achievements in electrical experiments. This translated extract from his Briefe aus England *is quoted from* A New Variorum Edition of Shakespeare, *Vol. IV,* Hamlet, Part 2 *(Philadelphia, 1877), pp. 269-271.*

HAMLET appears in black. Horatio and Marcellus are with him, in uniform; they are expecting the Ghost. Hamlet's arms are folded, and his hat overshadows his eyes: the theatre is darkened, and the whole audience of some thousands is as still and all faces are as immovable as if they were painted on the walls; one might hear a pin drop in the remotest part of the theatre. Suddenly, as Hamlet retires somewhat farther from the front to the left, turning his back upon the audience, Horatio starts, exclaiming, 'Look, my lord, it comes!' pointing to the right, where, without the spectators being aware of its coming, the Ghost is seen standing motionless. At these words Garrick turns suddenly about, at the same instant starting with trembling knees two or three steps backward; his hat falls off; his arms, especially the left, are extended straight out, the left hand as high as his head, the right arm is more bent, and the hand lower, the fingers are spread far apart; and the mouth open; thus he stands, one foot far advanced before the other, in a graceful attitude, as if petrified, supported by his friends, who, from having seen the apparition before, are less unprepared for it, and who fear that he will fall to the ground; so expressive of horror is his mien that a shudder seized me again and again even before he began to speak; the almost fearful stillness of the audience which preceded this scene, and made one feel that he was hardly sure of himself, contributed, I suppose, not a little to the effect. At last Hamlet exclaims, not at the beginning, but at the end of an expiration, and with an agitated voice: 'Angels and ministers of grace, defend us!'—words which complete all that this scene could want to render it one of the greatest and most terrible. His eyes are fixed upon the Ghost even while he speaks with his friends, from whom he struggles to free himself. But at last, as they will not let him go, he turns his face to them, tears himself violently from them, and with a quickness which makes one shudder draws his sword upon them: 'I'll make a ghost of him that lets me,' he exclaims. That is enough for them. He then extends his sword towards the Ghost: 'Go on, I'll follow thee.' The Ghost leads the way. Hamlet, with the sword still held before him, stands motionless in order to gain a wider interval. At last, when the Ghost is no longer visible to the spectators, he begins slowly to follow it, pausing, and then advancing, with the sword still extended, his eyes fixed upon the Ghost, his hair all disordered, and still breathless, until he disappears behind the scenes. In the soliloquy, 'O that this too too solid flesh,' &c., the tears of most righteous sorrow for a virtuous father, for whom a lightminded mother not only wears no mourning, but feels no grief,—of all tears the hardest, perhaps, to be kept back, as they are the sole solace of a true man in such a conflict of duties,—these tears completely overpower Garrick. Of the words, 'So excellent a king,' the last is uttered inaudibly; it is caught only from the movement of the lips, which close upon the word firmly and with a quiver, in order to suppress an expression of grief which might seem unmanly. Tears of this kind, revealing the whole weight of grief and the manly soul suffering beneath it, fell without cessation through the soliloquy. At the close, righteous indignation mingled with the sorrow, and once as his arm fell forcibly, as if giving a blow, in order to emphasize a word expressive of his indignation, this word, unexpectedly to the hearers, is choked by tears and is uttered only after some moments, with the tears at the same time flowing.

In the celebrated soliloquy, 'To be or not to be,' Hamlet, having already begun to assume the madman, appears with hair all in disorder, locks of it hanging down over one shoulder, one of his black stockings has fallen down, allowing the white understocking to be visible, and a loop of his red garter hangs down midway of the calf of his leg. Thus he slowly comes to the front, wrapt in thought, his chin resting on his right hand, and the elbow of the right arm in the left hand: his looks are bent, with great dignity, sideways to the ground. Taking his right hand from his chin, but holding the arm still supported by his left hand, he utters the words, 'To be or not to be,' &c., softly, but, on account of the profound stillness, audible all over the house.

Before the soliloquy begins which follows the Ghost's disclosure to Hamlet, Garrick stands as if he were Hamlet himself, stupefied almost to utter ruin, and when at last the stupor gradually ceases, into which yawning graves, horror without compare, and the cry of a father's blood, have cast the noble soul, and when, his pained, stupefied sensibilities awakening to thought and speech, Hamlet collects himself for secret resolves, Shakespeare has taken care that every thought and word shall bear witness to the depth and the tumult from which they burst forth, and Garrick also takes care that every gesture shall tell, even to a deaf spectator, of the earnestness and weight of the accompanying words. One only line excepted, which, according to my feeling as it was then spoken by Garrick, could not have satisfied either the dumb or the blind. He uttered the physiognomical remark, which he also noted down in his tablets, 'That one may smile, and smile, and be a villain,' with a look and tone of petty mimickry as if he would represent the man who always smiled, and smiled, and yet was a villain. Upon the second representation, however, he pronounced these words entirely in accordance with my idea of them—namely, *with the tone of a well-considered note for immediate use.* The smile of the villain, to which Hamlet alludes, was in his case too serious on the one side and too horrible on the other to permit him to relieve himself in a soliloquy with a mimicking mockery; the lips which had so smiled must be taught seriousness by death at Hamlet's hands, and by death only, and the sooner the better.

BIBLIOGRAPHY ENTRY FOR RESEARCH PAPERS:

Lichtenberg, Georg Christoph. *Briefe aus England.* October, 1775. Translated in *A New Variorum Edition of Shakespeare.* Philadelphia, 1877. Excerpt in *Interpreting Hamlet,* ed. Russell E. Leavenworth. San Francisco, 1960.

FIRST FOOTNOTE:

* Georg Christoph Lichtenberg. *Briefe aus England* (Oct., 1775), translated in *A New Variorum Edition of Shakespeare* (Philadelphia, 1877), excerpt in *Interpreting Hamlet,* ed. Russell E. Leavenworth (San Francisco, 1960), pp. 38-40.

SUBSEQUENT FOOTNOTES:

    * Lichtenberg, *op. cit., IH,* p. ■■.
    * Lichtenberg, *Briefe aus England, IH,* p. ■■.
    * Lichtenberg, *IH,* p. ■■.

In place of "*IH*," "ed. Leavenworth" may be used in these subsequent-footnote forms.

JOHANN WOLFGANG VON GOETHE

ON

the Character of Hamlet

Goethe's Wilhelm Meisters Lehrjahre, *the writing of which dates from 1778, is a novel which had a tremendous influence on German fiction and an even more notable influence on* Hamlet *criticism. The extract below catches the hero, a Hamlet-like character in search of himself, at a moment when he feels he has finally reached an understanding of the play. The translation is Thomas Carlyle's,* Wilhelm Meister's Apprenticeship *and Travels,* Book IV, Chapter 13 (London, 1851).

CONCEIVE A PRINCE such as I have painted him, and that his father suddenly dies. Ambition and the love of rule are not the passions that inspire him. As a king's son, he would have been contented; but now he is first constrained to consider the difference which separates a sovereign from a subject. The crown was not hereditary; yet a longer possession of it by his father would have strengthened the pretensions of an only son, and secured his hopes of the succession. In place of this, he now beholds himself excluded by his uncle, in spite of specious promises, most probably forever. He is now poor in goods and favor, and a stranger in the scene which from youth he had looked upon as his inheritance. His temper here assumes its first mournful tinge. He feels that now he is not more, that he is less, than a private nobleman; he offers himself as the servant of every one; he is not courteous and condescending, he is needy and degraded.

"His past condition he remembers as a vanished dream. It is in vain that his uncle strives to cheer him, to present his situation in another point of view. The feeling of his nothingness will not leave him.

"The second stroke that came upon him wounded deeper, bowed still more. It was the marriage of his mother. The faithful tender son had yet a mother, when his father passed away. He hoped, in the company of his surviving noble-minded parent, to reverence the heroic form of the departed; but his mother too he loses, and it is something worse than death that robs him of her. The trustful image, which a good child loves to form of its parents, is gone. With the dead there is no help, on the living no hold. She also is a woman, and her name is Frailty, like that of all her sex.

"Now first does he feel himself completely bent and orphaned; and no happiness of life can repay what he has lost. Not reflective or sorrowful by nature, reflection and sorrow have become for him a heavy obligation. It is thus that we see him first enter on the scene. I do not think that I have mixed aught foreign with the piece, or overcharged a single feature of it."

Serlo looked at his sister, and said, "Did I give thee a false picture of our friend? He begins well; he has still many things to tell us, many to persuade us of." Wilhelm asseverated loudly, that he meant not to persuade, but to convince; he begged for another moment's patience.

"Figure to yourselves this youth," cried he, "this son of princes; conceive him vividly, bring his state before your eyes, and then observe him when he learns that his father's spirit walks; stand by him in the terrors of the night, when the venerable ghost itself appears before him. A horrid shudder passes over him; he speaks to the mysterious form; he sees it beckon him; he follows it, and hears. The fearful accusation of his uncle rings in his ears; the summons to revenge, and the piercing oft-repeated prayer, Remember me!

"And when the ghost has vanished, who is it that stands before us? A young hero panting for vengeance? A prince by birth, rejoicing to be called to punish the usurper of his crown? No! trouble and astonishment take hold of the solitary young man: he grows bitter against smiling villains, swears that he will not forget the spirit, and concludes with the significant ejaculation: —

> The time is out of joint: O cursed spite,
> That ever I was born to set it right!

"In these words, I imagine, will be found the key to Hamlet's whole procedure. To me it is clear that Shakespeare meant, in the present case, to represent the effects of a great action laid upon a soul unfit for the performance of it. In this view the whole piece seems to me to be composed. There is an oak-tree planted in a costly jar, which should have borne only pleasant flowers in its bosom; the roots expand, the jar is shivered.

"A lovely, pure, noble, and most moral nature, without the strength of nerve which forms a hero, sinks beneath a burden which it cannot bear and must not cast away. All duties are holy for him; the present is too hard. Impossibilities have been required of him; not in themselves impossibilities, but such for him. He winds, and turns, and torments himself; he advances and recoils; is ever put in mind, ever puts himself in mind; at last does all but lose his purpose from his thoughts; yet still without recovering his peace of mind."

BIBLIOGRAPHY ENTRY FOR RESEARCH PAPERS:

> Goethe, Johann Wolfgang von. *Wilhelm Meister's Apprenticeship*. 1796. Tr. Thomas Carlyle. Bk. IV, ch. 13. London, 1851. Excerpt in *Interpreting Hamlet*, ed. Russell E. Leavenworth. San Francisco, 1960.

FIRST FOOTNOTE:

> * J. W. von Goethe, *Wilhelm Meister's Apprenticeship*, 1796, tr. Thomas Carlyle, Bk. IV, ch. 13, excerpt in *Interpreting Hamlet*, ed. Russell E. Leavenworth (San Francisco, 1960), pp. 42-44.

SUBSEQUENT FOOTNOTES:

> * Goethe, *op. cit.*, IH, p. ■■.
> * Goethe, *Wilhelm Meister's Apprenticeship*, IH, p. ■.
> * Goethe, IH, p. ■■.

In place of "*IH*," "ed. Leavenworth" may be used in these subsequent-footnote forms.

SAMUEL TAYLOR COLERIDGE

ON

the Character of Hamlet

Coleridge (1772–1834)—poet, philosopher, lecturer and conver-
sationalist extraordinary—combined an unalloyed appreciation
of Shakespeare with remarkable gifts for digging beneath the
surfaces of the plays. His comments on Shakespeare consist largely
of notes for unwritten essays and lectures, and records of con-
versations; but collected together they make a sizable volume of
criticism. The volume titled Notes and Lectures upon Shakespeare
and the Old Dramatists *was first published in London in 1849,*
edited by Sara Coleridge. The brief selection here is from an
American collected edition.

NOTES AND LECTURES UPON SHAKESPEARE

I BELIEVE the character of Hamlet may be traced to Shakespeare's
deep and accurate science in mental philosophy. Indeed, that this character
must have some connection with the common fundamental laws of our
nature may be assumed from the fact that Hamlet has been the darling of
every country in which the literature of England has been fostered. In
order to understand him, it is essential that we should reflect on the constitution of our own minds. Man is distinguished from the brute animals
in proportion as thought prevails over sense: but in the healthy processes
of the mind, a balance is constantly maintained between the impressions
from outward objects and the inward operations of the intellect:—for if
there be an overbalance in the contemplative faculty, man thereby

becomes the creature of mere meditation, and loses his natural power of action. Now one of Shakespeare's modes of creating characters is to conceive any one intellectual or moral faculty in morbid excess, and then to place himself, Shakespeare, thus mutilated or diseased, under given circumstances. In Hamlet he seems to have wished to exemplify the moral necessity of a due balance between our attention to the objects of our senses, and our meditation on the working of our minds,—an *equilibrium* between the real and the imaginary worlds. In Hamlet this balance is disturbed: his thoughts and the images of his fancy are far more vivid than his actual perceptions, and his very perceptions, instantly passing through the *medium* of his contemplations, acquire, as they pass, a form and a colour not naturally their own. Hence we see a great, an almost enormous, intellectual activity, and a proportionate aversion to real action consequent upon it, with all its symptoms and accompanying qualities. This character Shakespeare places in circumstances, under which it is obliged to act on the spur of the moment:—Hamlet is brave and careless of death; but he vacillates from sensibility, and procrastinates from thought, and loses the power of action in the energy of resolve. Thus it is that this tragedy presents a direct contrast to that of Macbeth; the one proceeds with the utmost slowness, the other with a crowded and breathless rapidity.

The effect of this overbalance of the imaginative power is beautifully illustrated in the everlasting broodings and superfluous activities of Hamlet's mind, which, unseated from its healthy relation, is constantly occupied with the world within, and abstracted from the world without,—giving substance to shadows, and throwing a mist over all commonplace actualities. It is the nature of thought to be indefinite:—definiteness belongs to external imagery alone. Hence it is that the sense of sublimity arises, not from the sight of an outward object, but from the beholder's reflection upon it;—not from the sensuous impression, but from the imaginative reflex. Few have seen a celebrated waterfall without feeling something akin to disappointment: it is only subsequently that the image comes back full into the mind, and brings with it a train of grand or beautiful associations. Hamlet feels this; his senses are in a state of trance, and he looks upon external things as hieroglyphics. His soliloquy—

Oh! that this too, too solid flesh would melt, &c.

springs from that craving after the indefinite—for that which is not—which most easily besets men of genius; and the self-delusion common to this temper of mind is finely exemplified in the character which Hamlet gives of himself:—

—It cannot be
But I am pigeon-livered, and lack gall
To make oppression bitter.

He mistakes the seeing of his chains for the breaking of them, delays
action till action is of no use, and dies the victim of mere circumstance
and accident.

BIBLIOGRAPHY ENTRY FOR RESEARCH PAPERS:

> Coleridge, Samuel Taylor. "Notes and Lectures upon Shakes-
> peare and the Old Dramatists," in *Complete Works of Samuel
> Taylor Coleridge,* Vol. IV, ed. Shedd, New York, 1853, pp.
> 145-146. Excerpt in *Interpreting Hamlet,* ed. Russell E. Leaven-
> worth. San Francisco, 1960.

FIRST FOOTNOTE:

> * S. T. Coleridge, "Notes and Lectures upon Shakespeare and
> the Old Dramatists," excerpt in *Interpreting Hamlet,* ed. Russell
> E. Leavenworth (San Francisco, 1960), pp. 45-47.

SUBSEQUENT FOOTNOTES:

> * Coleridge, *op. cit., IH,* p. ■■.
> * Coleridge, *Notes and Lectures, IH,* p. ■■.
> * Coleridge, *IH,* p. ■■.

In place of *"IH,"* "ed. Leavenworth" may be used in these
subsequent-footnote forms.

WILLIAM HAZLITT

ON

Edmund Kean as Hamlet

William Hazlitt (1778–1830) was a critic, essayist, and lecturer who, like Coleridge, idolized Shakespeare and sought artistic grounds for the justification of his every word. Unlike Coleridge, however, Hazlitt took the trouble to write out his thoughts in the form of finished essays. The review below appeared first in the London Morning Chronicle, *March 14, 1814, and is reprinted from the* Collected Works *(London, 1903).*

HIGH AS Mr. Kean stood in our opinion before, we have no hesitation in saying, that he stands higher in it (and, we think, will in that of the public), from the powers displayed in this last effort. If it was less perfect as a whole, there were parts in it of a higher cast of excellence than any part of his Richard. We will say at once, in what we think his general delineation of the character wrong. It was too strong and pointed. There was often a severity, approaching to virulence, in the common observations and answers. There is nothing of this in Hamlet. He is, as it were, wrapped up in the cloud of his reflections, and only thinks aloud. There should therefore be no attempt to impress what he says upon others by any exaggeration of emphasis or manner, no talking at his hearers. There should be as much of the gentleman and scholar as possible infused into the part, and as little of the actor. A pensive air of sadness should sit unwillingly upon his brow, but no appearance of fixed and sullen gloom. He is full of 'weakness and melancholy,' but there is no harshness in his nature. Hamlet should be the most amiable of misanthropes. There is no one line in this play, which should be spoken like any one line in Richard; yet Mr. Kean did not appear to us to keep the two characters always distinct. He was least happy in the last scene with Guildenstern and Rosencrantz. In some of these more familiar scenes he displayed more energy than was requisite; and in others where it would have been appropriate, did not rise equal to the exigency of the occasion. In particular, the scene with Laertes, where he leaps into the grave, and utters the exclamation, ' 'Tis I, Hamlet the Dane,' had not the tumultuous and overpowering effect we expected from it. To point out the defects of Mr. Kean's performance of the part, is a less grateful but a much shorter task, than to enumerate the many striking beauties which he gave to it, both by the power of his action and by the true feeling of nature. His surprise when he first sees the Ghost, his eagerness and filial confidence in following it, the impressive pathos of his action and voice in addressing it, 'I'll call thee Hamlet, Father, Royal Dane,' were admirable.

Mr. Kean has introduced in this part a new reading, as it is called, which we think perfectly correct. In the scene where he breaks from his friends to obey the command of his father, he keeps his sword pointed behind him, to prevent them from following him, instead of holding it before him to protect him from the Ghost. The manner of his taking Guildenstern and Rosencrantz under each arm, under pretence of communicating his secret to them, had the finest effect, and was, we conceive, exactly in the spirit of the character. So was the suppressed tone of irony in which he ridicules those who gave ducats for his uncle's picture, though they would 'make mouths at him,' while his father lived. Whether the way in which Mr. Kean hesitates in repeating the first line of the speech in the interview with the player, and then, after several ineffectual attempts to recollect it, suddenly hurries on with it, 'The rugged Pyrrhus,' etc. is in perfect keeping, we have some doubts: but there was great ingenuity in the thought; and the spirit and the life of the execution was beyond every thing. Hamlet's speech in describing his own melancholy, his instructions to the players, and the soliloquy on death, were all delivered by Mr. Kean in a tone of fine, clear, and natural recitation. His pronunciation of the word 'contumely' in the last of these, is, we apprehend, not authorized by custom, or by the metre.

Both the closet scene with his mother, and his remonstrances to Ophelia, were highly impressive. If there had been less vehemence of effort in the latter, it would not have lost any of its effect. But whatever nice faults might be found in this scene, they were amply redeemed by the manner of his coming back after he has gone to the extremity of the stage, from a pang of parting tenderness to press his lips to Ophelia's hand. It had an electrical effect on the house. It was the finest commentary that was ever made on Shakespeare. It explained the character at once (as he meant it), as one of disappointed hope, of bitter regret, of affection suspended, not obliterated by the distractions of the scene around him! The manner in which Mr. Kean acted in the scene of the Play before the King and Queen was the most daring of any, and the force and animation which he gave to it, cannot be too highly applauded. Its extreme boldness 'bordered on the verge of all we hate,' and the effect it produced, was a test of the extraordinary powers of this extraordinary actor.

BIBLIOGRAPHY ENTRY FOR RESEARCH PAPERS:

Hazlitt, William. Review of Kean's performance as Hamlet. *Morning Chronicle,* March 14, 1814. *Collected Works.* London, 1903. In *Interpreting Hamlet,* ed. Russell E. Leavenworth. San Francisco, 1960.

FIRST FOOTNOTE:

    * William Hazlitt, review of Kean's performance as Hamlet, *Morning Chronicle,* March 14, 1814, *Collected Works* (London, 1903), in *Interpreting Hamlet,* ed. Russell E. Leavenworth (San Francisco, 1960), pp. 48-50.

SUBSEQUENT FOOTNOTES:

    * Hazlitt, *op. cit., IH,* p. ■■.
    * Hazlitt, on Kean's Hamlet, *IH,* p. ■■.
    * Hazlitt, *IH,* p. ■■.

In place of *"IH,"* "ed. Leavenworth" may be used in these subsequent-footnote forms.

JOHN FORSTER

ON

William Charles Macready as Hamlet

John Forster (1812–1876) was a drama critic for the London Examiner *as well as a literary historian and the noted biographer of Dickens and other writers. This essay is quoted (omitting the editor's footnotes) from* Dramatic Essays, John Forster and G. H. Lewes, *edited by William Archer (London, 1896), pp. 7-12.*

MR. MACREADY'S Hamlet is a noble and a beautiful performance. It is infinitely finer than it used to be, more subtle and various, multiplied and deepened in its lights and shadows, with its sudden and brilliant effects harmonised to the expression of profound feeling, lofty yet gentle, the grandest sustainment of imagination and sensibility we have ever witnessed on the stage. We considered Mr. Macready highly successful in this character before seeing him last Wednesday, yet he illustrated then what it is to study Shakespeare with a love unwearied by success. But genius may well be its own rival, for it has no other. We venture to think, without a shade of misgiving, that this performance was the noblest approach that the *stage* can present to Hamlet, as he exists in the wonderful creativeness of Shakespeare's fancy. Vivid delineations of moments of passion, we have seen equally fine, fragments of possibly superior beauty in the acting of the late Mr. Kean—but never such a grasp of thought, never such a sustained exhibition of single, profound, and enduring passion, cast in the yielding and varying mould of imagination. Mr. Macready was indeed the princely and heart-broken philosopher, the irresolute avenger, the friend of Horatio, the lover of Ophelia.

Hamlet is more than this, it is true; but we must recollect the palpable intervention of the stage. Mr. Macready cannot exhibit that which 'passeth show.' We try in vain to conceive of an actor that should present with effect the exact Hamlet of Shakespeare. There is that in it, considered deeply in the closet, with which eye, and tone, and gesture have nothing to do. Supposing we had an actor who could subdue all sense of his art, could consent to sacrifice all dramatic point, all severe effect, all brilliant antitheses of action,—who, with grace, wit, chivalrous and princely bearing, profound intellect, and a high faculty of imagination, could yet merge all these in a struggle of sensibility, of weakness, and of melancholy, and bear them with him about the stage, 'like sweet bells jangled, out of tune and harsh,'—suppose such an actor upon the stage, who, with these accomplishments, chooses to show them only in such a struggle, using them unconsciously, and to himself not to others—who abstracts himself from the audience, the actors, and the theatre, and, wrapped in a veil of subtle intellectual refinement, only, as it were, reflects aloud,—supposing, we say, all this, which might alone serve the realisation of the book Hamlet, of his solitary musings, his silent thoughts, his 'light-and-noise-abhorring ruminations,' we are more than half-inclined to think that his audience might fancy he had little business where he was, and take to hissing the pointless and unprecise performance. We do not say they would be wrong. The necessities of his art limit the sway of the actor. It is evident to us that Mr. Macready has as true and profound a sense of the character of Hamlet as it would be possible to entertain, and that where he sacrifices anything of this, he is only surrendering to his art as much as is necessary to secure its own triumph. He is the Hamlet of our fancies reconciled to our waking thoughts. For this we pardon an occasional over-display of the resources of his art, such as Hamlet might never have indulged.

The impassioned and heart-breaking sorrow with which Mr. Macready opened the play in the first soliloquy was a noble foundation for the entire structure of the character. This quick and passionate sensibility he never lost sight of, whether under the influence of supernatural visiting, or goaded by the desire of earthly vengeance. If Mr. Macready's performance had suddenly closed in the soliloquy of 'Oh! what a rogue and peasant slave am I,' at the words—

> *Bloody, bawdy villain!*
> *Remorseless, treacherous, lecherous,* KINDLESS *villain!*

we should have needed no better assurance of the power of his genius to cope with this wonderful character. Where he tempers this quick sensibility during his intercourse with Horatio, with Rosencrantz and Guildenstern, and with Ophelia, by the gentleness of the scholar, the schoolfellow, the friend and the lover, we feel the apologies that are due for the weaknesses and inconsistencies of Hamlet. In all this Mr. Macready, as it seemed to us, touched the highest point of perfection. His affection for Horatio and his reliance on his judgment were marked and exclusive, and throughout excellently sustained—in the third act more especially, during the progress of the Play-scene, and at last in the agonies of his death, when his care is chiefly for him. In his intercourse with Rosencrantz and Guildenstern, Mr. Macready happily kept up the quiet demeanour of conscious detection, of cool observance yet friendly familiarity, hitting one of the very nicest points in Hamlet, without the intrusion of any violence or severe abruptness. We shall never forget the tone with which he broke into 'What a piece of work is a man!' so earnest in its faith, and so passionate in its sorrow. Here is the true Hamlet. No wonder the shock of this outraged sense of good should drive him nearly mad. 'That ever he was born to set it right!' No wonder his purpose failed by 'thinking too precisely on the event!' No wonder that, even with his motive and his cue for action, he should remain indolent and undecided, 'unpregnant of his cause and can do nothing'— excess of thought absorbing his faculty of action. If ever this was expressed on the stage, it was expressed by Mr. Macready. If ever the subtle madness of Hamlet, which is not madness, and yet not an assumption, which might rather stand for the over-subtle workings of the intellect, for the awful though quiet action of the *sources* of wit and madness, passing through the brain alone, and witnessed only in changes of metaphysical emotion, and in the dejected ruins of a noble presence and universal accomplishment, 'blasted by ecstasy'—if ever this was presented upon the stage, it was presented by this great actor. His scene with Ophelia was truly exquisite. It was the realisation of Mr. Lamb's opinion, that the scene is 'a profound artifice of love, to alienate Ophelia by affected discourtesies, so to prepare her mind for the breaking off of that loving intercourse, which can no longer find a place amidst business so serious as that which he has to do.' It was indeed not alienation, but distraction purely, and such it made itself felt by her—not anger, but grief assuming the appearance of anger—love awkwardly counterfeiting hate, 'as sweet countenances when they try to frown.'

In the scene with the Ghost, Mr. Macready still sustained the burthen of this surpassing character. Nothing could be more true than his restless walk up and down on the platform before the terrible appearance, or than the solemn and awful effect of his adjuration afterwards. He sinks before that preternatural visitation. The burst of human energy he gives way to, when his friends endeavour to oppose him, was, as a momentary wild relief, and in the bold and awful contrast into which it throws the 'Go on, I'll follow thee,' extremely grand and effective. The variety, the power, and the brilliant animation of the play-scene were daring and fine to the last degree. His manner of turning from Horatio, as he hears the approaching footsteps of the King—'They are coming to the play, I must be idle,'—his quick and salient walk up and down the front of the stage, waving his handkerchief as if in idle and gay indifference, but ill concealing, at that instant, the sense of an approaching triumph—was one of those things Shakespeare himself would have done had he acted Hamlet. The whole scene was masterly; its bitterness fearful—'your Majesty and we that have free souls, it touches *us* not!'—and its energy quite appalling. Mr. Macready made us feel, what is literally the case with Hamlet, that his power exhausts itself here. His attitude as the King hurries off, was a noble commentary on that subtle purpose of Shakespeare. As he stands there, in the flushed excitement of a triumph, we feel that he is satisfied with the discovery alone. It was an earnest to Horatio and to all, that that confirmation of his suspicions was all he sought, that the success of his experiment was his greatest aim, and that to *act* upon it was as far from his thoughts as ever. In the same exquisite apprehensiveness of Shakespeare was the loud bullying of himself to thrust down the thought which would at once have disabled his act, as he rushed to stab through the arras,—and his fine, breathless change of tone, as he rushes back with 'Is it the King?' This scene, and his conduct to his mother throughout, was marked by profound discrimination.

If we might hazard an objection to a performance so truly great as this, it would be to the delivery of the celebrated Soliloquy on Death, as too quiet and deliberate, and to the reception and intercourse with the players, as not sufficiently familiar. Why did not Mr. Macready recognise them cordially, at least his 'old friend,'—for does not Hamlet shake hands with his schoolfellows before the players enter, and assign as his reason, 'lest my extent to the players, which, I tell you, must show fairly outward, should more appear like entertainment than yours?' He has his reason for this familiarity, as he has reasons for all he does, and for all he does not do.

This praise of ours, which we have meant to be as enthusiastic as it is sincere, we have yet felt to be inadequate to the occasion. We conclude as we began by characterising Mr. Macready's performance of Hamlet as the most perfect achievement of the modern stage—in depth, in originality, in truth, in beauty, and in grandeur of sustainment. Its expression is altogether equal to its conception.

BIBLIOGRAPHY ENTRY FOR RESEARCH PAPERS:

Forster, John. Review of Macready's performance as Hamlet. *The Examiner,* October 11, 1835. From William Archer, ed., *Dramatic Essays, John Forster and G. H. Lewes.* London, 1896. In *Interpreting Hamlet,* ed. Russell E. Leavenworth. San Francisco, 1960.

FIRST FOOTNOTE:

* John Forster, review of Macready's performance as Hamlet, *The Examiner,* October 11, 1835, from William Archer, ed., *Dramatic Essays, John Forster and G. H. Lewes* (London, 1896), in *Interpreting Hamlet,* ed. Russell E. Leavenworth (San Francisco, 1960), pp. 51-55.

SUBSEQUENT FOOTNOTES:

* Forster, *op. cit., IH* p. ■■.
* Forster, on Macready's Hamlet, *IH,* p. ■■.
* Forster, *IH,* p. ■■.

In place of *"IH,"* "ed. Leavenworth" may be used in the subsequent-footnote forms. If your reader might assume that *The Examiner* is published in San Francisco, you can insert "London," in the bibliography entry or footnote after *The Examiner.*

WILLIAM WINTER

ON

Sir Henry Irving as Hamlet

<hr />

William Winter (1836–1917), historian and biographer of stage personalities, was the drama critic on the New York Tribune *for many years. This review of Sir Henry Irving's performance in New York in 1883 is quoted from Winter's* Henry Irving *(New York, 1885), pp. 84–96.*

HAMLET

NOVEMBER 27th.—Mr. Irving has crowned his noble series of perform-ances in this capital with his original, extraordinary, and deeply impressive impersonation of *Hamlet.* This was given last night before a numerous audience, enthusiastic but also thoughtful; and it was viewed with eager attention, sometimes with surprise, sometimes with delight, once in a while with consternation, more often with cordial plaudits, always with profound respect. Miss Ellen Terry appeared as *Ophelia,* and she dignified and adorned the occasion by a performance so radiant in beauty, so exquisite in grace, and so tender and lovely in pathos that simply "it paragons descrip-tion and wild fame." The sublime tragedy of "Hamlet" was set upon the stage in scenery remarkable for the rich quality of its sombre tone, and its several characters, judiciously distributed to suitable actors, were, with little exception, personated in a competent and effective manner. The night was a golden one, and it will long abide in the pleased and grateful remembrance of this community.

The character of *Hamlet* appears to be chosen, by common consent, as furnishing the standard by which every actor should be judged, with reference to his claim to a place in the front rank of the dramatic profession. It is not, indeed, so difficult a part to act as either *Macbeth* or *King Lear*— since it requires neither the lurid, overwhelming imagination of the fiend-driven murderer, nor the vast torrent of thwarted tenderness and shattered senile sensibility essential to the afflicted, insane monarch; neither does it exact such prodigious physical resource and exertion as are demanded in these characters. But it is a majestic and beautiful personality, richly fraught with intellect, sensibility, refinement, and grace, and displayed under circumstances of impressive mystery and romance; its thoroughly adequate representation is possible only to a nature of exquisite sensibility, hallowed by the charm of genius, matured by the experience of suffering, and dominated by an intellect that perfectly controls alike itself and the methods, expedients, and accomplishments of dramatic art; and hence it is reasoned that the actor who can endear himself to the world in the character of *Hamlet* is necessarily a great actor. In England, where they accept a new *Hamlet* about once every twenty years, and where the mantle of Garrick has fallen, successively, on Kemble, Kean, Young, Macready, and Fechter, Mr. Irving's embodiment of *Hamlet* was long since crowned with the laurel of renown. He has now placed this noble work for the first time before the public of New-York, and so at length the corner-stone of his great reputation stands fully disclosed.

The performance is one of the richest and most suggestive that have been presented on the contemporary stage, and one of the most difficult to analyse and describe. In ideal—in fidelity to Shakespeare's conception—it is almost entirely great. The proportion, indeed, is not strictly maintained. Certain attributes of the character are more amply, boldly, and truly presented than others. The feeling exceeds the mentality. The bitterness is more prominent than the charm. Of that lucid interval of lofty poise—that *Hamlet* who shines forth in the speech, to *Horatio*, about "passion's slave" and "fortune's finger"—there is scarcely a trace. But the *Hamlet* who looked into *Ophelia's* eyes as if he would read her very soul; the *Hamlet* who seemed to her "like sweet bells jangled, out of tune and harsh"; the *Hamlet* who thought he could be bounded in a nutshell and count himself king of infinite space, but that he had bad dreams; the *Hamlet* through the temple of whose soul streamed a hideous rout of foul and frightful shapes; the *Hamlet* who said "You would not think how ill all's here, about my heart"—this is thought, felt, understood, and interpreted with profound earnestness and remarkable beauty. And this is enough. The blemishes will not invalidate this. They are in the method and not in the substance. Yet they exist: for Mr. Irving has applied to *Hamlet* the same "natural" treatment and the same colloquial style that he employs for *Mathias* in "The Bells." They are, in that character, consummate; but they sometimes seemed enfeebled and inadequate, in contact with the towering magnitude of Shakespeare's thought and the stately pomp and sonority of his verse. Mr. Irving's *Hamlet* is great in ideal; but his expression of that ideal could be made, in some ways, more massive and more splendid. It is upon the substance, and not the manner, of the work, accordingly, that reflection will first repose and longest dwell.

The universal tendency of the human mind is to summarise. Almost every person likes to hear, and likes to make, comprehensive and positive statements upon all subjects of knowledge or thought. Hundreds of writers —pursuant to this usual impulse—have assumed to define *Hamlet*. No writer has entirely succeeded in doing it. There are subjects that cannot be summarised, and this is one of them. Much lucid and splendid thought upon it has been uttered, because many of the greatest minds which have existed within the last two hundred years have been attracted, aroused and inspired by its glory and its mystery. But the final elucidating word has never yet been found. Much, to be sure, is clear. There can be no doubt about the general drift. But what was left a secret remains a secret still. When the human soul and its relations to the universe are entirely understood, *Hamlet* will be entirely understood—and not till then.

Without presuming to undertake to define *Hamlet*, however, it may yet be said that certain illuminative facts about him are positively known. He is a prince, in a royal court; noble, gentle, and of perfect breeding; "the expectancy and rose of the fair state." He is thirty years old. He has been educated at the most famous university in Europe. He has been reared in the Catholic faith. He has lived a life, not of action but of thought. His intellect, vast, far-reaching, and conscious of its power, has been cultivated, by intense thinking, to the most extreme limit, so that now the idea of anything—no matter what—is more real to him than the thing itself; and he has lost the faculty, if ever he had it, of practical, continuous action, even while living at the height of mental activity and in a fever of destructive excitement. It seems to have been Shakespeare's intention to present a divinely gifted man, as representative of all that is highest and best in human nature; to place him at the pinnacle of worldly fortune; to make him great in himself and in his state; to give him honour, genius, love, friendship, power, wealth, popularity, every blessing; and then to overwhelm him with affliction, developing a latent strain of misery and taint of madness in his organisation, and thus, on the largest canvas and with the boldest colours ever used by mortal hand, to paint human life in the aspect of total failure.

For this, surely, is what the tragedy of "Hamlet" seems to say. However much mankind may close its eyes to the truth, the truth nevertheless remains, that mortality is a condition not of happiness but of sorrow. The protracted and cruel pain with which it begins, the uncertainty with which it is attended, the trouble with which it is burdened, the mystery with which it is surrounded, the mutability with which it is cursed, and the misery in which it ends unite to make it, for all who look beneath the surface, infinitely pathetic. Some of its pleasures, indeed, are very great; but all of them are evanescent. Everything breaks and dies—everything but memory, and that is the cruelest affliction of all. Poor Byron said the whole sad truth in four lines:

> "*Count o'er the joys thine hours have seen,*
> *Count o'er thy days from anguish free,*
> *And know, whatever thou hast been,*
> *'Tis something better not to be.*"

All this is implied in Mr. Irving's impersonation. He never misses the subtlety of the character. The misery of *Hamlet* is inherent misery. It is not, to any considerable extent, caused by his personal circumstances. "The uses of this world" are to him "weary, stale, flat, and unprofitable" long before he knows that his father was murdered, or that his mother's new husband is the murderer, or that his father's spirit is abroad. Grief at the death of his father, bitter resentment of his mother's ensuing hasty nuptials, dim suspicion of his uncle's wickedness, and presentiment and foreboding as to the love of *Ophelia* are the only sources of his wretchedness that can be distinctly stated. These are in part explanatory of his condition; but only in part. For the secret, profound cause of the overwhelming weight of his misery we must look into his soul. Self-disgust and disgust at the human race are properties of his mind. A sense of the awful grandeur and mystery of the universe and of the angelic and even godlike attributes that appertain to the nature of man abide with him, it is true; yet as he looks forth upon that universe he sees only "a foul and pestilent congregation of vapours"; and as he looks upon mankind he sees only the "quintessence of dust." Suicide has long been a familiar subject in his thoughts, and he would destroy his own life but that self-murder is forbidden, and—more important still—but that greater misery may await the soul, beyond the grave, than that which it suffers here.

Hamlet is the very genius of sorrow; born so, and not made so; and whatever his circumstances might have been he would have reacted on them to afflicting if not to tragical results. Upon this nature, thus saturated with gloom and predestined to anguish, falls the shock of a supernatural visitation and a heartrending disclosure of cruel and loathsome crime; and thus the will, already irresolute from baffled thinking and enfeebling grief, is shattered; the mind drifts from its moorings, and steadfast action becomes impossible. *Hamlet* is in a real delirium—to which Mr. Irving gives prominent and thrilling expression—after the disappearance of the *Ghost,* in the scene upon "the dreadful summit of the cliff"; and he then has the impulse to assume to be insane (in which device it is singular and significant to note that the *Ghost* appears to concur), because he is already deranged, and feels it, and wishes, in a certain blind way, to conceal it. He has no plan in his madness. Whenever there is an opportunity to act he will reason it away. He does not really wish to plunge the soul of *Claudius* into hell; but he can persuade himself to think, for the moment, that even this is needful, in order to free himself from the necessity of killing him, then and there, in the prayer scene. He can feel no personal experience without presently making it into a generalisation. This shattered condition—this incertitude —this desolate, drifting plight—is thoroughly realised in Mr. Irving's embodiment; and this is *Hamlet.*

Charles Knight's theory, that the play commonly referred to as "the old Hamlet" was, in fact, Shakespeare's "Hamlet" as it stood when first written (probably in 1589), and as it stands in the quarto piratically published in 1603, is a sagacious theory. The first authentic draft is the quarto of 1604; and—as readers doubtless know—it is from a comparison of this, and of the folio print of 1623, with the piratical copy, that Shakespeare scholars gain a peculiar knowledge of the astonishing growth of Shakespeare's mind, and, especially, derive instruction as to his drift in this tragedy. This drift was far more definitely expressed at first, but in a manner far less poetical, philosophical, eloquent, and profound. Great emphasis was laid on the madness of *Hamlet.* The *Queen* was distinctly declared to be innocent of complicity in the murder of her first husband. *Hamlet* himself was made more comprehensible every way—being less heavily freighted with the "large discourse of reason, looking before and after," less reflective upon mankind, and, especially, less interpenetrated with embittering sorrow. The lesson learned from this research, as applied to the acting of *Hamlet,* is that the character should be deduced from the play as it stands in its mature form; that, while the Prince must be presented as a man whose soul and body are steeped in hopeless misery, and who is sustained by proud, scornful, bitter, incessant, feverish, intellectual power, —the restless, terrible excitement of a great brain and heart surcharged with irremediable woe,—he must yet be presented with a certain vagueness. It is a great excellence of Mr. Irving's embodiment of *Hamlet* that it so presents him.

Observant persons who have ever heard Mr. Irving's recital of Hood's poem of "The Dream of Eugene Aram" had then a rare opportunity of studying his peculiar method of execution—which again forces itself upon attention in his performance of *Hamlet.* He begins with repose. His level speaking is clear, measured, even, precise, and always steadily effective. Soon his nervous forces become excited; the imagination, working upon the feelings, throws the whole system into a tremor of emotion; and thereupon both his walk and his enunciation are, in a peculiar way (peculiar and not disagreeable), constricted, in some slight degree, by a sort of inflexibility. He now moves a little stiffly; his words are spoken with monosyllabic ejaculation, and with an occasional cadence. At moments his tone is indistinct. The character and the feeling have obtained control of the man, and his intellectual will is forcing the man to become representative and expressive of them. If the character and the feeling be weird, grimly grotesque, or afflictively passionate, the intellectual will of the actor splendidly predominates over all his functions and makes him superlatively true and touchingly sympathetic. If the character and the feeling be stately, spiritualised, classical, philosophic, expressed within the formalism and inflexible lines of verse, and exacting of a body in which absolute symmetry is to be shown with absolute grace, the emotion of the actor responds less readily to his will, or does not yield at all, but carries all before it; and that which ought to be perfect in form and held in supreme poise with the iron grip of intellectual power is shattered and diffused, like a coruscation of ever-changing fires; and the eye knows not where to rest. This is shown in his embodiment of *Hamlet,* and this is why so many students of the work constantly speak of single features in it and not of the work as a whole. There are parts of *Hamlet* to which Mr. Irving's temperament and method are exactly fitted. No actor was ever truer or finer than he in denotement of the blending of assumed madness with involuntary derangement—the forlorn state of a wild, unsettled mind, protecting itself by simulated wildness. No actor ever better expressed the bitterness and sarcasm of a sweet nature, outraged, shocked, and turned back upon itself. In the play scene, in the ensuing colloquy with the two spaniel courtiers, as in the first talk with them, and in the last ghost scene, Mr. Irving's *Hamlet* is at its best; and its best is exceedingly beautiful. There was not a perfect correspondence between the actor's ideal of Shakespeare's conception and the actor's faculties of expressing it. There are defects of execution. But viewed as an ideal Mr. Irving's *Hamlet* is profoundly true on the side of the emotions; rightly saturated with sorrow; touched with glittering scorn and pathetic bitterness; tainted, as in Shakespeare's page, with the morbid tinge of mental disease; and, above all, and in spite of irregularities of form and excess of impulse over will, it is fused by passionate intensity into one continuous, fluent strain of vital personification.

Abstractly considered, however, what does it signify whether *Hamlet* is a character who feigns madness, or who really is mad? whether *Hamlet* loves *Ophelia,* or has ceased to love her? whether *Hamlet* has really seen his dead father's spirit, or a devil in that shape, or has imagined a vocal apparition that he never saw at all? whether his mother was privy to the murder of her husband, or guiltless of participation in that hideous crime? What signify any or all questions about the matter—unless the experience of *Hamlet* be viewed as something germane to the experience of every individual of the human race? If nothing more is to be considered than cleverness in acting—the adroit treatment of mooted points—sonority in soliloquies —flexibility in dialogue—grace or wildness of demeanour—felicity of stage-business—taste in dress—we may as well descant on the soap bubbles that a child blows from its pipe, at the nursery window. The important thing is to grasp *Hamlet's* experience as a whole, to absorb it into our knowledge, to bring it home to our own hearts; and surely the actor who enables us to accomplish this result, or who largely helps us toward it, has succeeded in *Hamlet,* no matter what, to individual taste, may be the defects of his technical mechanism. The execution, to be sure, is the art of acting. Drama being, first of all, for the eye, it is not so much what you do as how you do it that is your potent element of victory. Signor Salvini's embodiment of *Othello,* for example, is a great piece of acting, and one that exercises a prodigious power over an audience, although to a considerable extent it is a demonstrable perversion of Shakespeare. Mrs. Pritchard was esteemed, in the eighteenth century, a wonderful actress of *Lady Macbeth,* although she had never read the tragedy of "Macbeth," but only knew the part that she had to act; and Dr. Johnson called her an "inspired idiot." Her ideal may have been wrong; her execution, obviously, was magnificent. No thinker will deny or undervalue the prodigious influence of the art of expression in these matters. Yet what you do is also of great importance. In the last analysis of the subject, looking toward what remains with the spectator of a dramatic performance, it, indeed, transcends all the rest, being an element of permanent worth and an abiding result. A man who acts greatly is, doubtless, a great actor, without reference to what it is that his acting is specifically designed to exhibit; but the man who acts a great part, like *Hamlet,* so as to put us into possession of it, has accomplished more, and risen to a higher intellectual station, than is possible to even the most perfect executant. This is Mr. Irving's victory—and it is a brilliant one; unequivocal; permanent; not to be denied; and safe beyond the reach of disparagement.

The character of *Ophelia,* when first it dawns upon the apprehension of a reader of the tragedy of "Hamlet," appears to be all that is lovely. Its lack of strength is not perceived until the observer reflects that strength also is an element of loveliness in woman. *Ophelia* is exquisitely beautiful, soft, innocent, trustful, and fond. She loves with her whole heart—but her heart is neither resolute nor passionate. She instantly yields to the first touch of opposition and she is broken by the first blow of adversity. That blow, indeed, it must be admitted, is a heavy one—for it is her affrighted perception of what, in *Hamlet,* her lover, she can regard only as madness. Her description, to *Polonius,* of the visitation that she has received from the Prince is surely one of the most significant passages in the tragedy, with reference both to herself and him. *Hamlet* uses no guile with *Ophelia.* To others he may put on "an antic disposition"; to her he is himself. And the meaning of that deplorable spectacle is that, with everything else that has suffered shipwreck in the life of *Hamlet,* love also is destroyed and henceforth will exist only as a memory—now passionate, now meekly and mutely woful, but always agonising and bitter: for *Hamlet's* gaze has pierced through the loveliness of *Ophelia* to the frailness beneath it, and beneath all loveliness, and he knows that for him there is no dependence on a woman's heart and no refuge in love. His mind, in receiving its consecration to vengeance, has likewise received its death-blow from the spiritual world. *Ophelia,* incapable at any time of fully understanding *Hamlet,* does understand that his mind is distracted and that his love is dead; and this, doubtless, is the beginning of her own mental derangement, subsequently developed by the cruelty of *Hamlet's* rebuke and by the calamitous death of her father, slain by her frantic lover's hand. *Ophelia,* then, is an image or personification of innocent, delicious, feminine youth and beauty, and she passes before us in the two phases of sanity and delirium. Miss Ellen Terry presented her in this way. The embodiment is fully within her reach, and it is one of the few unmistakably perfect creations with which dramatic art has illumined literature and adorned the stage. Miss Terry was born to play such a part and she is perfect in it. There is no other word for such an achievement.

BIBLIOGRAPHY ENTRY FOR RESEARCH PAPERS:

Winter, William. "Hamlet," review of Irving's performance as Hamlet. New York *Tribune,* November 27, 1883. From his *Henry Irving.* New York, 1885. In *Interpreting Hamlet,* ed. Russell E. Leavenworth. San Francisco, 1960.

FIRST FOOTNOTE:

* William Winter, "Hamlet," review of Irving's performance as Hamlet, New York *Tribune,* November 27, 1883, from his *Henry Irving* (New York, 1885), in *Interpreting Hamlet,* ed. Russell E. Leavenworth (San Francisco, 1960), pp. 56-63.

SUBSEQUENT FOOTNOTES:

* Winter, *op. cit., IH,* p. ■■.
* Winter, "Hamlet," *IH,* p. ■■.
* Winter, *IH,* p. ■■.

In place of *"IH,"* "ed. Leavenworth" may be used in these subsequent-footnote forms.

GEORGE BERNARD SHAW

ON

Sir Johnston Forbes-Robertson as Hamlet

George Bernard Shaw (1856–1950) was well established both as a critic of music, drama, and society, and as a famous play-wright when he wrote this review of Sir Johnston Forbes-Robert-son's production of Hamlet *for the London* Saturday Review, *October 2, 1897.*

HAMLET

THE Forbes Robertson* 'Hamlet' at the Lyceum is, very unexpectedly at that address, really not at all unlike Shakespear's play of the same name. I am quite certain I saw Reynaldo in it for a moment; and possibly I may have seen Voltimand and Cornelius; but just as the time for their scene arrived, my eye fell on the word 'Fortinbras' in the programme, which so amazed me that I hardly know what I saw for the next ten minutes. Ophelia, instead of being a strenuously earnest and self-possessed young lady giving a concert and recitation for all she was worth, was mad— actually mad. The story of the play was perfectly intelligible, and quite took the attention of the audience off the principal actor at moments. What is the Lyceum coming to? Is it for this that Sir Henry Irving has invented a whole series of original romantic dramas, and given the credit of them without a murmur to the immortal bard whose profundity (as exemplified in the remark that good and evil are mingled in our natures) he has just been pointing out to the inhabitants of Cardiff, and whose

---

* [Shaw and Forbes-Robertson differed as to the hyphen in the actor's name.]

works have been no more to him than the word-quarry from which he has hewn and blasted the lines and titles of masterpieces which are really all his own? And now, when he has created by these means a reputation for Shakespear, he no sooner turns his back for a moment on London than Mr. Forbes Robertson competes with him on the boards of his own theatre by actually playing off against him the authentic Swan of Avon. Now if the result had been the utter exposure and collapse of that impostor, poetic justice must have proclaimed that it served Mr. Forbes Robertson right. But alas! the wily William, by literary tricks which our simple Sir Henry has never quite understood, has played into Mr. Forbes Robertson's hands so artfully that the scheme is a prodigious success. The effect of this success, coming after that of Mr. Alexander's experiment with a Shakespearean version of 'As You Like It,' makes it almost probable that we shall presently find managers vieing with each other in offering the public as much of the original Shakespearean stuff as possible, instead of, as heretofore, doing their utmost to reassure us that everything that the most modern resources can do to relieve the irreducible minimum of tedium inseparable from even the most heavily cut acting version will be lavished on their revivals. It is true that Mr. Beerbohm Tree still holds to the old scepticism, and calmly proposes to insult us by offering us Garrick's puerile and horribly caddish knockabout farce of "Katherine and Petruchio" for Shakespear's 'Taming of the Shrew'; but Mr. Tree, like all romantic actors, is incorrigible on the subject of Shakespear.

Mr. Forbes Robertson is essentially a classical actor, the only one, with the exception of Mr. Alexander, now established in London management. What I mean by classical is that he can present a dramatic hero as a man whose passions are those which have produced the philosophy, the poetry, the art, and the statecraft of the world, and not merely those which have produced its weddings, coroner's inquests, and executions. And that is just the sort of actor that Hamlet requires. A Hamlet who only understands his love for Ophelia, his grief for his father, his vindictive hatred of his uncle, his fear of ghosts, his impulse to snub Rosencrantz and Guildenstern, and the sportsman's excitement with which he lays the 'mouse-trap' for Claudius, can, with sufficient force or virtuosity of execution, get a great reputation in the part, even though the very intensity of his obsession by these sentiments (which are common not only to all men but to many animals), shows that the characteristic side of Hamlet, the side that differentiates him from Fortinbras, is absolutely outside the actor's consciousness. Such a reputation is the actor's, not Hamlet's. Hamlet is not a man in whom 'common humanity' is raised by great vital energy to a heroic pitch, like Coriolanus or Othello. On the contrary, he is a man in whom the common personal passions are so superseded by wider and rarer interests, and so discouraged by a degree of critical self-consciousness which makes the practical efficiency of the instinctive man on the lower plane impossible to him, that he finds the duties dictated by conventional revenge and ambition as disagreeable a burden as commerce is to a poet. Even his instinctive sexual impulses offend his intellect; so that when he meets the woman who excites them he invites her to join him in a bitter and scornful criticism of their joint absurdity, demanding 'What should such fellows as I do crawling between heaven and earth?' 'Why would'st thou be a breeder of sinners?' and so forth, all of which is so completely beyond the poor girl that she naturally thinks him mad. And, indeed, there is a sense in which Hamlet is insane; for he trips over the mistake which lies on the threshold of intellectual self-consciousness: that of bringing life to utilitarian or Hedonistic tests, thus treating it as a means instead of an end. Because Polonius is 'a foolish prating knave,' because Rosencrantz and Guildenstern are snobs, he kills them as remorselessly as he might kill a flea, showing that he has no real belief in the superstitious reason which he gives for not killing himself, and in fact anticipating exactly the whole course of the intellectual history of Western Europe until Schopenhauer found the clue that Shakespear missed. But to call Hamlet mad because he did not anticipate Schopenhauer is like calling Marcellus mad because he did not refer the Ghost to the Psychical Society. It is in fact not possible for any actor to represent Hamlet as mad. He may (and generally does) combine some notion of his own of a man who is the creature of affectionate sentiment with the figure drawn by the lines of Shakespear; but the result is not a madman, but simply one of those monsters produced by the imaginary combination of two normal species, such as sphinxes, mermaids, or centaurs. And this is the invariable resource of the instinctive, imaginative, romantic actor. You will see him weeping bucketsful of tears over Ophelia, and treating the players, the gravedigger, Horatio, Rosencrantz and Guildenstern as if they were mutes at his own funeral. But go and watch Mr. Forbes Robertson's Hamlet seizing delightedly on every opportunity for a bit of philosophic discussion or artistic recreation to escape from the 'cursed spite' of revenge and love and other common troubles; see how he brightens up when the players come; how he tries to talk philosophy with Rosencrantz and Guildenstern the moment they come into the room; how he stops on his country walk with Horatio to lean over the churchyard wall and draw out the gravedigger whom he sees

singing at his trade; how even his fits of excitement find expression in
declaiming scraps of poetry; how the shock of Ophelia's death relieves
itself in the fiercest intellectual contempt for Laertes's ranting, whilst an
hour afterwards, when Laertes stabs him, he bears no malice for that at
all, but embraces him gallantly and comradely; and how he dies as we
forgive everything to Charles II. for dying, and makes 'the rest is silence'
a touchingly humorous apology for not being able to finish his business.
See all that; and you have seen a true classical Hamlet. Nothing half
so charming has been seen by this generation. It will bear seeing again
and again.

And please observe that this is not a cold Hamlet. He is none of
your logicians who reason their way through the world because they
cannot feel their way through it: his intellect is the organ of his passion:
his eternal self-criticism is as alive and thrilling as it can possibly be.
The great soliloquy—no: I do NOT mean 'To be or not to be': I mean
the dramatic one, 'O what a rogue and peasant slave am I!'—is as passionate in its scorn of brute passion as the most bullnecked affirmation or
sentimental dilution of it could be. It comes out so without violence: Mr.
Forbes Robertson takes the part quite easily and spontaneously. There is
none of that strange Lyceum intensity which comes from the perpetual
struggle between Sir Henry Irving and Shakespear. The lines help Mr.
Forbes Robertson instead of getting in his way at every turn, because he
wants to play Hamlet, and not to slip into his inky cloak a changeling of
quite another race. We may miss the craft, the skill double-distilled by
constant peril, the subtlety, the dark rays of heat generated by intense
friction, the relentless parental tenacity and cunning with which Sir Henry
nurses his own pet creations on Shakespearean food like a fox rearing its
litter in the den of a lioness; but we get light, freedom, naturalness,
credibility, and Shakespear. It is wonderful how easily everything comes
right when you have the right man with the right mind for it—how the
story tells itself, how the characters come to life, how even the failures in
the cast cannot confuse you, though they may disappoint you. And Mr.
Forbes Robertson has certainly not escaped such failures, even in his own
family. I strongly urge him to take a hint from Claudius and make a real
ghost of Mr. Ian Robertson at once; for there is really no use in going
through that scene night after night with a Ghost who is so solidly, com-
fortably and dogmatically alive as his brother. The voice is not a bad
voice; but it is the voice of a man who does not believe in ghosts. Moreover, it is a hungry voice, not that of one who is past eating. There is
an indescribable little complacent drop at the end of every line which no

sooner calls up the image of purgatory by its words than by its smug elocution it convinces us that this particular penitent is cosily warming his shins and toasting his muffin at the flames instead of expiating his bad acting in the midst of them. His aspect and bearing are worse than his recitations. He beckons Hamlet away like a beadle summoning a timid candidate for the post of junior footman to the presence of the Lord Mayor. If I were Mr. Forbes Robertson I would not stand that from any brother: I would cleave the general ear with horrid speech at him first. It is a pity; for the Ghost's part is one of the wonders of the play. And yet, until Mr. Courtenay Thorpe divined it the other day, nobody seems to have had a glimpse of the reason why Shakespear would not trust any one else with it, and played it himself. The weird music of that long speech which should be the spectral wail of a soul's bitter wrong crying from one world to another in the extremity of its torment, is invariably handed over to the most squaretoed member of the company, who makes it sound, not like Rossetti's 'Sister Helen,' or even, to suggest a possible heavy treatment, like Mozart's statue-ghost, but like Chambers's Information for the People.

Still, I can understand Mr. Ian Robertson, by sheer force of a certain quality of sententiousness in him, overbearing the management into casting him for the Ghost. What I cannot understand is why Miss Granville was cast for the Queen. It is like setting a fashionable modern mandolinist to play Haydn's sonatas. She does her best under the circumstances; but she would have been more fortunate had she been in a position to refuse the part.

On the other hand, several of the impersonations are conspicuously successful. Mrs. Patrick Campbell's Ophelia is a surprise. The part is one which has hitherto seemed incapable of progress. From generation to generation actresses have, in the mad scene, exhausted their musical skill, their ingenuity in devising fantasias in the language of flowers, and their intensest powers of portraying anxiously earnest sanity. Mrs. Patrick Campbell, with that complacent audacity of hers which is so exasperating when she is doing the wrong thing, this time does the right thing by making Ophelia really mad. The resentment of the audience at this outrage is hardly to be described. They long for the strenuous mental grasp and attentive coherence of Miss Lily Hanbury's conception of maiden lunacy; and this wandering, silly, vague Ophelia, who no sooner catches an emotional impulse than it drifts away from her again, emptying her voice of its tone in a way that makes one shiver, makes them horribly uncomfortable. But the effect on the play is conclusive. The shrinking discomfort of the

King and Queen, the rankling grief of Laertes, are created by it at once; and the scene, instead of being a pretty interlude coming in just when a little relief from the inky cloak is welcome, touches us with a chill of the blood that gives it its right tragic power and dramatic significance. Playgoers naturally murmur when something that has always been pretty becomes painful; but the pain is good for them, good for the theatre, and good for the play. I doubt whether Mrs. Patrick Campbell fully appreciates the dramatic value of her quite simple and original sketch—it is only a sketch—of the part; but in spite of the occasional triviality of its execution and the petulance with which it has been received, it seems to me to finally settle in her favor the question of her right to the very important place which Mr. Forbes Robertson has assigned to her in his enterprises.

I did not see Mr. Bernard Gould play Laertes: he was indisposed when I returned to town and hastened to the Lyceum; but he was replaced very creditably by Mr. Frank Dyall. Mr. Martin Harvey is the best Osric I have seen: he plays Osric from Osric's own point of view, which is, that Osric is a gallant and distinguished courtier, and not, as usual, from Hamlet's, which is that Osric is 'a waterfly.' Mr. Harrison Hunter hits off the modest, honest Horatio capitally; and Mr. Willes is so good a Gravedigger that I venture to suggest to him that he should carry his work a little further, and not virtually cease to concern himself with the play when he has spoken his last line and handed Hamlet the skull. Mr. Cooper Cliffe is not exactly a subtle Claudius; but he looks as if he had stepped out of a picture by Madox Brown, and plays straightforwardly on his very successful appearance. Mr. Barnes makes Polonius robust and elderly instead of aged and garrulous. He is good in the scenes where Polonius appears as a man of character and experience; but the senile exhibitions of courtierly tact do not match these, and so seem forced and farcical.

Mr. Forbes Robertson's own performance has a continuous charm, interest and variety which are the result not only of his well-known familiar grace and accomplishment as an actor, but of a genuine delight —the rarest thing on our stage—in Shakespear's art, and a natural familiarity with the plane of his imagination. He does not superstitiously worship William: he enjoys him and understands his methods of expression. Instead of cutting every line that can possibly be spared, he retains every gem, in his own part or anyone else's, that he can make time for in a spiritedly brisk performance lasting three hours and a half with very short intervals. He does not utter half a line; then stop to act; then go on with another half line; and then stop to act again, with the clock running away with Shakespear's chances all the time. He plays as Shakespear should be played, on the line and to the line, with the utterance and acting simultaneous, inseparable and in fact identical. Not for a moment is he solemnly conscious of Shakespear's reputation, or of Hamlet's momentousness in literary history: on the contrary, he delivers us from all these boredoms instead of heaping them on us. We forgive him the platitudes, so engagingly are they delivered. His novel and astonishingly effective and touching treatment of the final scene is an inspiration, from the fencing match onward. If only Fortinbras could also be inspired with sufficient force and brilliancy to rise to the warlike splendor of his helmet, and make straight for that throne like a man who intended to keep it against all comers, he would leave nothing to be desired. How many generations of Hamlets, all thirsting to outshine their competitors in effect and originality, have regarded Fortinbras, and the clue he gives to this kingly death for Hamlet, as a wildly unpresentable blunder of the poor foolish old Swan, than whom they all knew so much better! How sweetly they have died in that faith to slow music, like Little Nell in 'The Old Curiosity Shop'! And now how completely Mr. Forbes Robertson has bowled them all out by being clever enough to be simple.

By the way, talking of slow music, the sooner Mr. Hamilton Clarke's romantic Irving music is stopped, the better. Its effect in this Shakespearean version of the play is absurd. The four Offenbachian young women in tights should also be abolished, and the part of the player-queen given to a man. The courtiers should be taught how flatteringly courtiers listen when a king shows off his wisdom in wise speeches to his nephew. And that nice wooden beach on which the ghost walks would be the better for a seaweedy-looking cloth on it, with a handful of shrimps and a pennorth of silver sand.

BIBLIOGRAPHY ENTRY FOR RESEARCH PAPERS:

Shaw, George Bernard. "Hamlet," review of Forbes-Robertson's performance as Hamlet. *Saturday Review* (London), October 2, 1897. From his *Dramatic Opinions and Essays.* New York, 1907. In *Interpreting Hamlet,* ed. Russell E. Leavenworth. San Francisco, 1960.

FIRST FOOTNOTE:

    * George Bernard Shaw, "Hamlet," review of Forbes-Robertson's performance as Hamlet, *Saturday Review* (London), October 2, 1897, from his *Dramatic Opinions and Essays* (New York, 1907), in *Interpreting Hamlet,* ed. Russell E. Leavenworth (San Francisco, 1960), pp. 65-71.

SUBSEQUENT FOOTNOTES:

    * Shaw, *op. cit., IH,* p. ■■.
    * Shaw, "Hamlet," *IH,* p. ■■.
    * Shaw, *IH,* p. ■■.

In place of *"IH,"* "ed. Leavenworth" may be used in these subsequent-footnote forms.

A. C. BRADLEY

ON

the Meaning of Hamlet

Andrew Cecil Bradley (1851–1935), Professor of Poetry at Oxford and brother of the neo-Hegelian philosopher, F. H. Bradley, wrote one of the great classics of Shakespeare criticism, Shakespearean Tragedy *(London, 1904). The two extracts reprinted here are taken from the third lecture, "Shakespeare's Tragic Period—Hamlet," pp. 108-117, 122-128, by permission of Macmillan and Company, Ltd. and St. Martin's Press.*

SHAKESPEARE'S TRAGIC PERIOD: HAMLET

3

LET US FIRST ask ourselves what we can gather from the play, immediately or by inference, concerning Hamlet as he was just before his father's death. And I begin by observing that the text does not bear out the idea that he was one-sidedly reflective and indisposed to action. Nobody who knew him seems to have noticed this weakness. Nobody regards him as a mere scholar who has 'never formed a resolution or executed a deed.' In a court which certainly would not much admire such a person he is the observed of all observers. Though he has been disappointed of the throne everyone shows him respect; and he is the favourite of the people, who are not given to worship philosophers. Fortinbras, a sufficiently practical man, considered that he was likely, had he been put on, to have proved most royally. He has Hamlet borne by four captains 'like a soldier' to his grave; and Ophelia says that Hamlet *was* a soldier. If he was fond of acting, an aesthetic pursuit, he was equally fond of fencing, an athletic one: he practised it assiduously even in his worst days.[1] So far as we can conjecture from what we see of him in those bad days, he must normally have been charmingly frank, courteous and kindly to everyone, of whatever rank, whom he liked or respected, but by no means timid or deferential to others; indeed, one would gather that he was rather the reverse, and also that he was apt to be decided and even imperious if thwarted or interfered with. He must always have been fearless,—in the play he appears insensible to fear of any ordinary kind. And, finally, he must have been quick and impetuous in action; for it is downright impossible that the man we see rushing after the Ghost, killing Polonius, dealing with the King's commission on the ship, boarding the pirate, leaping into the grave, executing his final vengeance, could *ever* have been shrinking or slow in an emergency. Imagine Coleridge doing any of these things!

If we consider all this, how can we accept the notion that Hamlet's was a weak and one-sided character? 'Oh, but he spent ten or twelve years at a University!' Well, even if he did, it is possible to do that without becoming the victim of excessive thought. But the statement that he did rests upon a most insecure foundation.[2]

Where then are we to look for the seeds of danger?

(1) Trying to reconstruct from the Hamlet of the play, one would not judge that his temperament was melancholy in the present sense of the word; there seems nothing to show that; but one would judge that by temperament he was inclined to nervous instability, to rapid and perhaps extreme changes of feeling and mood, and that he was disposed to be, for the time, absorbed in the feeling or mood that possessed him, whether it were joyous or depressed. This temperament the Elizabethans would have called melancholic; and Hamlet seems to be an example of it, as Lear is of a temperament mixedly choleric and sanguine. And the doctrine of temperaments was so familiar in Shakespeare's time—as Burton, and earlier prose-writers, and many of the dramatists show—that Shakespeare may quite well have given this temperament to Hamlet consciously and deliberately. Of melancholy in its developed form, a habit, not a mere temperament, he often speaks. He more than once laughs at the passing and half-fictitious melancholy of youth and love; in Don John in *Much Ado*

---

[1] He says so to Horatio, whom he has no motive for deceiving (v. ii. 218). His contrary statement (II. ii. 308) is made to Rosencrantz and Guildenstern.

[2] See Note B. [An appendix note, not included here, in which Bradley discusses where Hamlet could have been at the time his father was murdered.]

he had sketched the sour and surly melancholy of discontent; in Jaques
a whimsical self-pleasing melancholy; in Antonio in the *Merchant of
Venice* a quiet but deep melancholy, for which neither the victim nor his
friends can assign any cause.[3] He gives to Hamlet a temperament which
would not develop into melancholy unless under some exceptional strain,
but which still involved a danger. In the play we see the danger realised,
and find a melancholy quite unlike any that Shakespeare had as yet
depicted, because the temperament of Hamlet is quite different.

(2) Next, we cannot be mistaken in attributing to the Hamlet of
earlier days an exquisite sensibility, to which we may give the name 'moral,'
if that word is taken in the wide meaning it ought to bear. This, though
it suffers cruelly in later days, as we saw in criticising the sentimental
view of Hamlet, never deserts him; it makes all his cynicism, grossness
and hardness appear to us morbidities, and has an inexpressibly attractive
and pathetic effect. He had the soul of the youthful poet as Shelley and
Tennyson have described it, an unbounded delight and faith in everything
good and beautiful. We know this from himself. The world for him was
herrlich wie am ersten Tag—'this goodly frame the earth, this most excellent canopy the air, this brave o'erhanging firmament, this majestical roof
fretted with golden fire.' And not nature only: 'What a piece of work
is a man! how noble in reason! how infinite in faculty! in form and
moving how express and admirable! in action how like an angel! in apprehension how like a god!' This is no commonplace to Hamlet; it is the
language of a heart thrilled with wonder and swelling into ecstasy.

Doubtless it was with the same eager enthusiasm he turned to those
around him. Where else in Shakespeare is there anything like Hamlet's
adoration of his father? The words melt into music whenever he speaks
of him. And, if there are no signs of any such feeling towards his mother,
though many signs of love, it is characteristic that he evidently never
entertained a suspicion of anything unworthy in her,—characteristic, and
significant of his tendency to see only what is good unless he is forced
to see the reverse. For we find this tendency elsewhere, and find it going
so far that we must call it a disposition to idealise, to see something better
than what is there, or at least to ignore deficiencies. He says to Laertes,
'I loved you ever,' and he describes Laertes as a 'very noble youth,' which

---

[3] The critics have laboured to find a cause, but it seems to me Shakespeare
simply meant to portray a pathological condition; and a very touching picture he
draws. Antonio's sadness, which he describes in the opening lines of the play,
would never drive him to suicide, but it makes him indifferent to the issue of the
trial, as all his speeches in the trial-scene show.

he was far from being. In his first greeting of Rosencrantz and Guildenstern, where his old self revives, we trace the same affectionateness and
readiness to take men at their best. His love for Ophelia, too, which seems
strange to some, is surely the most natural thing in the world. He saw her
innocence, simplicity and sweetness, and it was like him to ask no more;
and it is noticeable that Horatio, though entirely worthy of his friendship,
is, like Ophelia, intellectually not remarkable. To the very end, however
clouded, this generous disposition, this 'free and open nature,' this unsus-
piciousness survive. They cost him his life; for the King knew them, and
was sure that he was too 'generous and free from all contriving' to 'peruse
the foils.' To the very end, his soul, however sick and tortured it may be,
answers instantaneously when good and evil are presented to it, loving
the one and hating the other. He is called a sceptic who has no firm belief
in anything, but he is never sceptical about *them*.

And the negative side of his idealism, the aversion to evil, is perhaps
even more developed in the hero of the tragedy than in the Hamlet of
earlier days. It is intensely characteristic. Nothing, I believe, is to be
found elsewhere in Shakespeare (unless in the rage of the disillusioned
idealist Timon) of quite the same kind as Hamlet's disgust at his uncle's
drunkenness, his loathing of his mother's sensuality, his astonishment and
horror at her shallowness, his contempt for everything pretentious or false,
his indifference to everything merely external. This last characteristic appears in his choice of the friend of his heart, and in a certain impatience
of distinctions of rank or wealth. When Horatio calls his father 'a goodly
king,' he answers, surely with an emphasis on 'man,'

> He was a man, take him for all in all,
> I shall not look upon his like again.

He will not listen to talk of Horatio being his 'servant.' When the others
speak of their 'duty' to him, he answers, 'Your love, as mine to you.' He
speaks to the actor precisely as he does to an honest courtier. He is not in
the least a revolutionary, but still, in effect, a king and a beggar are all
one to him. He cares for nothing but human worth, and his pitilessness
towards Polonius and Osric and his 'school-fellows' is not wholly due to
morbidity, but belongs in part to his original character.

Now, in Hamlet's moral sensibility there undoubtedly lay a danger.
Any great shock that life might inflict on it would be felt with extreme
intensity. Such a shock might even produce tragic results. And, in fact,
Hamlet deserves the title 'tragedy of moral idealism' quite as much as
the title 'tragedy of reflection.'

(3) With this temperament and this sensibility we find, lastly, in the Hamlet of earlier days, as of later, intellectual genius. It is chiefly this that makes him so different from all those about him, good and bad alike, and hardly less different from most of Shakespeare's other heroes. And this, though on the whole the most important trait in his nature, is also so obvious and so famous that I need not dwell on it at length. But against one prevalent misconception I must say a word of warning. Hamlet's intellectual power is not a specific gift, like a genius for music or mathematics or philosophy. It shows itself, fitfully, in the affairs of life as unusual quickness of perception, great agility in shifting the mental attitude, a striking rapidity and fertility in resource; so that, when his natural belief in others does not make him unwary, Hamlet easily sees through them and masters them, and no one can be much less like the typical helpless dreamer. It shows itself in conversation chiefly in the form of wit or humour; and, alike in conversation and in soliloquy, it shows itself in the form of imagination quite as much as in that of thought in the stricter sense. Further, where it takes the latter shape, as it very often does, it is not philosophic in the technical meaning of the word. There is really nothing in the play to show that Hamlet ever was 'a student of philosophies,' unless it be the famous lines which, comically enough, exhibit this supposed victim of philosophy as its critic:

> *There are more things in heaven and earth, Horatio,*
> *Than are dreamt of in your philosophy.*[4]

His philosophy, if the word is to be used, was, like Shakespeare's own, the immediate product of the wondering and meditating mind; and such thoughts as that celebrated one, 'There is nothing either good or bad but thinking makes it so,' surely needed no special training to produce them. Or does Portia's remark, 'Nothing is good without respect,' *i.e.,* out of relation, prove that she had studied metaphysics?

Still Hamlet had speculative genius without being a philosopher, just as he had imaginative genius without being a poet. Doubtless in happier days he was a close and constant observer of men and manners, noting his results in those tables which he afterwards snatched from his breast to make in wild irony his last note of all, that one may smile and smile and be a villain. Again and again we remark that passion for generalisation which so occupied him, for instance, in reflections suggested by the

---

[4] Of course 'your' does not mean Horatio's philosophy in particular. 'Your' is used as the Gravedigger uses it when he says that 'your water is a sore decayer of your . . . dead body.'

King's drunkenness that he quite forgot what it was he was waiting to meet upon the battlements. Doubtless, too, he was always considering things, as Horatio thought, too curiously. There was a necessity in his soul driving him to penetrate below the surface and to question what others took for granted. That fixed habitual look which the world wears for most men did not exist for him. He was for ever unmaking his world and rebuilding it in thought, dissolving what to others were solid facts, and discovering what to others were old truths. There were no old truths for Hamlet. It is for Horatio a thing of course that there's a divinity that shapes our ends, but for Hamlet it is a discovery hardly won. And throughout this kingdom of the mind, where he felt that man, who in action is only like an angel, is in apprehension like a god, he moved (we must imagine) more than content, so that even in his dark days he declares he could be bounded in a nutshell and yet count himself a king of infinite space, were it not that he had bad dreams.

If now we ask whether any special danger lurked *here*, how shall we answer? We must answer, it seems to me, 'Some danger, no doubt, but, granted the ordinary chances of life, not much.' For, in the first place, that idea which so many critics quietly take for granted—the idea that the gift and the habit of meditative and speculative thought tend to produce irresolution in the affairs of life—would be found by no means easy to verify. Can you verify it, for example, in the lives of the philosophers, or again in the lives of men whom you have personally known to be addicted to such speculation? I cannot. Of course, individual peculiarities being set apart, absorption in *any* intellectual interest, together with withdrawal from affairs, may make a man slow and unskilful in affairs; and doubtless, individual peculiarities being again set apart, a mere student is likely to be more at a loss in a sudden and great practical emergency than a soldier or a lawyer. But in all this there is no difference between a physicist, a historian, and a philosopher; and again, slowness, want of skill, and even helplessness are something totally different from the peculiar kind of irresolution that Hamlet shows. The notion that speculative thinking specially tends to produce *this* is really a mere illusion.

In the second place, even if this notion were true, it has appeared that Hamlet did *not* live the life of a mere student, much less of a mere dreamer, and that his nature was by no means simply or even one-sidedly intellectual, but was healthily active. Hence, granted the ordinary chances of life, there would seem to be no great danger in his intellectual tendency and his habit of speculation; and I would go further and say that there was nothing in them, taken alone, to unfit him even for the extraordinary call that was made upon him. In fact, if the message of the Ghost had come to him within a week of his father's death, I see no reason to doubt that he would have acted on it as decisively as Othello himself, though probably after a longer and more anxious deliberation. And therefore the Schlegel-Coleridge view (apart from its descriptive value) seems to me fatally untrue, for it implies that Hamlet's procrastination was the normal response of an over-speculative nature confronted with a difficult practical problem.

On the other hand, under conditions of a peculiar kind, Hamlet's reflectiveness certainly might prove dangerous to him, and his genius might even (to exaggerate a little) become his doom. Suppose that violent shock to his moral being of which I spoke; and suppose that under this shock, any possible action being denied to him, he began to sink into melancholy; then, no doubt, his imaginative and generalising habit of mind might extend the effects of this shock through his whole being and mental world. And if, the state of melancholy being thus deepened and fixed, a sudden demand for difficult and decisive action in a matter connected with the melancholy arose, this state might well have for one of its symptoms an endless and futile mental dissection of the required deed. And, finally, the futility of this process, and the shame of his delay, would further weaken him and enslave him to his melancholy still more. Thus the speculative habit would be *one* indirect cause of the morbid state which hindered action; and it would also reappear in a degenerate form as one of the *symptoms* of this morbid state.

*   *   *

4

'Melancholy,' I said, not dejection, nor yet insanity. That Hamlet was not far from insanity is very probable. His adoption of the pretence of madness may well have been due in part to fear of the reality; to an instinct of self-preservation, a fore-feeling that the pretence would enable him to give some utterance to the load that pressed on his heart and brain, and a fear that he would be unable altogether to repress such utterance. And if the pathologist calls his state melancholia, and even proceeds to determine its species, I see nothing to object to in that; I am grateful to him for emphasising the fact that Hamlet's melancholy was no mere common depression of spirits; and I have no doubt that many readers of the play would understand it better if they read an account of melancholia in a work on mental diseases. If we like to use the word 'disease' loosely, Hamlet's condition may truly be called diseased. No exertion of will could have dispelled it. Even if he had been able at once to do the bidding of the Ghost he would doubtless have still remained for some time under the cloud. It would be absurdly unjust to call *Hamlet* a study of melancholy, but it contains such a study.

But this melancholy is something very different from insanity, in anything like the usual meaning of that word. No doubt it might develop into insanity. The longing for death might become an irresistible impulse to self-destruction; the disorder of feeling and will might extend to sense and intellect; delusions might arise; and the man might become, as we say, incapable and irresponsible. But Hamlet's melancholy is some way from this condition. It is a totally different thing from the madness which he feigns; and he never, when alone or in company with Horatio alone, exhibits the signs of that madness. Nor is the dramatic use of this melancholy, again, open to the objections which would justly be made to the portrayal of an insanity which brought the hero to a tragic end. The man who suffers as Hamlet suffers—and thousands go about their business suffering thus in greater or less degree—is considered irresponsible neither by other people nor by himself: he is only too keenly conscious of his responsibility. He is therefore, so far, quite capable of being a tragic agent, which an insane person, at any rate according to Shakespeare's practice, is not.[1] And, finally, Hamlet's state is not one which a healthy mind is unable sufficiently to imagine. It is probably not further from average experience, nor more difficult to realise, than the great tragic passions of Othello, Antony or Macbeth.

Let me try to show now, briefly, how much this melancholy accounts for.

It accounts for the main fact, Hamlet's inaction. For the *immediate* cause of that is simply that his habitual feeling is one of disgust at life and everything in it, himself included,—a disgust which varies in intensity, rising at times into a longing for death, sinking often into weary apathy, but is never dispelled for more than brief intervals. Such a state of feeling is inevitably adverse to *any* kind of decided action; the body is inert, the mind indifferent or worse; its response is, 'it does not matter,' 'it is not worth while,' 'it is no good.' And the action required of Hamlet is very exceptional. It is violent, dangerous, difficult to accomplish perfectly, on one side repulsive to a man of honour and sensitive feeling, on another side involved in a certain mystery (here come in thus, in their subordinate place, various causes of inaction assigned by various theories). These

---

[1] [A cross reference to page 13 of Bradley's book, not included in this selection.]

obstacles would not suffice to prevent Hamlet from acting, if his state were normal; and against them there operate, even in his morbid state, healthy and positive feelings, love of his father, loathing of his uncle, desire of revenge, desire to do duty. But the retarding motives acquire an unnatural strength because they have an ally in something far stronger than themselves, the melancholic disgust and apathy; while the healthy motives, emerging with difficulty from the central mass of diseased feeling, rapidly sink back into it and 'lose the name of action.' We *see* them doing so; and sometimes the process is quite simple, no analytical reflection on the deed intervening between the outburst of passion and the relapse into melancholy.[2] But this melancholy is perfectly consistent also with that incessant dissection of the task assigned, of which the Schlegel-Coleridge theory makes so much. For those endless questions (as we may imagine them), 'Was I deceived by the Ghost? How am I to do the deed? When? Where? What will be the consequence of attempting it—success, my death, utter misunderstanding, mere mischief to the State? Can it be right to do it, or noble to kill a defenceless man? What is the good of doing it in such a world as this?'—all this, and whatever else passed in a sickening round through Hamlet's mind, was not the healthy and right deliberation of a man with such a task, but otiose thinking hardly deserving the name of thought, an unconscious weaving of pretexts for inaction, aimless tossings on a sick bed, symptoms of melancholy which only increased it by deepening self-contempt.

Again, (*a*) this state accounts for Hamlet's energy as well as for his lassitude, those quick decided actions of his being the outcome of a nature normally far from passive, now suddenly stimulated, and producing healthy impulses which work themselves out before they have time to subside. (*b*) It accounts for the evidently keen satisfaction which some of these actions give to him. He arranges the play-scene with lively interest, and exults in its success, not really because it brings him nearer to his goal, but partly because it has hurt his enemy and partly because it has demonstrated his own skill (III. ii. 286-304). He looks forward almost with glee to countermining the King's designs in sending him away (III. iv. 209), and looks back with obvious satisfaction, even with pride, to the address and vigour he displayed on the voyage (V. ii. 1-55). These were not *the* action on which his morbid self-feeling had centred; he feels

---

[2] *E.g.* in the transition, referred to above, from desire for vengeance into the wish never to have been born; in the soliloquy, 'O what a rogue'; in the scene at Ophelia's grave. The Schlegel-Coleridge theory does not account for the psychological movement in those passages.

in them his old force, and escapes in them from his disgust. (*c*) It accounts for the pleasure with which he meets old acquaintances, like his 'school-fellows' or the actors. The former observed (and we can observe) in him a 'kind of joy' at first, though it is followed by 'much forcing of his disposition' as he attempts to keep this joy and his courtesy alive in spite of the misery which so soon returns upon him and the suspicion he is forced to feel. (*d*) It accounts no less for the painful features of his character as seen in the play, his almost savage irritability on the one hand, and on the other his self-absorption, his callousness, his insensibility to the fates of those whom he despises, and to the feelings even of those whom he loves. These are frequent symptoms of such melancholy, and (*e*) they sometimes alternate, as they do in Hamlet, with bursts of transitory, almost hysterical, and quite fruitless emotion. It is to these last (of which a part of the soliloquy, 'O what a rogue,' gives a good example) that Hamlet alludes when, to the Ghost, he speaks of himself as 'lapsed in *passion*,' and it is doubtless partly his conscious weakness in regard to them that inspires his praise of Horatio as a man who is not 'passion's slave.'[3]

Finally, Hamlet's melancholy accounts for two things which seem to be explained by nothing else. The first of these is his apathy or 'lethargy.' We are bound to consider the evidence which the text supplies of this, though it is usual to ignore it. When Hamlet mentions, as one possible cause of his inaction, his 'thinking too precisely on the event,' he mentions another, 'bestial oblivion'; and the thing against which he inveighs in the greater part of that soliloquy (IV. iv.) is not the excess or the misuse of reason (which for him here and always is godlike), but this *bestial* oblivion or '*dullness*,' this 'letting all *sleep*,' this allowing of heaven-sent reason to 'fust unused':

> *What is a man,*
> *If his chief good and market of his time*
> *Be but to* sleep *and* feed? *a beast, no more.*[4]

---

[3] Hamlet's violence at Ophelia's grave, though probably intentionally exaggerated, is another example of this want of self-control. The Queen's description of him (v. i. 307),

> *This is mere madness;*
> *And thus awhile the fit will work on him;*
> *Anon, as patient as the female dove,*
> *When that her golden couplets are disclosed,*
> *His silence will sit drooping,*

may be true to life, though it is evidently prompted by anxiety to excuse his violence on the ground of his insanity. On this passage see further Note G. [Not included in this selection.]

[4] Throughout, I set in roman to show the connection of ideas.

So, in the soliloquy in II. ii. he accuses himself of being 'a *dull* and muddy-mettled rascal,' who 'peaks [mopes] like a John-a-dreams, unpregnant of his cause,' dully indifferent to his cause.[5] So, when the Ghost appears to him the second time, he accuses himself of being tardy and lapsed in *time;* and the Ghost speaks of his purpose being almost *blunted,* and bids him not to *forget* (cf. 'oblivion'). And so, what is emphasised in those undramatic but significant speeches of the player-king and of Claudius is the mere dying away of purpose or of love.[6] Surely what all this points to is not a condition of excessive but useless mental activity (indeed there is, in reality, curiously little about that in the text), but rather one of dull, apathetic, brooding gloom, in which Hamlet, so far from analysing his duty, is not thinking of it at all, but for the time literally *forgets* it. It seems to me we are driven to think of Hamlet *chiefly* thus during the long time which elapsed between the appearance of the Ghost and the events presented in the Second Act. The Ghost, in fact, had more reason than we suppose at first for leaving with Hamlet as his parting injunction the command, 'Remember me,' and for greeting him, on reappearing, with the command, 'Do not forget.'[7] These little things in Shakespeare are not accidents.

The second trait which is fully explained only by Hamlet's melancholy is his own inability to understand why he delays. This emerges in a marked degree when an occasion like the player's emotion or the sight of Fortinbras's army stings Hamlet into shame at his inaction. '*Why,*' he asks himself in genuine bewilderment, 'do I linger? Can the cause be cowardice? Can it be sloth? Can it be thinking too precisely of the event? And does *that* again mean cowardice? What is it that makes me sit idle when I feel it is shameful to do so, and when I have *cause, and will, and strength, and means, to act?*' A man irresolute merely because he was considering a proposed action too minutely would not feel this bewilderment. A man might feel it whose conscience secretly condemned the act which his explicit consciousness approved; but we have seen that there is no sufficient evidence to justify us in conceiving Hamlet thus. These are the

---

[5] Cf. *Measure for Measure,* IV. iv. 23, 'This deed . . . makes me unpregnant and dull to all proceedings.'

[6] III. ii. 196 ff., IV. vii. 111 ff.: *e.g.,*

> *Purpose is but the slave to memory,*
> *Of violent birth but poor validity.*

[7] So, before, he had said to him:

> *And duller should'st thou be than the fat weed*
> *That roots itself in ease on Lethe wharf,*
> *Would'st thou not stir in this.*

questions of a man stimulated for the moment to shake off the weight of his melancholy, and, because for the moment he is free from it, unable to understand the paralysing pressure which it exerts at other times.

I have dwelt thus at length on Hamlet's melancholy because, from the psychological point of view, it is the centre of the tragedy, and to omit it from consideration or to underrate its intensity is to make Shakespeare's story unintelligible. But the psychological point of view is not equivalent to the tragic; and, having once given its due weight to the fact of Hamlet's melancholy, we may freely admit, or rather may be anxious to insist, that this pathological condition would excite but little, if any, tragic interest if it were not the condition of a nature distinguished by that speculative genius on which the Schlegel-Coleridge type of theory lays stress. Such theories misinterpret the connection between that genius and Hamlet's failure, but still it is this connection which gives to his story its peculiar fascination and makes it appear (if the phrase may be allowed) as the symbol of a tragic mystery inherent in human nature. Wherever this mystery touches us, wherever we are forced to feel the wonder and awe of man's godlike 'apprehension' and his 'thoughts that wander through eternity,' and at the same time are forced to see him powerless in his petty sphere of action, and powerless (it would appear) from the very divinity of his thought, we remember Hamlet. And this is the reason why, in the great ideal movement which began towards the close of the eighteenth century, this tragedy acquired a position unique among Shakespeare's dramas, and shared only by Goethe's *Faust*. It was not that *Hamlet* is Shakespeare's greatest tragedy or most perfect work of art; it was that *Hamlet* most brings home to us at once the sense of the soul's infinity, and the sense of the doom which not only circumscribes that infinity but appears to be its offspring.

BIBLIOGRAPHY ENTRY FOR RESEARCH PAPERS:

Bradley, Andrew Cecil. *Shakespearean Tragedy*. London, 1904. Excerpt in *Interpreting Hamlet,* ed. Russell E. Leavenworth. San Francisco, 1960.

FIRST FOOTNOTE:

* Andrew Cecil Bradley, *Shakespearean Tragedy,* London, 1904, excerpt in *Interpreting Hamlet,* ed. Russell E. Leavenworth (San Francisco, 1960), pp. 73-84.

SUBSEQUENT FOOTNOTES:

* Bradley, *op. cit., IH*, p. ▮▮.
* Bradley, *Shakespearean Tragedy, IH*, p. ▮▮.
* Bradley, *IH*, p. ▮▮.

In place of "*IH*," "ed. Leavenworth" may be used in these subsequent-footnote forms.

T. S. ELIOT

ON

the Meaning of Hamlet

Thomas Stearns Eliot (b. 1888), poet, dramatist, essayist, has occupied a commanding critical influence ever since the publication of The Sacred Wood *(London, 1919), a collection of critical essays which included the one reprinted here. By permission of the author, Methuen and Company, and Harcourt, Brace and Company.*

HAMLET AND HIS PROBLEMS

FEW CRITICS have even admitted that *Hamlet* the play is the primary problem, and Hamlet the character only secondary. And Hamlet the character has had an especial temptation for the most dangerous type of critic: the critic with a mind which is naturally of the creative order, but which through some weakness in creative power exercises itself in criticism instead. These minds often find in Hamlet a vicarious existence for their own artistic realization. Such a mind had Goethe, who made of Hamlet a Werther; and such had Coleridge, who made of Hamlet a Coleridge; and probably neither of these men in writing about Hamlet remembered that his first business was to study a work of art. The kind of criticism that Goethe and Coleridge produced, in writing of Hamlet, is the most misleading kind possible. For they both possessed unquestionable critical insight, and both make their critical aberrations the more plausible by the substitution—of their own Hamlet for Shakespeare's—which their creative gift effects. We should be thankful that Walter Pater did not fix his attention on this play.

Two recent writers, Mr. J. M. Robertson and Professor Stoll of the University of Minnesota, have issued small books which can be praised for moving in the other direction. Mr. Stoll performs a service in recalling to our attention the labours of the critics of the seventeenth and eighteenth centuries,[1] observing that

> they knew less about psychology than more recent Hamlet critics, but they were nearer in spirit to Shakespeare's art; and as they insisted on the importance of the effect of the whole rather than on the importance of the leading character, they were nearer, in their old-fashioned way, to the secret of dramatic art in general.

Qua work of art, the work of art cannot be interpreted; there is nothing to interpret; we can only criticize it according to standards, in comparison to other works of art; and for 'interpretation' the chief task is the presentation of relevant historical facts which the reader is not assumed to know. Mr. Robertson points out, very pertinently, how critics have failed in their 'interpretation' of *Hamlet* by ignoring what ought to be very obvious: that *Hamlet* is a stratification, that it represents the efforts of a series of men, each making what he could out of the work of his predecessors. The *Hamlet* of Shakespeare will appear to us very differently if, instead of treating the whole action of the play as due to Shakespeare's design, we perceive his *Hamlet* to be superposed upon much cruder material which persists even in the final form.

We know that there was an older play by Thomas Kyd, that extraordinary dramatic (if not poetic) genius who was in all probability the author of two plays so dissimilar as the *Spanish Tragedy* and *Arden of Feversham;* and what this play was like we can guess from three clues: from the *Spanish Tragedy* itself, from the tale of Belleforest upon which Kyd's *Hamlet* must have been based, and from a version acted in Germany in Shakespeare's lifetime which bears strong evidence of having been adapted from the earlier, not from the later, play. From these three sources it is clear that in the earlier play the motive was a revenge-motive simply; that the action or delay is caused, as in the *Spanish Tragedy,* solely by the difficulty of assassinating a monarch surrounded by guards; and that the 'madness' of Hamlet was feigned in order to escape suspicion, and successfully. In the final play of Shakespeare, on the other hand, there is a

---

[1] I have never, by the way, seen a cogent refutation of Thomas Rymer's objections to *Othello.*

motive which is more important than that of revenge, and which explicitly 'blunts' the latter; the delay in revenge is unexplained on grounds of necessity or expediency; and the effect of the 'madness' is not to lull but to arouse the king's suspicion. The alteration is not complete enough, however, to be convincing. Furthermore, there are verbal parallels so close to the *Spanish Tragedy* as to leave no doubt that in places Shakespeare was merely *revising* the text of Kyd. And finally there are unexplained scenes—the Polonius-Laertes and the Polonius-Reynaldo scenes —for which there is little excuse; these scenes are not in the verse style of Kyd, and not beyond doubt in the style of Shakespeare. These Mr. Robertson believes to be scenes in the original play of Kyd reworked by a third hand, perhaps Chapman, before Shakespeare touched the play. And he concludes, with very strong show of reason, that the original play of Kyd was, like certain other revenge plays, in two parts of five acts each. The upshot of Mr. Robertson's examination is, we believe, irrefragable: that Shakespeare's *Hamlet,* so far as it is Shakespeare's, is a play dealing with the effect of a mother's guilt upon her son, and that Shakespeare was unable to impose this motive successfully upon the 'intractable' material of the old play.

Of the intractability there can be no doubt. So far from being Shakespeare's masterpiece, the play is most certainly an artistic failure. In several ways the play is puzzling, and disquieting as is none of the others. Of all the plays it is the longest and is possibly the one on which Shakespeare spent most pains; and yet he has left in it superfluous and inconsistent scenes which even hasty revision should have noticed. The versification is variable. Lines like

> *Look, the morn, in russet mantle clad,*
> *Walks o'er the dew of yon high eastern hill,*

are of the Shakespeare of *Romeo and Juliet.* The lines in Act v. sc. ii.,

> *Sir, in my heart there was a kind of fighting*
> *That would not let me sleep . . .*
> *Up from my cabin,*
> *My sea-gown scarf'd about me, in the dark*
> *Grop'd I to find out them: had my desire;*
> *Finger'd their packet;*

are of his quite mature. Both workmanship and thought are in an unstable condition. We are surely justified in attributing the play, with that other profoundly interesting play of 'intractable' material and astonishing versification, *Measure for Measure,* to a period of crisis, after which follow the tragic successes which culminate in *Coriolanus. Coriolanus* may be not as 'interesting' as *Hamlet,* but it is, with *Antony and Cleopatra,* Shakespeare's most assured artistic success. And probably more people have thought *Hamlet* a work of art because they found it interesting, than have found it interesting because it is a work of art. It is the 'Mona Lisa' of literature.

The grounds of *Hamlet's* failure are not immediately obvious. Mr. Robertson is undoubtedly correct in concluding that the essential emotion of the play is the feeling of a son towards a guilty mother:

> [Hamlet's] tone is that of one who has suffered tortures on the score of his mother's degradation. . . . The guilt of a mother is an almost intolerable motive for drama, but it had to be maintained and emphasized to supply a psychological solution, or rather a hint of one.

This, however, is by no means the whole story. It is not merely the 'guilt of a mother' that cannot be handled as Shakespeare handled the suspicion of Othello, the infatuation of Antony, or the pride of Coriolanus. The subject might conceivably have expanded into a tragedy like these, intelligible, self-complete, in the sunlight. *Hamlet,* like the sonnets, is full of some stuff that the writer could not drag to light, contemplate, or manipulate into art. And when we search for this feeling, we find it, as in the sonnets, very difficult to localize. You cannot point to it in the speeches; indeed, if you examine the two famous soliloquies you see the versification of Shakespeare, but a content which might be claimed by another, perhaps by the author of the *Revenge of Bussy d'Ambois,* Act v. sc. i. We find Shakespeare's *Hamlet* not in the action, not in any quotations that we might select, so much as in an unmistakable tone which is unmistakably not in the earlier play.

The only way of expressing emotion in the form of art is by finding an 'objective correlative'; in other words, a set of objects, a situation, a chain of events which shall be the formula of that *particular* emotion; such that when the external facts, which must terminate in sensory experience, are given, the emotion is immediately evoked. If you examine any of Shakespeare's more successful tragedies, you will find this exact equivalence; you will find that the state of mind of Lady Macbeth walking in her sleep has been communicated to you by a skilful accumulation of imagined sensory impressions; the words of Macbeth on hearing of his wife's death strike us as if, given the sequence of events, these words were automatically released by the last event in the series. The artistic 'inevitability' lies in this complete adequacy of the external to the emotion; and this is precisely what is deficient in *Hamlet*. Hamlet (the man) is dominated by an emotion which is inexpressible, because it is in *excess* of the facts as they appear. And the supposed identity of Hamlet with his author is genuine to this point: that Hamlet's bafflement at the absence of objective equivalent to his feelings is a prolongation of the bafflement of his creator in the face of his artistic problem. Hamlet is up against the difficulty that his disgust is occasioned by his mother, but that his mother is not an adequate equivalent for it; his disgust envelops and exceeds her. It is thus a feeling which he cannot understand; he cannot objectify it, and it therefore remains to poison life and obstruct action. None of the possible actions can satisfy it; and nothing that Shakespeare can do with the plot can express Hamlet for him. And it must be noticed that the very nature of the *données* of the problem precludes objective equivalence. To have heightened the criminality of Gertrude would have been to provide the formula for a totally different emotion in Hamlet; it is just *because* her character is so negative and insignificant that she arouses in Hamlet the feeling which she is incapable of representing.

The 'madness' of Hamlet lay to Shakespeare's hand; in the earlier play a simple ruse, and to the end, we may presume, understood as a ruse by the audience. For Shakespeare it is less than madness and more than feigned. The levity of Hamlet, his repetition of phrase, his puns, are not part of a deliberate plan of dissimulation, but a form of emotional relief. In the character Hamlet it is the buffoonery of an emotion which can find no outlet in action; in the dramatist it is the buffoonery of an emotion which he cannot express in art. The intense feeling, ecstatic or terrible, without an object or exceeding its object, is something which every person of sensibility has known; it is doubtless a study to pathologists. It often occurs in adolescence: the ordinary person puts these feelings to sleep, or trims down his feeling to fit the business world; the artist keeps it alive by his ability to intensify the world to his emotions. The Hamlet of Laforgue is an adolescent; the Hamlet of Shakespeare is not, he has not that explanation and excuse. We must simply admit that here Shakespeare tackled a problem which proved too much for him. Why he attempted it at all is an insoluble puzzle; under compulsion of what experience he attempted to express the inexpressibly horrible, we cannot ever know. We need a great many facts in his biography; and we should like to know whether, and when, and after or at the same time as what personal experience, he read Montaigne, II. xii., *Apologie de Raimond Sebond*. We should have, finally, to know something which is by hypothesis unknowable, for we assume it to be an experience which, in the manner indicated, exceeded the facts. We should have to understand things which Shakespeare did not understand himself.

BIBLIOGRAPHY ENTRY FOR RESEARCH PAPERS:

Eliot, Thomas Stearns. "Hamlet and His Problems." From his *The Sacred Wood*. London, 1919. In *Interpreting Hamlet*, ed. Russell E. Leavenworth. San Francisco, 1960.

FIRST FOOTNOTE:

* T. S. Eliot, "Hamlet and His Problems," from his *The Sacred Wood* (London, 1919), in *Interpreting Hamlet*, ed. Russell E. Leavenworth (San Francisco, 1960), pp. 86-91.

SUBSEQUENT FOOTNOTES:

* Eliot, *op. cit., IH*, p. ■■.
* Eliot, "Hamlet and His Problems," *IH*, p. ■■.
* Eliot, *IH*, p. ■■.

In place of *"IH,"* "ed. Leavenworth" may be used in these subsequent-footnote forms.

GEORGE WILSON KNIGHT

ON

the Meaning of Hamlet

George Wilson Knight (b. 1897), former Chancellor's Professor of English Literature at Trinity College, Toronto, and now Reader in English Literature at the University of Leeds, acted in and directed many productions of Shakespeare's plays. Of his numerous volumes of published criticism, five deal with Shakespeare, including The Wheel of Fire *(London, 1930, 1949), from which Part II of "The Embassy of Death: An Essay on* Hamlet" *is reprinted here. By permission of the author and Methuen and Company, Ltd.*

THE EMBASSY OF DEATH: AN ESSAY ON HAMLET

II

IT IS USUAL in Shakespeare's plays for the main theme to be reflected in subsidiary incidents, persons, and detailed suggestion throughout. Now the theme of *Hamlet* is death. Life that is bound for the disintegration of the grave, love that does not survive the loved one's life—both, in their insistence on death as the primary fact of nature, are branded on the mind of Hamlet, burned into it, searing it with agony. The bereavement of Hamlet and his consequent mental agony bordering on madness is mirrored in the bereavement of Ophelia and her madness. The death of the Queen's love is reflected in the swift passing of the love of the Player-Queen, in the 'Murder of Gonzago.' Death is over the whole play. Polonius and Ophelia die during the action, and Ophelia is buried before our eyes. Hamlet arranges the deaths of Rosencrantz and Guildenstern. The plot is set in motion by the murder of Hamlet's father, and the play opens with the apparition of the Ghost:

> *What may this mean,*
> *That thou, dead corse, again in complete steel*
> *Revisit'st thus the glimpses of the moon,*
> *Making night hideous; and we fools of nature*
> *So horridly to shake our dispositions*
> *With thoughts beyond the reaches of our souls?*   (I. iv. 51)

Those first scenes strike the note of the play—death. We hear of terrors beyond the grave, from the Ghost (I. v.) and from the meditations of Hamlet (III. i.). We hear of horrors in the grave from Hamlet whose mind is obsessed with hideous thoughts of the body's decay. Hamlet's dialogue with the King about the dead Polonius (IV. iii. 17) is painful; and the graveyard meditations, though often beautiful, are remorselessly realistic. Hamlet holds Yorick's skull:

> Hamlet. . . . . *Now, get you to my lady's chamber and tell her, let*
>   *her paint an inch thick, to this favour she must come; make her*
>   *laugh at that. Prithee, Horatio, tell me one thing.*
> Horatio. *What's that, my lord?*
> Hamlet. *Dost thou think Alexander looked o' this fashion i' the*
>   *earth?*
> Horatio, *E'en so.*
> Hamlet. *And smelt so? pah!*   (V. i. 211)

The general thought of death, intimately related to the predominating human theme, the pain in Hamlet's mind, is thus suffused through the whole play. And yet the play, as a whole, scarcely gives us that sense of blackness and the abysms of spiritual evil which we find in *Macbeth;* nor is there the universal gloom of *King Lear.* This is due partly to the difference in the technique of *Hamlet* from that of *Macbeth* or *King Lear.* Macbeth, the protagonist and heroic victim of evil, rises gigantic from the murk of an evil universe; Lear, the king of suffering, towers over a universe that itself toils in pain. Thus in *Macbeth* and *King Lear* the predominating imaginative atmospheres are used not to contrast with the mental universe of the hero, but to aid and support it, as it were, with similarity, to render realistic the extravagant and daring effects of volcanic passion to which the poet allows his protagonist to give voice. We are forced by the attendant personification, the verbal colour, the symbolism and events of the play as a whole, to feel the hero's suffering, to see with his eyes. But in *Hamlet* this is not so. We need not see through Hamlet's eyes. Though the idea of death is recurrent through the play, it is not implanted in the minds of other persons as is the consciousness of evil throughout *Macbeth* and the consciousness of suffering throughout *King Lear*. Except for the original murder of Hamlet's father, the *Hamlet* universe is one of healthy and robust life, good-nature, humour, romantic strength, and welfare: against this background is the figure of Hamlet pale with the consciousness of death. He is the ambassador of death walking amid life. The effect is at first primarily one of separation. But it is to be noted that the consciousness of death, and consequent bitterness, cruelty, and inaction, in Hamlet not only grows in his own mind disintegrating it as we watch, but also spreads its effects outward among the other persons like a blighting disease, and, as the play progresses, by its very passivity and negation of purpose, insidiously undermines the health of the state, and adds victim to victim until at the end the stage is filled with corpses. It is, as it were, a nihilistic birth in the consciousness of Hamlet that spreads its deadly venom around. That Hamlet is originally blameless, that the King is originally guilty, may well be granted. But, if we refuse to be diverted from a clear vision by questions of praise and blame, responsibility and causality, and watch only the actions and reactions of the persons as they appear, we shall observe a striking reversal of the usual commentary.

If we are to attain a true interpretation of Shakespeare we must work from a centre of consciousness near that of the creative instinct of the poet. We must think less in terms of causality and more in terms of imaginative impact. Now Claudius is not drawn as wholly evil—far from it. We see the government of Denmark working smoothly. Claudius shows every sign of being an excellent diplomatist and king. He is troubled by young Fortinbras, and dispatches ambassadors to the sick King of Norway demanding that he suppress the raids of his nephew. His speech to the ambassadors bears the stamp of clear and exact thought and an efficient and confident control of affairs:

> *. . . and we here dispatch*
> *You, good Cornelius, and you, Voltimand,*
> *For bearers of this greeting to old Norway;*
> *Giving to you no further personal power*
> *To business with the king, more than the scope*
> *Of these delated articles allow.*
> *Farewell, and let your haste commend your duty.*   (I. ii. 33)

The ambassadors soon return successful. Claudius listens to their reply, receives the King of Norway's letter, and hears that young Fortinbras desires a free pass through Denmark to lead his soldiers against the Poles. Claudius answers:

> *It likes us well;*
> *And at our more consider'd time we'll read,*
> *Answer, and think upon this business.*
> *Meantime we thank you for your well-took labour:*
> *Go to your rest; at night we'll feast together:*
> *Most welcome home!*   (II. ii. 80)

Tact has found an easy settlement where arms and opposition might have wasted the strength of Denmark. Notice his reservation of detailed attention when once he knows the main issues are clear; the courteous yet dignified attitude to his subordinates and the true leader's consideration for their comfort; and the invitation to the feast. The impression given by these speeches is one of quick efficiency—the efficiency of the man who can dispose of business without unnecessary circumstance, and so leaves himself time for enjoying the good things of life: a man kindly, confident, and fond of pleasure.

Throughout the first half of the play Claudius is the typical kindly uncle, besides being a good king. His advice to Hamlet about his exaggerated mourning for his father's death is admirable common sense:

> *Fie! 'Tis a fault to Heaven,*
> *A fault against the dead, a fault to nature,*
> *To reason most absurd; whose common theme*
> *Is death of fathers, and who still hath cried,*
> *From the first corse, till he that died to-day,*
> *'This must be so.'*   (I. ii. 101)

It is the advice of worldly common sense opposed to the extreme misery of a sensitive nature paralysed by the facts of death and unfaithfulness. This contrast points the relative significance of the King and his court to Hamlet. They are of the world—with their crimes, their follies, their shallownesses, their pomp and glitter; they are of humanity, with all its failings, it is true, but yet of humanity. They assert the importance of human life, they believe in it, in themselves. Whereas Hamlet is inhuman, since he has seen through the tinsel of life and love, he believes in nothing, not even himself, except the memory of a ghost, and his black-robed presence is a reminder to everyone of the fact of death. There is no question but that Hamlet is right. The King's smiles hide murder, his mother's love for her new consort is unfaithfulness to Hamlet's father, Ophelia has deserted Hamlet at the hour of his need. Hamlet's philosophy may be inevitable, blameless, and irrefutable. But it is the negation of life. It is death. Hence Hamlet is a continual fear to Claudius, a reminder of his crime. It is a mistake to consider Claudius as a hardened criminal. When Polonius remarks on the hypocrisy of mankind, he murmurs to himself:

> *O, 'tis too true!*
> *How smart a lash that speech doth give my conscience!*
> *The harlot's cheek, beautied with plastering art,*
> *Is not more ugly to the thing that helps it*
> *Than is my deed to my most painted word:*
> *O heavy burthen!*   (III. i. 49)

Again, Hamlet's play wrenches his soul with remorse—primarily not fear of Hamlet, as one might expect, but a genuine remorse—and gives us that most beautiful prayer of a stricken soul beginning, 'O, my offence is rank, it smells to Heaven' (III. iii. 36):

> *. . . What if this cursed hand*
> *Were thicker than itself with brother's blood,*
> *Is there not rain enough in the sweet heavens*
> *To wash it white as snow? Whereto serves mercy*
> *But to confront the visage of offence?*

He fears that his prayer is worthless. He is still trammelled by the enjoyment of the fruits of his crime. 'My fault is past,' he cries. But what does that avail, since he has his crown and his queen still, the prizes of murder? His dilemma is profound and raises the problem I am pointing in this essay. Claudius, as he appears in the play, is not a criminal. He is—strange as it may seem—a good and gentle king, enmeshed by the chain of causality linking him with his crime. And this chain he might, perhaps, have broken except for Hamlet, and all would have been well. But, granted the presence of Hamlet—which Claudius at first genuinely desired, persuading him not to return to Wittenberg as he wished—and granted the fact of his original crime which cannot now be altered, Claudius can hardly be blamed for his later actions. They are forced on him. As King, he could scarcely be expected to do otherwise. Hamlet is a danger to the state, even apart from his knowledge of Claudius' guilt. He is an inhuman—or superhuman—presence, whose consciousness—somewhat like Dostoievsky's Stavrogin—is centred on death. Like Stavrogin, he is feared by those around him. They are always trying in vain to find out what is wrong with him. They cannot understand him. He is a creature of another world. As King of Denmark he would have been a

thousand times more dangerous than Claudius. The end of Claudius' ✗
prayer is pathetic:

> *What then? What rests?*
> *Try what repentance can: what can it not?*
> *Yet what can it when one can not repent?*
> *O wretched state! O bosom black as death!*
> *O limed soul, that, struggling to be free,*
> *Art more engaged! Help, angels! make assay!*
> *Bow, stubborn knees; and, heart with strings of steel,*
> *Be soft as sinews of the new-born babe!*
> *All may be well.*   (III. iii. 64)

Set against this lovely prayer—the fine flower of a human soul in anguish
—is the entrance of Hamlet, the late joy of torturing the King's conscience
still written on his face, his eye a-glitter with the intoxication of conquest,
vengeance in his mind; his purpose altered only by the devilish hope of
finding a more damning moment in which to slaughter the King, next
hastening to his mother to wring her soul too. Which then, at this moment
in the play, is nearer the Kingdom of Heaven? Whose words would be
more acceptable of Jesus' God? Which is the embodiment of spiritual
good, which of evil? The question of the relative morality of Hamlet and
Claudius reflects the ultimate problem of this play.

Other eminently pleasant traits can be found in Claudius. He hears
of Hamlet's murder of Polonius:

> *O Gertrude, come away!*
> *The sun no sooner shall the mountains touch,*
> *But we will ship him hence: and this vile deed*
> *We must, with all our majesty and skill,*
> *Both countenance and excuse.*   (IV. i. 28)

Though a murderer himself, he has a genuine horror of murder. This does
not ring hypocritical. He takes the only possible course. Hamlet is a
danger:

> *His liberty is full of threats to all.*   (IV. i. 14)

To hurry him from Denmark is indeed necessary: it is the only way of
saving himself, and, incidentally, the best line of action in the interests of
the state. During the scene of Ophelia's madness (IV. v.) Claudius shows
a true and sensitive concern, exclaiming, 'How do you, pretty lady?' and
'Pretty Ophelia!' and after he has told Horatio to look after her, he speaks
in all sincerity to his Queen:

> O, this is the poison of deep grief; it springs
> All from her father's death. O Gertrude, Gertrude,
> When sorrows come, they come not single spies,
> But in battalions. First, her father slain:
> Next, your son gone; and he most violent author
> Of his most just remove . . .   (IV. v. 76)

He continues the catalogue of ills. The people are dissatisfied, Laertes has returned. The problems are indeed overwhelming. When Laertes enters, Claudius rouses our admiration by his cool reception of him:

> What is the cause, Laertes,
> That thy rebellion looks so giant-like?
> Let him go, Gertrude; do not fear our person:
> There's such divinity doth hedge a king,
> That treason can but peep to what it would,
> Acts little of its will. Tell me, Laertes,
> Why thou art thus incensed. Let him go, Gertrude.
> Speak, man.   (IV. v. 120)

When he hears of Hamlet's return he plots treachery with Laertes. Everything considered, one can hardly blame him. He has, it is true, committed a dastardly murder, but in the play he gives us the impression of genuine penitence and a host of good qualities. After the murder of Polonius we certainly feel that both the King and the Queen are sane and doing their level best to restrain the activities of a madman. That is the impression given by the play at this point, as we read. If we think in terms of logic, we remember at once that we must side with Hamlet; and we perhaps remember the continual and sudden emergences of a different Hamlet, a Hamlet loving and noble and sane. But intermittent madness is more dangerous by far than obvious insanity. At the best we only prove that Hamlet's madness is justifiable, a statement which makes nonsense; for Hamlet's behaviour, so utterly out of harmony with his environment of eminently likeable people, in that relation may well be called a kind of madness. Whatever it is, it is extremely dangerous and powerful.

I have concentrated on Claudius' virtues. They are manifest. So are his faults—his original crime, his skill in the less admirable kind of policy, treachery, and intrigue. But I would point clearly that, in the movement of the play, his faults are forced on him, and he is distinguished by creative and wise action, a sense of purpose, benevolence, a faith in himself and those around him, by love of his Queen:

> ... *and for myself—*
> *My virtue or my plague, be it either which—*
> *She's so conjunctive to my life and soul,*
> *That as the star moves not but in his sphere,*
> *I could not but by her.* (IV. vii. 12)

In short he is very human. Now these are the very qualities Hamlet lacks. Hamlet is inhuman. He has seen through humanity. And this inhuman cynicism, however justifiable in this case on the plane of causality and individual responsibility, is a deadly and venomous thing. Instinctively the creatures of earth, Laertes, Polonius, Ophelia, Rosencrantz and Guildenstern, league themselves with Claudius: they are of his kind. They sever themselves from Hamlet. Laertes sternly warns Ophelia against her intimacy with Hamlet, so does Polonius. They are, in fact, all leagued against him, they are puzzled by him or fear him: he has no friend except Horatio, and Horatio, after the Ghost scenes, becomes a queer shadowy character who rarely gets beyond 'E'en so, my lord', 'My lord——', and such-like phrases. The other persons are firmly drawn, in the round, creatures of flesh and blood. But Hamlet is not of flesh and blood, he is a spirit of penetrating intellect and cynicism and misery, without faith in himself or anyone else, murdering his love of Ophelia, on the brink of insanity, taking delight in cruelty, torturing Claudius, wringing his mother's heart, a poison in the midst of the healthy bustle of the court. He is a superman among men. And he is a superman because he has walked and held converse with death, and his consciousness works in terms of death and the negation of cynicism. He has seen the truth, not alone of Denmark, but of humanity, of the universe: and the truth is evil. Thus Hamlet is an element of evil in the state of Denmark. The poison of his mental existence spreads outwards among things of flesh and blood, like acid eating into metal. They are helpless before his very inactivity and fall one after the other, like victims of an infectious disease. They are strong with the strength of health—but the demon of Hamlet's mind is a stronger thing than they. Futilely they try to get him out of their country; anything to get rid of him, he is not safe. But he goes with a cynical smile, and is no sooner gone than he is back again in their midst, meditating in graveyards, at home with death. Not till it has slain all, is the demon that grips Hamlet satisfied. And last it slays Hamlet himself:

> *The spirit that I have seen*
> *May be the Devil . . .* (II. ii. 635)

It was.

It was the devil of the knowledge of death, which possesses Hamlet and drives him from misery and pain to increasing bitterness, cynicism, murder, and madness. He has indeed bought converse with his father's spirit at the price of enduring and spreading Hell on earth. But however much we may sympathize with Ophelia, with Polonius, Rosencrantz, Guildenstern, the Queen, and Claudius, there is one reservation to be made. It is Hamlet who is right. What he says and thinks of them is true, and there is no fault in his logic. His own mother is indeed faithless, and the prettiness of Ophelia does in truth enclose a spirit as fragile and untrustworthy as her earthly beauty; Polonius is 'a foolish prating knave'; Rosencrantz and Guildenstern are time-servers and flatterers; Claudius, whose benevolence hides the guilt of murder, is, by virtue of that fact, 'a damned smiling villain'. In the same way the demon of cynicism which is in the mind of the poet and expresses itself in the figures of this play, has always this characteristic: it is right. One cannot argue with the cynic. It is unwise to offer him battle. For in the warfare of logic it will be found that he has all the guns.

In this play we are confronted by a curious problem of technique. I pointed out early in this section that the effects are gained by contrast, and it will be seen from my analysis that this contrast has its powerful imaginative effects. But it is also disconcerting. Though we instinctively tend at first to adopt the view-point of Hamlet himself, we are not forced to do so throughout. My analysis has shown that other methods of approach are possible; and, if they are possible, they are, in objective drama, legitimate. It is, indeed, necessary that we should be equally prepared to adopt the point of view of either side, otherwise we are offering a biassed interpretation. And though the Hamlet-theme preponderates over that of any one other individual in the play, it will be clear that Hamlet has set in contrast to him all the other persons: they are massed against him. In the universe of this play—whatever may have happened in the past—he is the only discordant element, the only hindrance to happiness, health, and prosperity: a living death in the midst of life. Therefore a balanced judgement is forced to pronounce ultimately in favour of life as contrasted with death, for optimism and the healthily second-rate, rather than the nihilism of the superman: for he is not, as the plot shows, safe; and he is not safe, primarily because he is right—otherwise Claudius could soon have swept him from his path. If we think primarily of the state of Denmark during the action of the play, we are bound to applaud Claudius, as he appears before us: he acts throughout with a fine steadiness of purpose. By creating normal and healthy and lovable persons around

his protagonist, whose chief peculiarity is the abnormality of extreme melancholia, the poet divides our sympathies. The villain has become a kindly
uncle, the princely hero is the incarnation of cynicism. It is true that if
Hamlet had promptly avenged his father, taken the throne, forgotten his
troubles, resumed a healthy outlook on life, he would have all our acclama-
tions. Laertes entering in wrath at the death of his father, daring 'damna-
tion' (IV. v. 132) and threatening Claudius, comes on us like a blast of
fresh air, after the stifling, poisonous atmosphere of Hamlet's mind.
Laertes and Hamlet struggling at Ophelia's grave are like symbols of life
and death contending for the prize of love. Laertes is brave in his course
of loyalty. But to expect such a course from Hamlet is to misunderstand
him quite and his place in the play. The time is out of joint, he is thrown
out of any significant relation with his world. He cannot bridge the gulf
by rational action. Nor can he understand the rest any more than they
understand him. His ideals—which include an insistent memory of death
—are worth nothing to them, and, most maddening fact of all, they get
on perfectly well as they are—or would do if Hamlet were out of the
way. Thus, through no fault of his own, Hamlet has been forced into a
state of evil: Claudius, whose crime originally placed him there, is in a
state of healthy and robust spiritual life. Hamlet, and we too, are perplexed.

Thus Hamlet spends a great part of his time watching, analysing,
and probing others. He unhesitatingly lances each in turn in his weakest
spot. He is usually quite merciless. But all he actually accomplishes is to
torment them all, terrorize them. They are dreadfully afraid of him. Hamlet is so powerful. He is, as it were, the channel of a mysterious force,
a force which derives largely from his having seen through them all. In
contact with him they know their own faults; neither they nor we should
know them otherwise. He exposes faults everywhere. But he is not tragic
in the usual Shakespearian sense; there is no surge and swell of passion
pressing onward through the play to leave us, as in *King Lear,* with the
mighty crash and backwash of a tragic peace. There is not this direct
rhythm in Hamlet—there is no straight course. Instead of being dynamic,
the force of Hamlet is, paradoxically, static. Its poison is the poison of
negation, nothingness, threatening a world of positive assertion. But even
this element is not the whole of Hamlet. He can speak lovingly to his
mother at one moment, and the next, in an excess of revulsion, torment
her with a withering and brutal sarcasm. One moment he can cry:

> *I loved Ophelia: forty thousand brothers*
> *Could not, with all their quantity of love,*
> *Make up my sum.*   (V. i. 291)

Shortly after he scorns himself for his outbreak. His mind reflects swift changes. He may for a moment or two see with the eyes of humour, gentleness, love—then suddenly the whole universe is blackened, goes out, leaves utter vacancy. This is, indeed, the secret of the play's fascination and its lack of unified and concise poetic statement. Hamlet is a dualized personality, wavering, oscillating between grace and the hell of cynicism. The plot reflects this see-saw motion; it lacks direction, pivoting on Hamlet's incertitude, and analysis holds the fascination of giddiness. Nor can Hamlet feel anything passionately for long, since passion implies purpose, and he has no one purpose for any length of time. One element in Hamlet, and that a very important one, is the negation of any passion whatsoever. His disease—or vision—is primarily one of negation, of death. Hamlet is a living death in the midst of life; that is why the play sounds the note of death so strong and sombre at the start. The Ghost was conceived throughout as a portent not kind but sinister. That sepulchral cataclysm at the beginning is the key to the whole play. *Hamlet* begins with an explosion in the first act; the rest of the play is the reverberation thereof. From the first act onwards Hamlet is, as it were, blackened, scorched by that shattering revelation. The usual process is reversed and the climax is at the start. Hamlet, already in despair, converses early with death: through the remaining acts he lives within that death, remembering the Ghost, spreading destruction wherever he goes, adding crime to crime,[1] like Macbeth, and becoming more and more callous, until his detestable act of sending his former friends to unmerited death 'not shriving-time allow'd' (v. ii. 47). Finally 'this fell sergeant, death' (v. ii. 350) arrests him too. This is his mysterious strength, ghost-begotten, before which the rest succumb. That is why this play is so rich in death— why its meaning is analysed by Hamlet in soliloquy, why Hamlet is so fascinated by the skulls the Grave-digger unearths; why so many 'casual slaughters' and 'deaths put on by cunning and forced cause' (v. ii. 393) disrupt the action, till we are propelled to the last holocaust of mortality and Fortinbras' comment:

> *This quarry cries on havoc. O proud death,*
> *What feast is toward in thine eternal cell,*
> *That thou so many princes at a shot*
> *So bloodily hast struck?*   (v. ii. 378)

The Ghost may or may not have been a 'goblin damned'; it certainly was

---

[1] An exaggeration. Hamlet's 'crimes' are, properly, two only. See my essay *'Hamlet* Reconsidered' (1947).

no 'spirit of health' (I. iv. 40). The play ends with a dead march. The action grows out of eternity, closes in it. The ominous discharge of ordnance thus reverberates three times: once, before Hamlet sees the Ghost, and twice in Act v. The eternity of death falls as an abyss at either end, and Hamlet crosses the stage of life aureoled in its ghostly luminance.

BIBLIOGRAPHY ENTRY FOR RESEARCH PAPERS:

Knight, George Wilson. "The Embassy of Death: An Essay on *Hamlet,*" Part II. From his *The Wheel of Fire.* London, 1930, 1949. In *Interpreting Hamlet,* ed. Russell E. Leavenworth. San Francisco, 1960.

FIRST FOOTNOTE:

* George Wilson Knight, "The Embassy of Death: An Essay on *Hamlet,*" Part II, from his *The Wheel of Fire* (London, 1930, 1949), in *Interpreting Hamlet,* ed. Russell E. Leavenworth (San Francisco, 1960), pp. 92-103.

SUBSEQUENT FOOTNOTES:

* Knight, *op. cit., IH,* p. ■■.
* Knight, "Embassy," *IH,* p. ■■.
* Knight, *IH,* p. ■■.

In place of *"IH,"* "ed. Leavenworth" may be used in these subsequent-footnote forms.

E. E. STOLL

ON

the Meaning of Hamlet

Elmer Edgar Stoll (1874–1959) was for many years Professor of English at the University of Minnesota. A bibliography of his published criticism would be a long one, and largely on Shake-spearean subjects. The essay reprinted here, which follows a dis-cussion of Othello, *is from Chapter V of his* Art and Artifice in Shakespeare *(Cambridge, 1933), by permission of Cambridge University Press. We omit the last section.*

HAMLET

§ 1

IN HAMLET, also, though in a different manner, the hero is put in a plight—made superior to his conduct and somewhat averse to it. Again the highly effective situation is brought about by external means—by the ghost, which is, of course, no figment of the hero's imagination, and no more an allegory or symbol than is the goddess Athena in the epic or the Weird Sisters in the tragedy, who perform much the same dramatic function. And again the improbabilities are allayed by the reality of the characterization, the interest of a quickly moving story, a veiled confusion of motive, and the all-reconciling power of poetry.

Of the dramatist's particular purpose, however, and his success in achieving it, we are here less able rightly to judge because the original *Hamlet* is lost; though of this we indirectly know enough (that is, through the sister play *The Spanish Tragedy,* by the same author; the German *Hamlet;* and Quarto I, which is Shakespeare's first revision, piratically printed and inadequately reported)[1] to be sure that for the resulting obscurity it was much to blame. This rudely written but cunningly constructed Senecan melodrama of Kyd's was popular—hence the two revisions of it by the most popular dramatist of the London stage; and yielding to the demand of his company and their public, the poet was not free, if indeed, in view of the practical necessities and advantages, he was much disposed, to make sweeping changes. Until his life-giving hand retouched it the play had not been so popular as *The Spanish Tragedy,* which had, in the last months, taken a new lease of life from the mad-scenes added by Jonson; it was this success that the Chamberlain's company was now emulating; and since the most unreasonable features of the Danish tragedy, shared by the Spanish, were its most unmistakable attractions, they must be not only retained but, in Jonson's fashion, heightened and set off. The story must in general be the same story, though better told, or both company and public would be disappointed; and the principal improvement expected was no doubt in style and metre.

With merely that Shakespeare could not have contented himself, but just how far was he to go? Because not only of the popular demand but of dramatic requirements, the ghost must still appear at the beginning, and the tragic deed be accomplished, as in all good revenge plays, ancient or modern, at the end. How, then, was the revenger to be occupied in the meantime? As in the old *Hamlet,* of course—secretly, with intrigue and melancholy meditation, which to us seem not greatly to advance the business in hand (but must needs not too greatly advance it); and publicly, with a pretence of madness, which to us seems only to thwart it. But there these matters were, superficially at least, less unplausible. There the delay, though like Hieronimo, in *The Spanish Tragedy,* the hero reproached himself for it, was attributed to the King's being difficult of access; and the feigned madness was represented as a means to reach him. These motives, like others that the dramatist found in his sources, he

---

[1] The dates of *The Spanish Tragedy* and the old *Hamlet* are prior to 1589; and the old *Hamlet* is probably previous to the other play for the simple reason that the story of the latter is the Belleforest Hamlet story transposed, a father revenging instead of the son. That Kyd was the author of the old *Hamlet* is as certain as any attribution founded on indirect evidence can be. The First Quarto was published in 1603; *Der Bestrafte Brudermord* is in a MS. of 1710, though it must have been written much earlier, and is based either on Kyd direct or Quarto I. Marston's *Antonio's Revenge* (c. 1599-1600), being, like his other tragedies, under Kyd's influence, repeats *Hamlet* situations and follows its technique.

deliberately omitted (for a poor explanation only creates a need of explanation); and, as in *Othello* and *Macbeth,* he had recourse to manœuvring. In a play that bore such a title, and kept to the old story, he could not, without the plainest indication, which he has not provided, shake off the Senecan tradition;[1] and, prompted by his usual opportunism, he turned that tradition to account. Profiting by the familiarity of feigned madness as an artifice and a natural employment of the revenger at Court, not only in the old *Hamlet, The Spanish Tragedy,* and his own *Titus Andronicus,* but also in the legends of the elder Brutus at the Court of Tarquin, and of David at that of Achish, King of Gath—"And he changed his behaviour before them, and feigned himself mad in their hands"—he passed lightly, carrying his audience with him, over the reasons for it here:

> *As I perchance hereafter shall think meet*
> *To put an antic disposition on,—*

and by the time they are to see him again the hero has put it on already. The dramatist taking it as a matter of course, the audience would so take it; and not, like the critics, scratch their heads, and cunningly conclude (as a generation ago) that it is a "safety-valve", or (as nowadays) a case of "double consciousness", or any of the numerous other things it has been thought to be, and still less, that the man is crazy in reality. Thus, and by his subtler treatment and phrasing, he intensified an effect of contrast provided in the melodrama, similar (as we shall see) to that later invented for Othello, and, however improbable, too precious to be surrendered. And profiting by the familiarity of the rest of the intrigue— the baffling of the spies, the doubt of the ghost and the theatrical performance to satisfy it, the sparing of the King at his devotions, the killing

---

[1] This point is what many critics wholly literary in their interests do not see. They are shocked and indignant at the old *Hamlet* (and *The Spanish Tragedy*) being spoken of in the same breath with Shakespeare's, and at the heroes at all resembling each other; and they more than intimate that such comparisons argue an insensibility in the speaker. They rush to the conclusion that he discerns little difference between them in quality, as well as kind. They do not realize that Shakespeare, writing for an audience, and a company, not for them, had not a free hand, if really he desired it; that since the audience remembered the old *Hamlet,* and other plays like it now on the stage, he, writing apparently only another *Hamlet,* must constantly remember the earlier too; and that his critics, to understand him, must as well. Writing for print and two thousand years after, Racine could make a *Phaedra* rather different from that of Euripides, and Goethe, a different *Iphigenia;* but *not* so different as this *Hamlet* expected by the critics of Shakespeare, when the other was not a dozen years old and recently was still on the stage. And still less do the critics realize that in keeping the story and character fairly intact lay the Elizabethan dramatist's advantage.

of him (as is intended) behind the arras and the reproachful conference
with his mother, the trip to England—the dramatist (to judge by the
changes from Quarto I to Quarto II and the Folio) subdued, instead of
emphasizing, its irrelevance, but accentuated and complicated its dangers;
letting Hamlet perilously play the King's game (but beat him at it) as if
it were his own, and, unlike Kyd's Hamlet, keep the secret of his revengeful purpose from his friends, his mother, and even from Horatio until
near the end of the tragedy, and his plan to the very end.[1] Thus he
heightened the suspense and mystery, imparted to the hero dignity, delicacy, and pathos, and threw the whole burden of motivation, or explanation, upon his self-reproaches.

§ 2

These, I cannot but think, are not meant to hurt him in our opinion,
are merely to explain and justify the story. Here we are at the heart and
core of the character; and even if Shakespeare had desired it, he could
scarcely, on the contemporary stage, have introduced so fundamental an
innovation as, in the place of a popular heroic revenger, a procrastinator,
lost in thought and weak of will. Thereby he would have both disappointed and bewildered the company and audience he had undertaken to
please. Rather, he kept Hamlet as he found him, only manipulating him
more deftly. The audience were accustomed to the revenger beating about
the bush but reproaching himself for it, and even being reproached by his
confidants for it (as our Hamlet is not), without loss of prestige in their
eyes. They knew Hieronimo, in *The Spanish Tragedy;* they knew the hero
of Marston's *Antonio's Revenge* (1599–1600), and, in translation (as the
authors did in the original), Seneca's Atreus, Medea, and Clytaemnestra,
who, all of them, act and speak after much the same fashion. In effect
the reproaches are, as often in ancient and Renaissance soliloquy, exhorta-
tions, addressed by the character to himself. They motive the delay, not
in the sense of grounding it in character, but of explaining it and bridging
it over; they motive it by reminding the audience that the main business
in hand, though retarded, is not lost to view. They provide an epical
motive, if I may so call it—a *ficelle,* as Mr Walkley[2] called it—rather
than a dramatic one. In all the instances above mentioned, as well as

---

[1] My *Hamlet* (1919), pp. 40-3. [*Hamlet: An Historical and Comparative
Study* (*Research Publications of the University of Minnesota, Studies in Language
and Literature, No. 7,* Minneapolis, 1919)] In Quarto I, the Queen is plainly told
that her first husband was murdered, is requested to "assist me in revenge", and
agrees to do her best.

[2] *Drama and Life* (1908), p. 151.

many others in the Renaissance drama, reproaches beforehand for failure to act do not discredit the hero or reveal an inner flaw.[1] And, indeed, is not this simpler technique more in keeping with the surface and common course of life? "Yea, a man will pause", replies the Chorus to the complaint of Sophocles' Electra against Hamlet's prototype, Orestes, "on the verge of a great work". Who does not?

This is a case where what the character says of himself in soliloquy, even though (as with both Sophocles and Kyd) his confidants say it too, is not, according to the usual expectation of the dramatist, to be taken at its face value; or, we might better say, it is to be taken at that and no more, being the sort of charge that Elizabethan and ancient tragedy, concerned with ethical rather than psychical defects, made no further account of. In those days not everything in conduct was reduced to a psychological or sociological phenomenon, or was given an inner meaning, even as it is not by ordinary people in ours; and, in particular, not such a matter as the pausing or hesitating which holds the situation, which prolongs the story. But, it may be objected, the Elizabethan revenge plays being crude affairs, all we can be sure of is that Shakespeare could have profited by this tradition if he chose. In his play the fact of the murder and the project of revenge are, as we have seen, kept a secret; and this may be, apart from the reasons above given, simply in order to spare the hero the blame of his friends. Yet what counts in drama is the positive; and Hamlet not only is never blamed or criticized but is esteemed and openly praised on every hand. If at any other time he had shown himself a procrastinator or a weakling, Horatio or Laertes, the King or the Queen could have said or hinted as much; and by the laws of dramatic technique, both in that day and in this, they were under a heavy necessity of saying it, and not the contrary, now. A villain who reveals his inner nature in soliloquy may conceal it from the world until the end; but Hamlet, if he has anything worth concealing, does so even beyond the end, while Fortinbras is declaring he would have made a kingly king. The tradition of the stage, then, the admiration of others, his own intrepid and precipitate activity on many occasions[2]—the effect of all these readily

---

[1] See [Stoll's] *Hamlet*, pp. 14-19 for the evidence.

[2] This is ordinarily interpreted as a spasmodic and frantic "compensation", and really part of his disease. Why then does Hamlet, in his ruminations, never remark upon the matter, or a little wonder at himself after killing the man behind the arras, or after his trip to England, above all after the prodigies of his prowess at the fencing-match? What an audience the critics have been presupposing at the Globe, or, for that matter, anywhere!

overcomes, certainly in those days (and for long after) overcame, that of the vague and conflicting charges which, in his noble solicitude, he brings against himself; and as Swinburne truly says, "A man whose natural temptation was to swerve, whose inborn inclination was to shrink and skulk aside from duty and from action, would hardly be the first and last person to suspect his own weakness, the one only unbiased judge and witness of sufficiently sharp-sighted candour and accuracy to estimate aright his poverty of nature and the malformation of his mind".[1] At least in drama—popular Elizabethan drama, especially—he would not. Where else in Shakespeare is any secret, needful for the comprehension of the action, kept from the other characters—and really from the audience too!—for good and all?

And what of the reproaches in themselves? Here the dramatist is devious still, but to the same effect and tenor. There is, indeed, analysis, such as is not to be found in the other Elizabethan revenge plays; but with a "veiled confusion" that reminds one of Macbeth, yet more particularly of Iago. Both the Ancient and the Prince raise the question of this motive or that, but leave it unanswered. None of the motives at which Iago glances—the grievance in the matter of the promotion, or his lust for Desdemona, or his fancy that Othello or Cassio may have played him foul with Emilia—is sufficient for the vast villainy of his nature, as we already know it, and of his conduct, as we are about to know it; and his cool and cynical survey only indicts him the more deeply. He is a son of Belial, he is a limb of Satan. None of the motives which Hamlet considers—cowardice, melancholy, bestial oblivion, or thinking too precisely on the event—fits his noble nature, as we already know it, and his failure to act; and they fairly cancel one another. In the first soliloquy on the subject, "O what a rogue", he scornfully rejects the imputation of cowardice, afterwards, in ironical self-laceration, accepts it;[2] but he resolves upon the play. In the second, "How all occasions", he confesses that why he has delayed he "does not know"; but he resolves on bloody deeds. So similar a method with the two characters, and so dissimilar a result? But that is Shakespeare; and really, when the manner and spirit are allowed for, the result is much the same. In one case the motives are made up; in the other they are sought. In one case the consideration is accompanied with a jest or a jeer; in the other with chidings and amends. But in both

---

[1] *A Study of Shakespeare* (1895), p. 168.

[2] Mr Clutton-Brock (*Shakespeare's Hamlet*, 1922), p. 121, takes the acceptance seriously—and the Prince sinks to the level of Parolles!

cases the audience is thrown back upon the introspective speaker[1]—already revealed to it as ignoble and hateful, or as noble and lovable. In one case, after each doubtful consideration, he holds his course with unabated zest; in the other, he changes it. But he does not change it again.

Only twice does Hamlet reproach himself—in the soliloquies just mentioned, at the end of the second act, and in the fourth scene of Act IV. The first is provoked by the example of the player's passion; the second, by the example of Fortinbras' martial activity. For the first there is the occasion of the hero's failure, so far, to do anything but feign madness and baffle hostile curiosity; for the second, to do anything but confirm the ghost's report. In either the reproaches arise naturally, and are needed to satisfy the audience, to point and justify the story. And that they are not needed afterwards is simply owing to the fact that, now more than ever, Claudius takes the offensive—more than ever the game is his. Further explanations are not necessary, though no more than hitherto does Hamlet take the lead. But in life such a defect as the critics presume is not cured save by heroic measures, and in drama must not simply drop out of sight; it may drop out only if it be not momentous. To most critics the trip itself is an evasion, and the man is quite aimless now. Yet by Hamlet's previous remarks it is made abundantly clear that in going to England he is but turning the plan of the King and Rosencrantz and Guildenstern into his own—"I see a cherub that sees them", " 'tis sport to have the enginer hoist with his own petar", etc.; and before and after his reappearance we learn that, by fingering his custodians' packet and boarding the Pirate, he has been as good as his word. What little he is suffered to say on the subject of his purpose thereafter is in a tone of cool and quiet confidence. The news, he says, will soon be out—

> It will be short; the interim is mine.
> I shall win at the odds.

And by the second soliloquy, about Fortinbras, before embarkation, added in Quarto II, Shakespeare shows more clearly than elsewhere, not, as has been thought, that Hamlet is of a procrastinating nature, but that his "tardiness" is not a sin or a disease, not a taint in the blood or a clot on the brain, but simply, as he and the ghost both say, a case of "forgetting", in other words, remissness, neglect, or "almost blunted pur-

---

[1] Or else into the arms of the critics; who for Iago, too, have found new motives, under the surface. For a fuller discussion of this character cf. *Shakespeare Studies*, pp. 382-90 [E. E. Stoll, *Shakespeare Studies*, New York, 1927]; and similar opinions, in a book of the same year, *Studies in the Contemporary Theatre*, pp. 77-8, by a critic who is not misled by philosophy and psychology, Mr John Palmer.

pose", for that Hamlet does not forget is plain as day. These are not damaging charges, and, for an ordinary audience like that expected, as at the Globe, have no necessary psychological significance. They serve for the narrative—so Edgar, Albany, and the rest "forget" King Lear and Cordelia, until she is hanged.[1] And now the neglect and delay are over and done with: this soliloquy, with its final resolution, is there, if for nothing else, to show it; his conduct on the trip sets the seal upon it. It is unthinkable, otherwise, that the hero should never, in the two acts which follow, utter a word of complaint or self-reproach again. Evidently the soliloquy was put in, not as an indictment, but to make clear what was the trouble and end it. In that which closes Act II he has reproached himself with the duty undone, and, a doubt of the Ghost arising, he has resolved upon the play to catch the King. In this of Act IV he finds that still for some reason the duty is undone, and resolves on bloody deeds. "Thoughts", to be sure, is what he says; but that does not much matter, since these are thoughts that bring deeds in their trail. His words in both soliloquies are made good; both soliloquies are landmarks in the drama.

As psychology, certainly, the trouble is not made clear; yet, depending upon the success with which the character has already been enforced upon the audience, the dramatist avails himself of the familiar fact that the most practical person in the world may, sometime or other, say "I don't know why I haven't done that", only telling the truth. His friends press him no further, and Hamlet's friends in the theatre should not either. It is action, indeed, and little more, that he now engages in— check-mating the King, not killing him; but Shakespeare is again manœuvring, and making the best of a picturesque and exciting but irrational old plot. Here, as at the end of "O what a rogue", he is counting on the audience being, in their familiarity with the circuitous movement of revenge plays, satisfied with any action against the murderer. And only this defensive movement it must as yet be, for to resolve upon immediately killing him, and not kill him (as indeed by the requirements of the story, until the last act, he cannot) would make the Prince look more futile than ever.

---

[1] See below, Chap VI, p. 143. [Not included in this selection.] For other examples of "forgetting" (and the like) as a device of dramatic retardation, see [Stoll's] *Hamlet*, pp. 17-19. It is worth noting that when the Ghost appears in the bedchamber, Hamlet is made to anticipate the rebuke. Here was the chance for speaking plainly to him and clearly to the audience, if they needed it. But the warrior-king, little concerned about his son's degeneracy, bids him comfort his mother.

In both cases it is action, not collapse; in both cases it is action which has to do with the King and with thwarting him; what is more, in both cases it is action which wholly satisfies the speaker himself. After the second soliloquy he complains of himself, questions himself, no more. And that the audience will observe, and are meant to observe, much more readily than the circumstance that the action is not the supreme one demanded. So the dramatist is enabled to content his audience, shield his hero, and still prolong his play.[1]

A mechanical matter again, which, however, should not surprise us in a crude old play rewritten. The effort to postpone the catastrophe is apparent in some of the greatest tragedies, like the *Oedipus,* apart from those which deal with revenge.

§ 3

In sum and substance, then, we have no right, as the critics ever since the days of Romanticism have been doing (and not only in this play but in most of the others), to interpret the character by way of the plot instead of at first hand. "To save the story, the dramatist lets the hero heap upon himself reproaches for his inaction; to save the character, he counteracts the effect of these by his own words, those of others, and the whole impression of his conduct."[2] And this pretence of action of the dramatist's is not a pretence of the character's. Shakespeare's evasion of the revenge, or of plans for it, is not Hamlet's own. It has been demonstrated that his doubt of the Ghost is an honest doubt, that the sparing of the King at prayer is for the reason given; and there is no indication that anything else Hamlet does is more of an evasion than these.[3] On the stage, even more than in life, pretences and excuses should appear to be lugged in or snatched at, and evasions should look like evasions, as, indeed, for two centuries Hamlet's (if such they be) did not; and if the supreme dramatist's art in this matter is with our critics a success, with his audience, of which alone he was thinking, it was a failure! Certainly

---

[1] [Stoll's] *Hamlet,* p. 25.

[2] *Shakespeare Studies,* p. 132.

[3] [Stoll's] *Hamlet,* Chap. IV, "The Hero's Self-Deception"; for the doubt of the Ghost, pp. 47-51. That Hamlet should suspect the Ghost to be the devil is quite in accord with the orthodox Protestant opinion of the day. And that he should not be willing to send his victim to Heaven is in accord with the principles of the vendetta in tragedy and *novella* at the Renaissance, English and Continental; in Senecan tragedy; and even in the *Iliad,* as Hector wreaks himself on the body (and thus on the departed spirit) of Patroclus, and Achilles on that of Hector, mutilating it and refusing it burial. Neither motive could, without explicit indication, seem to the Elizabethan audience a pretext.

the hero's going off to England, which has been taken particularly ill, is least to be reckoned against him, as Swinburne insisted long ago:

> The compulsory expedition of Hamlet to England, his discovery, by the way, of the plot laid against his life, his interception of the King's letter and his forgery of a substitute for it against the lives of the King's agents, the ensuing adventure of the sea-fight, with Hamlet's daring act of hot-headed personal intrepidity, his capture and subsequent release on terms giving no less patent proof of ready-witted courage and resource than the attack had afforded of his physically impulsive and even impetuous hardihood—all this serves no purpose whatever but that of exhibiting the instant and almost unscrupulous resolution of Hamlet's character in time of practical need. But for all that he has got by it, Shakespeare might too evidently have spared his pains; and for all this voice as of one crying in the wilderness, etc.[1]

The trip to England, like the doubt of the Ghost and the sparing of the King at prayer, is, though for the Elizabethan stage adequately motived, a deliberate prolongation of the situation, an artful postponement of the catastrophe, such as is, for that matter, to be found in Homer. Above we have noticed the kinship of Shakespeare's tragic method to the Greek; but at this point the ancient epics offer a better comparison than do the tragedies, since the latter, keeping to the unities, contain, save in retrospect, little in the way of story, or incident, which we are now discussing. In the *Iliad,* too, the principal characters must be kept alive and active, and (as far as may be) with reputation untarnished, till near the end; and this is done not only by the intervention of the deities (as we have seen), and many other expedients (such as a marksmanship whereby generally not a hero is hit but his comrade or charioteer or companion, on one hand, or as an extraordinary proficiency in dodging, on the other, not to mention the timely discovery of guest-friendship, the interposition of heralds, the coming of night, or the breaking of weapons) but also, even in the case of the most redoubtable warriors, save Achilles alone, by

---

[1] *Op. cit.,* pp. 167-8. Shakespearean criticism is like the theological; and the great and formidable heretics, like Swinburne and Shaw, Walkley and Bridges, pass unscathed, untouched. Upon their want of perception there are no sarcasms, nor any strictures upon their opinions; though those of the last three, certainly, lay within the scope of Professor Herford's Sketch (1893-1923), and all four within that of Mr Clutton-Brock, as well as of the reviewers of books in which they are cited as authoritative. And, like other great heretics, again, these are little heeded. Swinburne wrote the words in 1879.

sudden, though not untimely, accesses of fear or promptings to "avoid fate". So Hector is saved on at least four several occasions,[1] not to mention those whereon he bows to the will of a god, yields to "a weakling heart" put within him, or gives way with all the host. Yet, unquestionably, he is no coward: by his tone and bearing, both his conduct and his reputation, he is to be judged. Neither is Odysseus one, in the later epic, nor Aeneas, in that to follow, amid their apprehensions, as, time and again, fate bids fair to overwhelm them. Moreover, these demonstrations, like the tears of Romeo, the lamentations of Troilus and Antony, the trepidations of Macbeth and his momentary refusal to fight Macduff, serve to mark and measure for us the tragic effect. So, at the end of Act I, does Hamlet's own outcry, "O cursed spite".

By his tone and bearing, likewise, and a conduct that is (if we be not cavilling) irreproachable, and a reputation that is stainless, is Hamlet to be judged. Even early in the play, as, in the soliloquy "O what a rogue", he looks forward to the Mousetrap, the tone is exactly the same that we have already noticed when he is looking forward to the fencing-match:

> *I'll tent him to the quick; if he but blench,*
> *I know my course.*

Such accents (unless I be utterly blind to the finer shades of expression, and deaf to the differences in rhythm of verse and speech) are not meant for those of irresolution or shiftiness, apathy or frailty;[2] and one's ear, not one's reason, is the best judge of Shakespeare's characters, as of Milton's likewise—not my ear, certainly, but Swinburne's, or Coleridge's (when he trusts it), yet even my own humble organ, for which the plastic dramatist wrote, I would boldly pit against the psychological ratiocinations of all the critics, which he never considered. In the form and fashion of Hamlet's speech there is no trace of uncertainty or fatuity, as there is no trace of suspiciousness or childishness, before he falls into the human

---

[1] *Iliad,* XI, 360; XIV, 408; XVII, 129; XXII, 136. In books VII and XXII Hector is afraid as Ajax and Achilles approach; in one case he would flee if he could, in the other he does.

[2] [Stoll's] *Hamlet,* pp. 38-9. Mr Clutton-Brock, indeed, finds (like others before him, I suppose) such qualities even in the cast of the hero's speech, and thinks that "he rambles on and on in a manner peculiar to himself among Shakespeare's characters" (p. 119), for example in the last soliloquy. If discursiveness were a test of irrelevance and irresolution in the text of Shakespeare, how many of his characters must needs suffer from the charge! The only place where Hamlet really is irrelevant is that which no psychological theory can justify, his discussion of theatrical art and business.

devil's clutches, in Othello's. And after one's ear (for are we not at the theatre?) one's simple wits. In this case, as at the fencing-match and on the trip to England, and in the same way, he makes his previous words good; for he kills the man he thinks to be the King. What is plainer still, he thus makes good the words he had uttered as he withheld his hand from the fratricide a minute or so before. Here, indeed, is the "more horrid hent", to "trip him that his heels may kick at heaven", as he catches the murderer spying upon him. And these plain and tangible things, this record of promise and fulfilment, the audience would notice, and were meant to notice; and if few of them stopped to think that in keeping the great deed to the last he was like the heroes of all revenge tragedies they knew of, including Achilles, still, they were used to that, and would instinctively approve of it. It is both the traditional form and the natural procedure; obviously, the deed done, the tragedy is over. To interpret Hamlet's conduct against him to the point of taking his delay or his aversion for a psychical defect, is somewhat like taking Othello's trustfulness for mental paralysis or stupidity.

And really Hamlet's case is much the same as Othello's and Macbeth's; only, the material being different, and the old play intervening, the treatment must be a little different too. The Weird Sisters and the villain alike touch responsive chords; but in Hamlet the chord struck by the Ghost is the noblest within him, his love for his father. His vengeance, unlike the Moor's and unlike the regicide at Glamis, is a duty; and his aversion, unlike theirs, is not a virtue, although no flagrant fault. It serves to motive the circuitousness of the plot, and, when there is no more need of it, disappears. Not far from the end it vanishes, like Lear's irascibility and Macbeth's ambition shortly after the beginning. "That was what it was for", says Professor Mackail of the latter; "it has served its purpose, and is dropped."[1] A *ficelle,* again. Here it does not furnish the central tragic contrast of the play; that is provided by something equally un-psychological, the madness feigned. For Hamlet, not unlike the others in error, is, like Romeo, a victim of circumstances.

And of Fate, like his enemies. The tragedy is one of intrigue and irony, according to James Drake (1699), who wrote the first extended criticism:

> The Criminals are not only brought to execution but they are taken in their own Toyls, their own Stratagems recoyl upon

---

[1] *Approach to Shakespeare* (1930), p. 22.

'em, and they are involved themselves in that mischief and ruine which they had projected for Hamlet.[1]

The author of *Some Remarks* (1736) says something to the same effect, particularly in connection with Laertes and the Queen.

> The Death of the Queen is particularly according to the strictest rules of Justice; for she loses her life by the villainy of the very Person who had been the Cause of all her Crimes.
>
> p. 48.

And unlike most criticism of the tragedy since, this finds ample warrant in the text. There are Hamlet's own words about the enginer hoist with his own petar, and two crafts directly meeting; Laertes' about a woodcock to his own springe, and the poison tempered by the King; and Horatio's at the end, as he anticipates the story he is to tell. How strange that this bosom friend of his, neither through confession, on the one hand, nor observation, on the other, has any inkling of the Prince's mental malady; and it is not to deal with him alone, and not at all with his dilatoriness, *his* story "of carnal, bloody, and unnatural acts", "of deaths put on by cunning and forc'd cause",

> *And, in this upshot, purposes mistook*
> *Fallen on the inventors' heads!*

How strange that Horatio, like Fortinbras, misses the point of the tragedy! Indeed, so strange a drama (if such there be) would be inconceivable on the stage. But from these and the other frequent discussions, down to the time of the Scottish—untheatrical—Richardson and Mackenzie, as well as from the play's continual popularity, it is apparent that Shakespeare had not misjudged his theatrical public, contemporary or posthumous. These only delighted in the intrigue, circuitous but cunning, bloody but poetically "just", and took it for what he intended it to be, a story, not of Hamlet's procrastination—that they would not have taken for a story!—but of a prolonged and artful struggle between him and the King. How far from the conception of present-day critics, that "Hamlet the man is *Hamlet* the play . . . the play itself, not a conflict of persons, but a conflict within the mind of Hamlet! The King and all the other persons of the play are almost passive spectators of the drama of Hamlet's mind, which they

---

[1] *Allusion-Book*, ii, 424-5.

cannot understand",[1]—which is just the thing, indeed, that Hamlet is taking every convenient or inconvenient measure to prevent or hinder!

In all that period no fault was found in him. The author of *Some Remarks* thinks Shakespeare "should have contrived some good reason" for his delay, but—"so brave and careless of his own life"—discovers none. In all that period the play was, as the Earl of Shaftesbury, in 1711, justly recognized, "that piece of his which appears to have most affected English hearts, and has been oftenest acted of any which have come upon our stage"—something it could not have been if the leading character had been represented as a hesitant weakling, a psychopathic case. Once he was so represented, he gradually retreated from the theatre, now a stranger to it; but before that he was probably, as he was in Germany indubitably, acted as a conquering hero. "So much the worse for those times", says even the historical-minded M. Legouis. But others may hesitate so lightly to reverse the verdict of two centuries of popular opinion and applause in the theatre, concerning a play written for the theatre, not published with the author's consent, and in both Quartos garbled, in favour of the judgment of Scotch professors and sentimentalists, Romantic poets and German philosophers, and present-day psychologists and psycho-analysts, exploring their own consciousness, in the study. Others still may have misgivings in acknowledging in a popular hero a tragic fault not discovered by a moral philosopher like Shaftesbury, or by neo-classical dramatists and critics, professionally on the alert for it, such as Nicholas Rowe, Fielding, Dennis, Tom Davies, Malone, Aaron Hill, Voltaire, and above all Johnson (who sought for it and was troubled by the lack of it), and first revealed to those who knew not and loved not the stage or its ways. The dramatic idiom[2] is not one of words and phrases merely, but of traditions and conventions; and why should not these successive generations of dramatists, actors, and spectators have far better understood it?

---

[1] Clutton-Brock, p. 95, etc. The conception here is not absolutely representative of present-day criticism, but it is the logical outcome of the prevailing psychological distortion of the drama. The little book here cited, by a sensitive and brilliant critic, is in some respects also an instance of the modern critic going sadly astray without the guidance of a dramatic tradition. (cf. above, p. 31). [Not included in this selection.] Mr Clutton-Brock does not, as many literary critics do, neglect the text, but he seems unable to read it. The dramatic idiom which I speak of in the next paragraph is foreign to him—he reads the words, but in another sense. And yet when the book appeared—such is the state of Shakespeare scholarship when it is not a matter of dates and sources and glosses—it was generally acclaimed. In dealing with individual words and phrases the learned have a standard—the dramatist's meaning; in dealing with the play as a whole they have none.

[2] Cf. above, p. 108 [the preceding footnote], note, and p. 49 [not included in this selection].

A novel or a poem may, in its own time and after, be neglected because misunderstood, but criticism should be wary of finding this to be the case with an extraordinarily popular play by an expert playwright; and of stepping into the breach itself, when the idiom has grown unfamiliar, with an interpretation diametrically opposed.

§ 4

There is not the usual refuge of muddled minds, a "middle ground". Hamlet, like Shylock and Falstaff, cannot conceivably be both what England for nearly two centuries with one consent took him for and also what critics take him for to-day, whether the later conception be thought to be intended or half intended, provided for "the judicious" of 1603 or of the nineteenth century and after. The two conceptions are antagonistic and incompatible, still more so than in the case of Shylock or Falstaff. Certainly Mr Dover Wilson's recent solution[1] for the Venetian usurer's is unsatisfactory: that, of the alternatives—"a great tragic figure, representative of the suffering Hebrew race", and "a comic character, of a devil in the likeness of an old Jew, a crafty, blood-thirsty villain crying out for revenge upon a decent Christian gentleman, and, at the last moment, hoist with his own petar"—"Shakespeare intended both". This the critic calls an example of "tragic balance"; but if he is echoing Coleridge's dictum cited above, there is no "reconcilement", either attempted or imaginable. The effect of the combination would be neither tragic nor comic, neither moral nor aesthetic, but chaotic or null. And the only acceptable mediation, I think, between the romantic conception of Shylock or Falstaff, and the earlier, lies in the recognition of the fact that the aesthetic ambiguity, in so far as it exists, was not intended, but is owing to the largeness of Shakespeare's sympathy, which would not suffer him, like Jonson or Molière, to keep sternly to a satirical rôle.[2] But like Mr Wilson's two-headed Shylock would be a Hamlet both morbid and healthy, weak and strong, irresolute and resolute, procrastinating and not procrastinating—contradictions, alike, in the world of fact, not of fiction, and not reconciled, as are those in Othello and Macbeth, by a conventional mechanism. And for me the balance in favour of the people and the stage, and against the critics and the study, is tipped decisively by three improbable implications of the current theory, already touched upon:

---

1 *The Essential Shakespeare* (1932), p. 81.
2 See *Shakespeare Studies*, pp. 302-36 and the chapter on Falstaff. And see below, Chap. IX, pp. 157-8. [Not included in this selection.]

(1) That Shakespeare, rewriting in response to popular demand a Senecan revenge-play, should have kept the story and so much of its spirit and method, without clearly indicating this wholly different turn which he is supposed to give the character. To have done so, of course, would have disappointed the audience; *famam sequere* then held good even more than now; and as Mr Archer observes, "a hero must be (more or less) a hero, a villain (more or less) a villain, if accepted tradition so decrees it". But if, as the critics would have him, Shakespeare was a dramatic dissenter and iconoclast, a Bernard Shaw from Nature's womb untimely ripped; and moulded a Hamlet, and a Shylock, and a Falstaff, in defiance of tradition and expectation; why then he must each time have flown and flaunted his colours like the Irishman, without possible mistake. He must have expatiated in prefaces, and descanted in italics. He must have penned prologues at least. Actually, however, they don't think him a Shaw, but, in some vague way, a "genius", exalted above the stage, tradition, and every obstacle (and therefore every means) of expression.

(2) That Shakespeare, designing innovation, should, on the other hand, have, out of the mouths of all the chief characters, praised the hero instead. If the dramatist had intended the flaw, he must by their comment have indicated it; as he does elsewhere, witness Othello[1] and Macbeth, Brutus, Antony, and Coriolanus. How amply is the much simpler mind of the Patrician general analysed, by friend and foe! That the hero must keep his secret does not matter—in drama still less than in life can he keep his character to himself. His failing, constitutional or newly developed, must have been made clear. Even by more difficult, modern dramatists, like Schiller in *Wallenstein,* and Ibsen in the *Wild Duck, Peer Gynt, The Master Builder,* and *Borkman,* apt critical comment upon it is found indispensable. But that, instead of criticism, he should have had nothing but praise and admiration poured upon him, is simply beyond my logical reach or aesthetic grasp. A problem-play and nobody aware of the problem, and in their admiration all of one accord?

For if this praise was mistaken, somehow, but unmistakably, the fact must be disclosed. Or if the subconscious (as has been thought) be here involved, through some prescience of the dramatist, why, even nowadays, when that entity is, as a notion, fairly familiar, it must, in the pages of Hervieu or O'Neill, whether by others or (subsequently) by the character himself, be explicitly recognized. How much the more *then*—when it wasn't and couldn't be! It scarcely matters that such psychology, of the

---

[1] That is, as in Iago's dictum, which must be taken for granted. See above, p. 18. [Not included in this section.]

subconscious, not only unsupported by comment but running counter to it, is both a scientific and a dramatic anachronism: it is, what is worse, a solecism, and upsets the play.

And what can Shakespeare ever have meant by the dénouement? (Is it better that he should play the psychologist, or remain a dramatist, an artist?) There is the hero, outfencing Laertes, killing the King, wresting the cup out of Horatio's hand. There is Horatio, ready to die with the wounded Prince out of sheer admiration and devotion; and Fortinbras, burying him "like a soldier", and declaring he would have "proved most royally". And what is he himself thinking, now as his life-blood is ebbing? Not a thought has he for any fault or defect such as Othello reveals in his last words for his own.[1] Not a thought, either, for his triumph over it. "Done after all", is what, infallibly, he should say to himself, if he were the crippled, aspiring but despairing, spirit the critics have taken him to be. Dramatic art—even common human nature—would demand no less. If the tragedy be, as the critics maintain, internal, here, if nowhere else—and since nowhere else—the fact must come to light. The audience must be permitted to see it, if the other characters do not. But Hamlet's only interests now are in things external—his name, the news, his father's crown.

And if plain (though the noblest) English means anything, he is not, as Mr Clutton-Brock would have it, "insisting that all through the play he has been misexpressing himself",[2] and both has not a doubt, but has every reason to believe, that Horatio can tell whatever he himself has left untold. Need I quote them, the dying but deathless words?

> *O good Horatio, what a wounded name,*
> *Things standing thus unknown, shall live behind me!*
> *If thou didst ever hold me in thy heart,*
> *Absent thee from felicity awhile,*
> *And in this harsh world draw thy breath in pain,*
> *To tell my story.*

"His anxiety cannot be merely that Horatio shall explain the external facts", declares the same critic, ". . . which could be done in a few words. . . . Dying himself, his last desire is that Horatio shall set him right with the world. The play ends with this desire unfulfilled; and the entry of Fortinbras tells that it is over and that life remains for good common-

---

1 That is, according to the sophistical premise (see above, p. 18) [not included in this selection]: "one that loved not wisely but too well", "one not easily jealous", etc.

2 [*Shakespeare's Hamlet*, 1922] Pp. 38, 81, including the citation below.

place people, such as Horatio, who certainly cannot explain Hamlet." Not
that of Mr Clutton-Brock, certainly, who well says that Hamlet himself
cannot explain him—a state of affairs (since nobody else can either)
that is acceptable in life or in Freud, but not in any conceivable drama!
Though (after forty more lines) the *play* is over, the *story* is not, and if
Horatio's and Fortinbras' promises count for anything, the "unsatisfied"
at once "shall hear" and Hamlet's desire be fulfilled. Any reader who
rouses from his dogmatic slumber and remembers that he is not conning
the text of James or construing that of Joyce, but (really) witnessing a
stage-fit theatrical performance, is well enough aware why neither Hamlet
nor Horatio is here at the end permitted to tell the audience what they,
if not the Danes (before them) already know.

Thus there is less point, to be sure, to the words "in this harsh world
draw thy breath in pain". The frail and shrinking spirit of the accepted
Hamlet has found the world harsher than has ours. But why should *he*
have his story told, or have Horatio draw his breath in pain to tell it?
If all of it were to be told, surely he had rather draw the veil—had rather
let Horatio drain the cup. Fine and reticent as he too must certainly be,
he would not, like a nineteenth-century Romantic poet, lay bare his bleed-
ing heart—exhibit his palsied will—to the curious and unfeeling world.
But for our Hamlet the story is only not long enough, and he yearns to
live a bit longer in the telling of it by his friend. He is a lord of the
Renaissance, and loves name and fame. He dies young, dies in the moment
of his triumph, dies, as it must seem to others, with all this blood on his
head. This is his triple tragedy, as Shakespeare, I think, intended it—a
simpler and nobler, possibly less interesting and piquant, conception than
the usual one, though one not less appealing. To some it may even be
more interesting because it seems to be more nearly what Shakespeare
intended—more like him and his age.

And why for the Prince, as for no one else in death, has Shakespeare
let the trumpets blare, the drums rattle, and the cannon thunder, as not for
Macbeth or Othello, who were warriors, nor for Lear, who was a king?
Why, even, the final abrupt and energetic half-line,

> *Go bid the soldiers shoot,*

instead of the couplet (as Mr Rylands points out[1]) in all the other
tragedies save *Timon of Athens* and *Coriolanus,* if Hamlet were in the
quality so unlike the other heroes and least of all like these? As a stage-

---

[1] *Words and Poetry* (1928), p. 169.

manager, and (of all things!) as a metrist, Shakespeare misses the point of his own play still more than as a dramatist, or than his ill-instructed raisonneur, Horatio! But the line—the salute—like the very Hamlet it was meant for, have long since quitted the stage! The producers, like the theorists, are not much troubled by the text.

(3) That Shakespeare should, in response to popular demand, but in defiance of such a taste, have best of all succeeded in satisfying both with what is an Elizabethan anomaly. There are other Hamlets[1] in Elizabethan times; but none of this modern complexion, and scarcely any, for that matter, even to-day. An irresolute hero is too unexhilarating a subject; but Hamlet, rightly interpreted, is (witness the past, whether on the stage or in the closet!) not unexhilarating. Elizabethan tragedy is romantic, heroic; and in the leading rôle there are no weaklings, save historical kings like Richard II, and Edward II, these erring through sentimentality rather than irresolution, and, anyway, not, like the Prince, held up to our admiration. Both friend and foe speak plainly, even in the presence. Only in comedy could such a character have then been acceptable—it is his rank and the dire consequences to the country that keep Richard at times from being comic himself—and there Hamlet, with the repeated pretexts and evasions attributed to him, might have done well enough. These, if recognized as such, could not then have been tragic; only by dint of great precaution could they, on the stage, before an uninstructed audience, be tragic even now. Mr Clutton-Brock has called the play a "tragedy of irrelevance"; which, on the Elizabethan or any other popular stage, would be, if anything, a contradiction in terms.

§ 5

What, now, of the present interpretation? Hamlet's madness, at least, is more nearly comprehensible. It is really feigned, not partly involuntary; and this is in keeping with Hamlet's words as he announces his intention, and with his perfect sanity when alone or with his friend. So, though less psychological, it is much more dramatic than if it were the presentation of a "disordered mind". It certainly is not a case of "double consciousness"; and the hero "misexpresses himself" only "under a compulsion" which he *does* understand, as, if simple and heedful, we also do.[2] For

---

[1] Apart from Kyd's Hieronimo and Marston's Antonio, Chapman's Clermont (*Revenge of Bussy d'Ambois, c.* 1604), who delays the deed like Hamlet, with no inner reason, for dramatic effect.

[2] Cf. Clutton-Brock, *op. cit.* Chap. II, *passim,* and p. 67: "misexpresses himself under a compulsion he does not understand".

himself it offers present liberty and saftey. For the drama it provides a contrast—the high-spirited Prince saying under a mask pretty much what he means (not ignominiously playing the friend or flatterer like the conspirators in *Julius Caesar,* the Greek Orestes plays, and the *Cinna* of Corneille[1]), and yet by no means betraying himself. Functionally, it is such a contrast as we have found in the other tragedies—between Othello jealous and noble, between Macbeth and his Lady engaged in murder and overwhelmed by conscience; but it is still more like the use of disguise, with its explicit ironies, as in *King Lear, As You Like It,* and *Twelfth Night;* indeed, in some other Elizabethan revenge plays, like Marston's *Malcontent,* it is by disguise replaced. In the matter of motivation, movement, and aesthetic result, however, *Othello* is still the best parallel. Without hesitation or struggle, without the clear presentation of processes or developments which would show how they arrived at this dire pass, the Moor, who lacks a jealous or a gullible nature, and the Dane, who has no sufficient reason to feign or dissemble, are nevertheless attended by all the authentic effects of tragedy, as, in the brothel scene of the one play and the nunnery scene of the other, they utter a mingled emotion, delight turned to anguish, love putting on the poisoned mask of bitterness or hate.[2]

Also, this playing of a part arouses suspense—we apprehend and dread the Prince's betrayal of his purpose. Not "double consciousness", of which the audience would comprehend nothing, it is a double situation, whereof they would comprehend the whole; the spies and his enemies are sounding the hero, and the hero them, and the limelight is not forever fixed on one melancholy figure's face and brain. Even in itself how much more acceptable is this madness as a ruse, though (on reflection) unplausible, than a madness half or wholly real, springing out of grief for a father's death and a mother's frailty—*that* is a thing more unplausible still! Hamlet has latterly been taken to be more fragile than Ophelia: she, within a day or so, fairly with her own eyes, had seen her lover lose his wits and kill her father. By some of the best critics[3] he is supposed to be suffering from "nervous shock", or "a wound in his mind", upon the Ghost's disclosures, as the Moorish general is supposed to be "stunned"

---

[1] On a speech, II, i, Mornet remarks "Cinna devient odieux". And here in general there is the same objection to the active conspirator in the leading rôle. See below, p. 124. [Not included in this selection.]

[2] My *Poets and Playwrights* (1930), p. 94.

[3] Bradley (pp. 113-28); Clutton-Brock, pp. 44, 45, 51, 75; and others. Cf. *Othello,* p. 32. [Stoll's *Othello, An Historical and Comparative Study* (Minneapolis, 1913)]

upon the ensign's—heroes, both, in that robust and bloody age and drama! Words—mere breath—are too much for them! The ramparts and defences of their characters tumble down about them like the walls of Jericho. In this degenerate day, we who make no heroic pretensions, and never faced or wielded a weapon, are stouter and tougher than that; and better an unplausible though effective dramatic device than a mythical psychology! How much more acceptable, too, this scorn and mockery of the folly and corruption, weakness and treachery, which compass him about, from one who has no touch of it himself! In justice, our present-day Hamlet cannot, as he does, rebuke the frailty of the Queen. To many of the critics, to be sure, that is no drawback, for they would have the Prince infected and poisoned by the air about him, his environment. Sociology must have its innings too! But to the dramatist the moral and emotional aspect is uppermost; and the isolation—and opposition—of the youthful hero is part of his tragedy.

He is melancholy, however, owing to his grief for his father's death and his mother's inconstancy; and like the other Elizabethan revengers, who are melancholy also, but not diseased or really deranged, he is, at certain moments, even when not in the presence of his enemies (or, for no reason, in their presence), nervously excited and demonstrative—as after the disclosures of the Ghost and *The Murder of Gonzago,* and at Ophelia's funeral. These contradictory extremes of conduct were recognized in the Elizabethan accounts of melancholy, and (what is more important) were, just at this time, being presented on the stage, as in *The Malcontent* (c. 1600); and on these extraordinary occasions Hamlet acts more like Marston's Malevole and Antonio (1599) than like any other of Shakespeare's characters. Whether the poet was at such moments under this influence, or merely that of the old play, or was even attempting an approach to a morbid psychology, cannot be determined. The first two instances of Hamlet's demonstrativeness, indeed, are by the occasion warranted; but his extravagant conduct at the funeral, where his enemies are present, seems to be the fruit of that Elizabethan infirmity of not knowing when to stop, or, as Dryden says, to "give over", treating the stage attraction of feigned madness, the late Mr Walkley observes, "for all it was worth",[1] as is done in *The Spanish Tragedy* and in Shakespeare's own *Titus Andronicus.* Why, though, undertake any explanation when Hamlet's own to Horatio contradicts his later one to Laertes himself?

---

[1] *Drama and Life* (1908): "Professor Bradley's Hamlet".

By the present interpretation, then, some matters remain unexplained, but not the character as a whole. The difficulties seem to be owing to two hurried and ill-printed revisions of a crude old play and to the complicated theatrical conditions of the time. And whatever other mystery there is in the character is that of great but irregular art, not—begging the question—the mystery of *life* itself. It is not that of the still prevailing doctrine, literalism blent with mysticism, whereby we treat Shakespeare's characters as if they were real persons, whom we know but cannot explain —and therefore we are sure that we know them!—or whom we then freely psychologize and psycho-analyse, to so little artistic or scientific profit.[1]

Whatever may be thought of him, such an heroic but pathetic Hamlet as (in barest outline, simply for the situation) I have been presenting, has the advantage over the morbid one of being stage-fit and fairly intelligible, which the psychologists have never made him; and of being in keeping with the text, the times, and the dramatic tradition and theatrical favour of two centuries; and that outweighs, I take it, the critical tradition of a century and a half. Such a Hamlet, above all, is in keeping with the whole play, of which he is only an inseparable component, and with the nature of drama. He is part of the structure, upholding and upheld by the other parts; and some of the mystery in him is only that of plot, some of it, a matter of emotional effect, as his reticence and dignity. He is a dramatic figure, not a psychological study. And if as such he could be accepted as the real Hamlet, he would then, by that very fact, have the greatest advantage attainable, that of relieving a long since weary world —in a play written in comprehensible English, for the popular stage—of the necessity, every little season, of coping with another.

But he will not be accepted, as Swinburne foretold. He has no "tragic fault", which is demanded, though not by Aristotle. (But so he is like Othello, Romeo, even King Lear, as, for that matter, Orestes, Oedipus, Iphigeneia, and Antigone). His tragedy, then, in which the hero is not the cause of his own undoing, must needs be "a melodrama".[2] (But in

---

[1] I cannot enter into the subject again—I have discussed it several times before, but most fully in *Shakespeare Studies,* pp. 120-5.

[2] Clutton-Brock, p. 120. See above, pp. 42, 58, note [not included in this selection], for the somewhat disputable ancient conception of the *hamartia.* If in life the Greeks considered motives less than we do, they did not in poetry ignore them; as appears, not only in Aeschylus and Sophocles, but in Aristotle himself, where he insists that the deed of horror should be done in ignorance (§14). [Not included in this selection.]

that case the tragedies, where figure the Greek heroes just mentioned, must be melodramas too.) And what of all the maxims and allusions in modern English and German—certainly our Hamlet must stay as he is! Indeed, he has of late taken on our dress, superfluously.

BIBLIOGRAPHY ENTRY FOR RESEARCH PAPERS:

Stoll, Elmer Edgar. "Hamlet." Ch. V from his *Art and Artifice in Shakespeare*. Cambridge, 1933. In part in *Interpreting Hamlet*, ed. Russell E. Leavenworth. San Francisco, 1960.

FIRST FOOTNOTE:

* Edgar Elmer Stoll, "Hamlet," ch. V from his *Art and Artifice in Shakespeare* (Cambridge, 1933), in part in *Interpreting Hamlet*, ed. Russell E. Leavenworth (San Francisco, 1960), pp. 104-126.

SUBSEQUENT FOOTNOTES:

* Stoll, *op. cit., IH*, p. ■■.
* Stoll, "Hamlet," *IH*, p. ■■.
* Stoll, *IH*, p. ■■.

In place of *"IH,"* "ed. Leavenworth" may be used in these subsequent-footnote forms.

ROSAMOND GILDER

ON

John Gielgud as Hamlet

Rosamond Gilder is a drama critic, Lecturer at Barnard College, and former editor of Theatre Arts Magazine. *Her* John Gielgud's Hamlet *(New York: copyright 1957 by Rosamond Gilder) is a line-by-line record of a distinguished performance; we reprint here Miss Gilder's introduction, also titled* "John Gielgud's Hamlet," *by permission of the author.*

JOHN GIELGUD'S HAMLET

I

FOR OVER three hundred and thirty years *Hamlet* has held the world in thrall. A stage success when it was written, the 'Standing Room Only' sign records its drawing power today. It triumphs over time and change because, more than any other single creation of man's mind, it is a living organism, complex and passionate, ugly and exalted, defying final analysis and permitting each succeeding generation to re-create it in its own image. The theatre grapples with it continuously, dressing it in every conceivable garb, ancient, modern and imaginary. Every actor, man or woman, lusts for it. The scholars snatch it from the players and retire with it like quarrelsome bears into remote fortresses of words, definitions, factual and fantastic interpretations. Children feed their love of beautiful sounds on its music and wise men spend their lives analyzing the meaning of a single phrase.

Yet *Hamlet* survives them all, survives the fleshly tragedienne as well as the desiccated pedant, survives the experiments of directors, the fantasies of designers, the virulent attacks of the smart young things, the dullness of the classroom, the weight of legendary reputation. It survives because Hamlet himself has never yet been caught, because he springs from the pins with which the pedant would fix him on the dissecting board, breaks the mould in which the critic would cast him, and refuses to conform to any formula yet proposed by any one age or generation. The most self-explanatory and generally talkative of young men, he yet does not tell us clearly such major things about himself as his age, his mental health, his feelings about his sweetheart, his morals, his religious beliefs, his political opinions. A library of documentation has failed to reveal what he actually says at certain crucial moments, or what he does at others. By the happy accident that Shakespeare never wrote a well-made play, that he forbore prefaces and never bothered to edit his own texts, *Hamlet* remains flexible and alive, various and variable. To each generation it is a different thing, and fortunate indeed is that generation which has its Hamlet made articulate for it by the genius of an actor who is kin both to the poet of Elizabeth's London and to the average man of his own day.

John Gielgud is such a Hamlet and by that he takes his place in the brief roll-call of the actors who have incarnated the Prince so completely for their day that they have become permanently associated with the part: Burbage for whom the role was written, Betterton who could make even his fellow actors' hair to stand on end, Garrick who held London in fee for years, Kean who revealed Shakespeare by flashes of lightning, Booth whose memory is cherished by our own parents and grandparents. The written records show that these men and the other great Hamlets of the past spoke directly and with no uncertain voice to the mind and heart of their own generation. In their presence the mystery of Hamlet was for the moment solved as it is solved to-day by Gielgud's performance. The creative genius of the actor, by its kinship with the creative genius of the poet, sheds a light on the text that the most fervid words, the most astute analysis of writer or scholar can never equal.

Two things must inevitably be said of any Hamlet worthy of his metal: this is Shakespeare's Prince—this is our own. Gielgud's fulfills both requirements—granting always that we can know either Shakespeare or ourselves! The play as he gives it is more nearly textually complete than we are accustomed to seeing it, and for this reason it is a more difficult, complex and startling Prince than the one, for instance, with which Booth fascinated and awed our forebears. Gielgud has been accused of not giving a unified impersonation. It is easy to see that the comment stems from a conception of the part based on versions delicately pruned to create the image of a princely youth of heroic mould who does, of course, exist in the text, but who is also doubled by a sardonic, virulent and cruel young man, a young man who talks bawdry to Ophelia, baits her father, sends his ex-friends to death without a scruple and kills without compunction once his blood is up. Hamlet, as Shakespeare wrote him, was a Renaissance youth to whom philosophy, poetry and violence were familiar. He lacked a decent sense of modern stage conventions, of climax and dénouement, of time-relationships and the proper conduct of a plot. He has a way of not remaining consistent that is disconcerting to the theorist.

To unify and simplify the role, Booth, for instance, omitted the most unappetizing of Hamlet's comments on his mother's behaviour, such as the 'incestuous sheets' of the first soliloquy, the 'most pernicious woman' of the speech that follows immediately on the ghostly interview. He left out all the coarse banter with Ophelia and large sections of the closet scene which were apparently not considered fit talk for a prince and certainly inconceivable for a son. Shakespeare, however, did write these things, if we are to trust the quartos and folios, and Gielgud plays them as integral to the role, and with shattering effect on those who cherish an image of Hamlet as all 'sweet Prince' in the modern and not in the Renaissance sense.

Shakespeare also provided Burbage with the Fortinbras soliloquy as well as the preceding soliloquies and the numberless elaborate set-pieces such as the speech to the players, and the graveyard passages. The Fortinbras soliloquy has usually been omitted, thereby depriving Hamlet of one of the telling facets of his multi-sided character. Another simplification has been to end the closet scene with the mood of reconciliation reached after storm and stress, in the rhymed couplet beginning 'I must be cruel only to be kind.' Actually, the scene at this point veers back again to the opening mood of violence and invective. By the elimination of this anticlimax a far smoother and more heroic Prince emerges from the text, but a Prince of less profoundly human proportions. Gielgud plays the scene through to the end, bringing it to a fresh and poignant climax with the one word 'mother' thrown after the retreating figure of the woman who carries away his last anchorage, his last security.

Gielgud has chosen to play Hamlet whole because he can accept and understand him whole. The generation he has grown up in is one which knew in its childhood that nobility and brutality were not legends but common facts recorded for four years in daily torrents of blood and printers' ink. Modern psychology must be as much a part of his thinking as the Darwinian theory was of our fathers'. The Freudian aspects of Hamlet's character are not startling for those to whom the revelations of the psycho-analytical technique are an accepted part of thought and experience. He can see and understand as perfectly sound and accurate portraiture Hamlet's split personality, his mother-fixation, his sense of guilt, his battles that will not stay won, his desperate efforts to reconcile the conflicting elements in his psychic make-up, his tendency to unpack his heart in words, his heroism and cowardice, his final integration. Shakespeare saw, understood and by a miracle of grace set down the detailed portrait of the 'modern man' of his day. Gielgud, speaking his words, fills them to the brim with the life blood of the 'modern man' of ours.

II

Gielgud's characterization is clear and convincing throughout, for though he shows a Hamlet, complex, moody—by turns furious and dejected, violent and indifferent—his concept is never blurred. He gives us at once, on our first sight of him, a picture of frustrated energy, of force held in check: force of grief curbed by lack of sympathy, force of filial love curbed by his mother's betrayal, force of ambition curbed by his uncle's usurpation, force of intellect curbed by surrounding stupidity. Hamlet sits frozen in grief, rage and futility. He has not been able to move forward from his father's death. His very natural grief, emphasized in Gielgud's performance, is denied its release in responsible action. He cannot take up the burden of his manhood, comfort himself by comforting his mother, heal the shock of his first severance from dependent childhood by assuming a role of leadership in family and state. His uncle has done more than pop in between the election and his hopes. Claudius has deprived him of the normal activities which would have permitted him to grow out of his state of shocked adolescence into maturity. In addition he has struck at his deepest physiological and psychological tie—his relation to his mother. Hamlet's profound trauma is disclosed in no uncertain terms in the virulent disgust of his first soliloquy.

To grief, frustration and psychic shock is added the burden of the ghostly visitation with its treble load of walking death, murder and revenge. Gielgud's performance gives a sense of an almost intolerable tension. Starting at the level of a sorrow which 'passeth show' in the opening of the first act, waves of emotion mount in a continuous progression. In the following scenes they gather momentum, rise to a climax, break and subside only to start again with accumulated force toward another intensity, until finally in the closet scene the last crest is reached, the last crash carries all before it.

These successive climaxes, so characteristic of Gielgud's interpretation, are the outward sign of Hamlet's basic difficulty. The driving force of his emotion, his power to imagine, suffer, act, runs head on against the other motivating element of his nature, his contemplative, questioning, rational mind. The onrush of emotion is suddenly stopped, with the inevitable drop to profound despair and a sense of nullity, exhaustion. On the upward sweep Hamlet may be hysterical, on the downward drop morbidly depressed, but these are the alternations of mood resulting from a psychological conflict, not the manifestations of a diseased mind. Gielgud's Hamlet is not mad. His antic disposition is always a deliberate mask. Excitable and highstrung, occasionally dominated by a force within himself that he cannot master and does not know how to canalize, Hamlet erupts now and again into speech and action which startle even himself— but if that should be taken as an indication of insanity, who among us would escape the straitjacket?

Hamlet's problem as Gielgud presents it is not a matter of lack of will, courage or determination—'Sith I have cause and will and strength and means'—but of an unresolved discord within himself. The resolution of such a discord does not come about by taking thought, since thought itself is a causative factor. Rather it comes by a releasing emotional experience, either actual or relived in words. In Hamlet we see this release take place in the closet scene. Here, suddenly, the deadlock is broken by an action so instinctive that there is no time for thought, followed immediately by an outpouring in words of the very dregs of Hamlet's mind. This is the climax, the turning point of the play. From then on Hamlet is changed, though the transformation is not instantly evident. The Hamlet which Gielgud gives us by including the Fortinbras soliloquy is already on the way to becoming captain of his soul. By the time he has returned from the abortive trip to England, he is an integrated personality. Quiet, courteous, occasionally almost gay, with the tender lightness of those who, loving life, have accepted death, the Hamlet of the last scenes has discovered the springs of his own being.

Gielgud shows, however, that though Hamlet's conflict has been resolved and his way to action discovered, his personality is untouched. He flares into a rage at Laertes, throws an enigmatic taunt at the King, indulges in fantastic quibbles with Osric, talks philosophy with Horatio as of old. But through all this he walks forward, his eyes open on a foreseen and calamitous end. In every gesture, every intonation, every quiet word and relaxed pose, this Hamlet is a contrast to the tense, tormented creature of the first scenes. Emotion and will are at last fused. When this happens to any one of us, such inner power as exists is released. In Hamlet that power is great, for it is intellectual and spiritual as well as physical and emotional. He is sure of his strength, because he is healed within: 'I do not fear it, I shall win at the odds.' But—there is also the prescience of disaster. As Gielgud turns to Horatio and speaks the two words 'Let be' with complete, quiet acceptance, the human race seems for a moment redeemed from its hopelessness. The theatre, which is poet-actor-artist in one, has made manifest before our eyes that noble particle which leavens the lump and makes hope possible.

Hamlet's psychological graph is but one element in the rich texture of his theatrical being. It must inevitably be the warp upon which any characterization is woven, since action, tone, tempo, mood and every detail of reading, every item of business, costume and make-up are based upon it, but it is only a part of the living whole, a largely unconscious part of the actor's apprehension of the role. It is Gielgud's ability to grasp this basic structure and express it in terms of a convincing theatricality that makes his performance illuminating. He combines the power to convey subtle movements of the spirit, delicate shades of thought, the inner workings of mind and heart, with a knowledge of theatrical technique and an ability to go 'to 't like French falconers' and tear off 'a passionate speech' with the best of them as occasion requires. He is not in the least afraid of the words he must handle, neither the poetry that pours in such beauty from his lips nor the invectives with which he attacks the foulness of the world and of those nearest him. He can fence with words as lightly and humourously as he can bludgeon with them.

He has above all an ever-renewed freshness of attack. In his hands Hamlet seems born again every night. He hears for the first time what is said to him, feels freshly his grief and bitter disgust, thinks through the torturing problems that beset him as though they had never been presented to him before. The movements of his thought and of his feeling are registered in expression, gesture, pause and intonation. Though listener and speaker alike may know to a syllable exactly what is coming, Gielgud's mastery of one of the cardinal technical mysteries of the actor's craft—'the illusion of the first time'—is so complete that he holds his audience suspended in breathless attention watching to see how his mental process or his emotional experience will evolve into speech or action.

He brings to the part a continuous flow of life. Thoughtful, philosophic and unhappy as this Prince may be, he is also keenly, almost painfully, alive. Though absorbed by his inner conflict he reacts to every impact from the unsympathetic world around him. This aliveness is expressed in every fibre of Gielgud's performance and is part of its dominant quality of young sensitiveness. For his Hamlet is the revolt of youth at the destruction of its faith in truth and decency and love. His Hamlet is also youth itself, with its intolerance, ruthlessness, arrogance and self-absorption. Gielgud is willing to play him both nobly and angrily, extenuating nothing of his harshnesses but painting so clearly the picture of his outraged purity, his sorrow and his spiritual isolation, that Hamlet becomes in his hands the prototype of all lost and lonely souls, as well as a prince most royal, the 'unmatch'd form and feature of blown youth.'

III

The outstanding elements of Gielgud's playing are its power, its subtlety, its variety, its physical beauty in movement, mask and voice. Slight and young as he seems, his Hamlet has a formidable force. 'Beautiful, bad, and dangerous to know' Caroline Lamb said of Byron. And the Hamlet who rouses himself from his first mood of brooding melancholy gives just this impression of latent menace. Gielgud moves on the stage with swift strength. He is a master of his body, using it with a consummate technical precision. *Hamlet* is so often discussed as a psychological and philological problem that the fact that it is a play and as such a matter of movement in space is sometimes forgotten. Gielgud does not forget it.

His Hamlet is three-dimensional as well as mobile, effectively related to the planes and solids about him. In the more active scenes it is a pattern of fluid movement, in moments of stillness a visible expression of mood. From his elaborate pose during the opening scene when he sits exuding disgust for the King, through the intricacies of the play scene when every event is commented by the soaring action of his black figure, to the moment of relaxation when, standing beside Horatio but, as ever, quite alone, he sees the coming end, Gielgud runs the gamut of action and reaction, of movement balanced against pause. This feeling for spatial relationship is like the painter's or the sculptor's instinct for composition. In an actor it is most effective when it is joined as in Gielgud with an accurate sense of timing. Throughout the play this expert handling of tempo and movement is evident, giving the observer, often unconsciously, the sense of satisfaction derived from watching a dance movement or an acrobatic performance.

The pattern of his action is carried through to every detail of his use of costume and properties. Whether he inherited the trick from his actor-forebears or learned to swing cloak and sword in his drama school days, his ability to handle all the adjuncts of his trade add immeasurably to such dramatic moments as that in which he flings off his friends and with them his enveloping cloak to follow the Ghost on the parapet, or when he reveals himself—'this is I, Hamlet the Dane'—from a swirl of folds in the grave-yard scene. In the details of living at Elsinore he is entirely at home. He wears his clothes, either formal or antic with equal ease, handles a book or a snuff box, a handkerchief or a rapier, with authority, using them to underline the thought or action of which they form an integral part and not merely to give himself something to do. He is chary in his use of proper-ties, even omitting such time-honoured accessories as the tablets on which Claudius' villainy is usually inscribed and the miniatures in the scene with Gertrude.

If his body as a whole is trained, his face and his hands are equally under the control of a guiding dramatic intention. The theatric effectiveness of the tragic mask which has served the Terry family so well is raised to extraordinary power and delicacy in Gielgud. Finely modelled throughout, the bony structure of his face has a ruggedness and prominence which gives it on the stage a hawk-like force and aggressiveness. His profile cuts through space. In such a scene as the one in which Horatio and the two soldiers tell of the visitations of the Ghost, or in the various scenes with Rosencrantz and Guildenstern there is a sweep as of a scimitar when he turns sharply from one to the other. Again and again as the light catches his face, its architecture shows that this Hamlet is a man of action, its expression that he is a man of thought and acute sensitivity.

A dramatic mask is a vehicle to convey the working of mind and emo-tion. It is theatrically worthless unless it is transparent. In this quality Gielgud is well endowed. Every thought or intention he wishes to express on the stage is written in his face before the words are spoken. It is possible to watch the successive ideas which pass through Hamlet's mind as he re-ceives, holds uncomprehendingly for a moment and then finally grasps the astounding news of his father's ghostly return. He says only two words during this heartshaking interval, yet between his polite, abstracted and slightly bored 'Saw' to the incredulous, explosive 'Who?' with which he challenges Horatio's statement he has travelled the whole road from per-sonal grief and self-absorption to the threshold of death and disaster.

Gielgud's ability to listen, always a sign of mastery on the stage, is continuously fascinating. It reaches a climax in the scene with the Ghost, where, with almost no lines to speak he seems to carry on a dialogue of truly unearthly horror. His occasional strangled exclamation, his gestures of protest and revolt, reinforce the succession of shattering emotions his face records. His whole body is intent. Here too, his hands, strong, expressive, flexible, help to build the crises. He uses both hands with equal and unconscious ease. Though sparing of anything approaching gesticulation, he will point a line, underscore a phrase, emphasize an idea, by a perfectly timed turn of finger, thumb and wrist, gestures which range all the way from the delicate irony of the 'moult no feather' remark addressed to Rosencrantz and Guildenstern to the sombre brushing of dust and corruption from his fingers after he has returned Yorick's skull to the gravedigger.

The supreme weapon in the actor's arsenal is his voice. Bernhardt, physically reduced to a thing of pity, could still enthrall with the magnificent cascade of her speech and Duse's voice will ring forever in the ears that have heard it. Gielgud brings again to the stage something of this lost beauty. The range and quality of his voice is not more remarkable than his control of its possibilities. Even more than his face it registers the constant movement of his mind so that a single phrase, even a single word or exclamation, can convey a whole range of experience. The demands of Hamlet on the voice are formidable. Not only does he talk continuously for hours, but again and again throughout the play the actor is called on for what is actually a spoken aria, a building of tonal harmonies to greater and greater heights. In such elaborate passages as 'what a piece of work is a man!' the vocal music has the quality of mounting chords, each phrase rising above its predecessor in majestic progression, yet the effect is never oratorical. Rather, Hamlet seems himself caught up in the excitement of a mental adventure in which his own words engender a sort of poetic intoxication.

The tonal quality of each of the four chief soliloquies is markedly different, since each is based on a different mental and emotional climate—anguished in the first, frenzied in the second, searching in the third, determined in the fourth. All of these speeches, however, require an equal technical force and control, as, in fact, does the entire gigantic role. Ultimately such force depends, as in singing, on the proper placing of the voice and on breath. The smooth transition from one register to another, the dramatic use of head tones, the absolute control of the breathing apparatus which permits a rising emphasis with increase of volume at the end of a long phrase, are indications of Gielgud's proficiency in the use of this essential element of technical equipment.

Though highly individual in timbre and quality, his voice is free of mannerisms, devoid of that rotund quality which the reading of Shakespeare so often engenders. Fatigue will occasionally make it husky or an irresistible impulse toward experimentation lead to the use of vocal pyrotechnics, but this is quickly disciplined. His voice is unusually clear of such impedimenta. It is an instrument delicately attuned to his intention and responsive to his will.

The various registers are used throughout the play in connection with various types of thought and action, though probably not schematically planned. The meditative, sorrowful or philosophic mood generally uses a lower register supported by a stronger breath than, for instance, the scenes of feigned madness or the light give and take with the 'good lads' from Wittenberg. In the use of resonant head tones lies the effectiveness of his occasional outbursts of sound and fury. This strong, hard note is struck in moments of high excitement, as in the Hecuba speech, the close of the nunnery scene, the climax of the rant at the grave of Ophelia. It is one of the many stops Gielgud can sound at will. These tonal and quantitive variations are so closely woven into the pattern of his playing that the need for some sort of musical notation becomes evident to anyone attempting to make a record of his performance.

This is particularly true when discussing the fundamental problem in Shakespeare, the reading of verse. How, for instance, is it possible to convey in words the effect of Gielgud's delivery of 'To be, or not to be' beyond the bare statement that the quality of voice, the sound of the words, the poetic and emotional content of the passage were one in sensuous and spiritual beauty? The prompt-book from which the detailed description of Gielgud's performance has been made is marked throughout with indications of where he paused, the approximate length of those pauses, where he changed from one register to another, where the inflection rose, where it fell, the weight of certain words, the relative tempi of certain passages, the stress on a vowel or consonant, where the rhythm was retarded, where it was speeded. Yet all this means nothing except to those in whose ear the living voice has rung. Phonograph records of speeches are even more unsatisfactory. The essential movement is lacking. They may recreate a memory; they cannot create a fact.

Gielgud's reading of verse is based on the dramatic and intellectual content of the line and tuned to the poet's deepest rhythm, the rhythm of the play itself. *Hamlet* as a play has already advanced both from Shakespeare's own early essays in dramatic writing and from the more ornate and elaborate style of his contemporaries. Rich and intricate as the pattern is, it is not so frequently embroidered with passages of poetic rhetoric as is *King Richard II,* for instance. The formal rhythms of the lines themselves are often shaken by the force of the emotion they contain, or again, a change of idea or direction breaks a line in two to start in mid-stream on a new tempo as in the speech to Horatio before the Gonzago play begins.

Most important of all, Hamlet himself, as Shakespeare has created him, is a man of words, a poet, often to his own despair. In Gielgud's reading, the creative poetic process of thought is felt throughout. The rhythm of the verse, and of the prose as well, is present as a strong sustaining pulse. The pauses accentuate the process of thought but do not break this underlying beat. Granville-Barker in his preface to *Hamlet* makes the statement that the verse in this play will always respond better to a dramatic than to a prosodic analysis. Gielgud approaches the problem from this angle and it is his dramatic analysis that gives his reading its sustained power and authority.

The various elements of Gielgud's craftsmanship are the means by which he obtains his objective, the projection of his characterization across the footlights. Yet no analysis of technical methods can explain the result. The ability to convey to the audience, often without words, the total being of the character which the actor is at the moment impersonating is the basic ingredient of all great acting. It has to do not only with technical skill but also with inner conviction. Gielgud's power of projection is strong; his concentration, the freshness and conviction of his attack, are matched by his gift of conveying his emotion directly to each member of his audience. He can, as one New York critic expressed it, 'fling his feeling across the footlights stirring the emotions of the audience, establishing and maintaining a tension—in them—that leaves him free to go on building to superb and superbly simple climaxes.' It is no wonder that an audience so moved comes again and again to see a performance which in beauty and distinction is not unworthy of the theatre's greatest masterpiece.

BIBLIOGRAPHY ENTRY FOR RESEARCH PAPERS:

Gilder, Rosamond. "John Gielgud's Hamlet." From her *John Gielgud's Hamlet*. New York, 1937. In *Interpreting Hamlet*, ed. Russell E. Leavenworth. San Francisco, 1960.

FIRST FOOTNOTE:

* Rosamond Gilder, "John Gielgud's Hamlet," from her *John Gielgud's Hamlet* (New York, 1937), in *Interpreting Hamlet*, ed. Russell E. Leavenworth (San Francisco, 1960), pp. 127-137.

SUBSEQUENT FOOTNOTES:

* Gilder, *op. cit.*, *IH*, p. ■■.
* Gilder, "John Gielgud's Hamlet," *IH*, p. ■■.
* Gilder, *IH*, p. ■■.

In place of "*IH*," "ed. Leavenworth" may be used in these subsequent-footnote forms.

JOHN GIELGUD

ON

the Hamlet Stage Tradition

Sir John Gielgud (b. 1904) was knighted in 1953 for his achievements as actor and producer. His essay reprinted here was written for Rosamond Gilder's John Gielgud's Hamlet *(New York: copyright 1957 by Rosamond Gilder). By permission of the author and Rosamond Gilder.*

THE HAMLET TRADITION—SOME NOTES ON COSTUME, SCENERY AND STAGE BUSINESS

ELLEN TERRY describes Henry Irving's appearance as Hamlet minutely in her memoirs, and speaks of it as if it were revolutionary and original at the time he produced *Hamlet* at the Lyceum in 1874. The pale face, disordered black hair, simple tunic edged with fur: 'No bugles, no order of the Danish Elephant—he did not wear the miniature of his father obtrusively round his neck.' Perhaps she was thinking of Fechter, who played Hamlet with Ellen's sister Kate (my grandmother) as Ophelia. He was a fair Dane, and a print I have of him in the part certainly looks elaborate, though vaguely Nordic and barbarian.

If Irving's Hamlet broke one tradition, it certainly started another, which has varied but little in continental or American representations of the part from that day to this. Of an earlier date is the famous portrait by Lawrence of John Philip Kemble with his hat of plumed feathers and long cloak. There are curious prints of Macready, Forrest and others in which the miniature is usually predominant, if not the bugles. Following Sir Henry, his son, H. B. Irving, naturally copied his father's make-up and costume, and looked extremely like him. Forbes-Robertson, who had played continually with Irving, also wore much the same attire. Booth wore cross-garterings instead of plain black tights. Salvini, Moissi, Katchalov, Kainz, from the continent—and, of course, Sarah Bernhardt; Booth, Sothern, Hampden in America; and in more recent times Tree, Wilson Barrett, Ainley, Barrymore, Martin-Harvey, Milton, Swinley and Tearle—all these famous Hamlets conformed more or less to the traditional appearance of the prince. Tree wore a fair wig and beard, in which unkind people said he looked like a German Professor, and Wilson Barrett was extremely décolleté. Basil Sydney in America, Colin Keith-Johnston in London and Moissi in Vienna played the part in modern dress.

The first production to make a stir in England in sixteenth century costume was that of the late J. B. Fagan at Oxford in 1924. This was an amateur performance by the Oxford University Dramatic Society in which Gyles Isham made a great success as Hamlet. The costumes were of the Dürer period, and the men wore puffed sleeves, short surcoats and slashed tights. The Ophelia was not assisted by a hat with a very long and ridiculous feather (in the play scene); otherwise the costuming was strikingly effective.

The late William Poel presented *Hamlet,* among many other Shakespeare plays, for the first time in Elizabethan dress. His experiments began as early as 1881. An even earlier attempt had been made by Benjamin Webster in 1844. Since Poel's productions the method had been followed at the Old Vic and elsewhere on various occasions. The first time I played Hamlet (1929) at the Vic, Harcourt Williams used this period for his production. The most practical drawback to it is that the women are not sympathetic dressed in farthingales, which seem to be stiff and ugly in an emotional or pathetic scene, nor are the men helped in tragic or exciting scenes by the short cloaks and bolstered trunks of the period. Besides, the actors find these clothes very hot and tight to act in.

The archaeological period—Saxo Grammaticus—which is the traditional theatrical and historically accurate period for the play, has the opposite disadvantage. The women look like virgin heroines from grand opera, with plaits, girdles and straight dresses with key-pattern borders, and the men are hampered and made absurd by war-like studded breastplates, thongs and winged helmets, contradicted by skinny arms and smooth faces, or 'dreadfully attended' by voluminous wigs and beards.

Gertrude and Claudius are liable to resemble the King and Queen in a pack of cards, and Polonius, in a pale blue gown, very long beard, and white staff of office, is boring before he has even opened his mouth. The key-pattern is sadly echoed in the scenery, climbing around doors, pillars and arches, and the furniture, in trying to be primitive, usually looks uncomfortable and lonely, in spite of the skins draped hopefully about. The period can be strikingly handled as in the recent *Hamlet* of Leslie Howard, which I am told was beautifully set and costumed by Stewart Chaney, but I have a very real and vivid reminiscence of H. B. Irving's archaeological production—the first I ever saw. I suppose I was about twelve at the time, and it made an unforgettable impression upon me. In this performance, Ophelia, played by Lady Forbes-Robertson, was introduced, dripping, on a bier at the end of the Queen's willow speech, to make an effective curtain—a very favourite Edwardian device to gain applause.

To return to Hamlet and his clothes. There is no doubt that the traditional costume of the Prince is becoming, loose, and comfortable— three essentials for such a long and exacting role. Long hair is apt to be more difficult to wear on the stage nowadays than short, but otherwise the dress is admirable to look at and easy to act in. Personally, however, I have always had a feeling that it is almost too much steeped in tradition, and therefore I have never worn it in the part. I like the more definite lines of the sixteenth century dress, which I have always worn (with slight modifications—as my own production was set in 1520, and the one in New York in 1620!). I feel the Renaissance costume suggests the scholar, the poet, the prince, the courtier, and the gentleman; that it is more youthful and at the same time more sophisticated than the Gothic Peter Pan of the traditional theatre. Probably if I had ever played in the cooler and more comfortable Saxon dress I should change my opinion.

Modern commentators seem to think that much should be made of Hamlet's appearance and costume after he feigns madness. Mr. Granville-Barker even thinks he should wear colours in this middle section of the play. This innovation has never, I believe, been tried, partly, perhaps, because we actors know that black is becoming and dignified, and partly because the sympathy of the audience towards Hamlet on account of his love for his father's memory would be jarred by such an emphatic deviation from mourning. There is also the practical question of effort. Hamlet is on the stage nearly all the evening, and a change of costume is an added labour for the actor. I have tried changing into a violet and grey travelling dress for the last act, thinking it would be a great innovation, and no one even

noticed it (this was at the Old Vic). As to the 'mad' scenes, it is dangerous to overdo a fantastically disordered appearance—and almost impossible, in any costume, to follow Ophelia's detailed account of 'stockings
foul'd, ungarter'd and down-gyved to his ankle,' without continually distracting the audience. An old print shows one actor who attempted this,
Henry E. Johnstone (1777-1845). One stocking is half way down a
muscular leg, the other definitely 'ungarter'd,' but the expression on his
face is quite calm.

Ophelia's costume in the mad scene presents another vexed question
of tradition. Walter Lacy, Henry Irving's adviser on his Shakespearian
productions, undoubtedly voiced Irving's own opinion when he said to
Ellen Terry who planned a black dress for the mad scene: 'My God,
Madam, there must be only one black figure in this play and that's Hamlet!' So in Irving's production and many others before and since, we have
the white robe, tousled hair, and generally conventional appearance of
Ophelia, with or without her flowers, which would pass equally well for
Margaret in the last act of *Faust*. She has variously been played since in
black, red and yellow. Mr. Granville-Barker thinks she should have a lute
in the first half of the scene, and in the second part herbs picked from
the garden which she delivers to the other characters as at a funeral. It
was apparently the Elizabethan custom to distribute them so and it would
certainly be appropriate and effective. Played by an actress in an Elizabethan dress (but not necessarily in a farthingale) carelessly worn and
soiled with mud and dirt, her hair dressed wildly but not altogether loose,
Ophelia might become a stranger and more poignant figure than she usually presents in theatrical usage.

Two other points in costuming: now that audiences are intelligent
enough not to feel that 'there must be only one black figure in the play'
there is no reason why both Ophelia and Laertes too should not wear
black for their father. Not only does this mark the similarity and contrast
of the two revenge stories, but it is particularly effective, in my opinion,
in the final scene of the duel, when the two young men stand pitted against
one another, fighting to the death for a similar cause. There is one other
innovation I have never seen attempted on the stage, which is suggested
strongly by the text. In the closet scene, the Ghost should appear 'in his
habit as he liv'd,' i.e., in a cap and nightgown—or some kind of crown
and robe—in contrast to his war-like appearance on the battlements. I
believe the effect would be a fine one in so domestic a scene, and that
Shakespeare intended it. It seems to be an impossibility to design 'silent'
armour for the Ghost, and consequently he is always dressed extremely

vaguely and underlighted almost out of all recognition, and therefore cannot make the impression intended in any of the scenes in which he appears. I consider this was a bad failing in my own production, as well as in every other I have seen or appeared in, and I commend it as one of the important details worth study and solution in any future performance of the play.

As regards scenery: it is important, of course, in this play, that the sense of pictorial richness and sensuous decadence of a Renaissance court should be somehow combined and contrasted with the feeling of a 'warlike state,' where ghosts and horror haunt the battlements by night; where armies are marshalling for war, graves give up their dead and a barbaric Northern feeling of cold and grimness cuts across the luxurious court life of the murderous poisoner and his shallow Queen. A pretty big problem, this, for any scene designer and director. The unlocalized setting, originally conceived and devised by Gordon Craig, and carried out by him with varying success in Stanislavsky's Moscow production in 1911, has of course influenced later productions tremendously. There was a violent reaction against the old-fashioned realistic settings. In Martin-Harvey's production, and in Arthur Hopkins' *Hamlet* designed by Robert Edmond Jones for John Barrymore, and later in my own, the influence of Craig was apparent. The chief danger in these unlocalized settings is the temptation to use steps and platforms to excess. The groupings and static pictures are greatly assisted by this means, but audiences quickly tire of looking at actors continually leaping up and down stairs that lead nowhere. The solidity of such settings enforces a minimum of variations. If the interiors are impressively majestic, the scenes of the battlements and the graveyard are seldom equally convincing. Finally, the necessity of using drop curtains, near the front of the stage (in a totally different stage convention) for short scenes during which furniture is being moved on the main stage, is most unsatisfactory.

ACT I—SCENE 1
The Sentinel's Platform before the Royal Palace / [1](*Act I, Scene I*)

This, one of the finest and most famous of all Shakespeare openings, is usually unimpressive on the stage. There are many technical reasons for this. Audiences will not be punctual, and, knowing the play well

---

[1] These notes are arranged according to the scene sequence of the London and New York productions printed in this volume [*John Gielgud's Hamlet*]. The act and scene notations given in parentheses are those of the standard editions.

enough to remember that the principal characters do not appear until the second scene, fidget inattentively and do not encourage the atmosphere the actors need. In order to help the appearance of the Ghost, the stage is usually very darkly lit, and the scenery is either a drop-cloth, to allow of an easy and quick change of scene, or else a permanent set, which the producer bathes in deepest shadow, so that it may look different when used as an interior a few moments later. In addition to these drawbacks, the actors are all 'small part' men, with the exception of Horatio, and seldom capable of expressing by their voices and emotional power the great range and quality of the poet's invention.

The scene has been played high on a rostrum, down on an apron close to the audience, with wind, bells, clocks, twinkling stars and music to heighten the effect. (The cock crowing, by the way, which I tried in my own production, had never to my knowledge been used before, and was remarkably atmospheric.) But the tremendously dramatic and staccato opening, the dramatic rhythm of the scene as it varies so markedly between the two entrances of the Ghost and moves towards its beautiful and poetic close, these beauties have not been apparent in performances I have seen.

With one exception: the production, in German, in which Alexander Moissi played in London in 1929, which was, I believe, an old one, originally Reinhardt's. The company was not outstanding, and there were many strange and ineffective innovations, but this opening scene was played better than I have ever seen it before or since. On a flat stage the soldiers waited, warming their hands over a brazier of coals. They were not raw young actors, but old and bearded veterans, whose terror at the sight of the martial figure of their old master, coming from such simple men of obvious physical hardihood, was moving and convincing in the extreme. Their trust in the wisdom of the young student Horatio seemed real and probable—he was cleverer than they and would interpret their fears. The disturbed feeling of imminent wars and horrors lurking about the castle communicated itself immediately to the audience, and, when Horatio spoke the famous lines about the dawn, his own relief and its effect upon the other actors made one feel as if a great curtain of darkness which had hung over them during a long sleepless night had rolled away at last to let in the fresh air of a cold morning and another day.

One wonders how this scene can have been played effectively when it was originally written. A noisy, fidgeting, mostly standing audience, no darkness, afternoon sunshine streaming on to a tidy little platform. But then we must remember that to know the play beforehand is a great loss for us today. It cramps our imaginations and our enjoyment of the thrilling drama of the scene, while demanding at the same time far greater conviction in the playing of it. No doubt first class actors and simple production (with enough light to see every expression clearly) is all that is really needed to make it as effective as it should be, and so seldom is.

Notes: 'Who's there?' I wonder whether Francisco is not meant to mistake Bernardo for the Ghost.

The cutting of the long speech of Horatio which is customary in the modern theatre has the disadvantage of making the second entrance of the Ghost far too quick upon the first, which does not therefore take the audience by surprise as the author seems to have intended.

'I'll cross it, though it blast me.' Horatio sometimes moves across the path of the Ghost on this line; alternatively he holds up the cross-hilt of his sword and makes a cross in the air with it towards the Ghost.

SCENE 2

The Council Chamber in the Castle / The First Soliloquy; the scene with Horatio and the Soldiers / (Act I, Scene II)

Commentators seem to agree that this represents the first privy council meeting held after the accession of Claudius as elective king. The more traditional stage usage has always been to place it in a throne room or a hall in the castle with the monarchs on their thrones, a crowd of soldiers, ladies and attendants, and Hamlet seated on a stool apart or standing sadly below the chairs of state. Henry Irving, in stricter obedience to the text, had a long procession, at the end of which came Hamlet. Ellen Terry says, 'The lights were lowered at his entrance, another stage trick,' but this must have been cunningly contrived, and seems rather a curious artifice to resort to so early in a play which is often hampered in performance by too many dark scenes. On the other hand, I once saw a Hamlet who made a 'star' entrance, centre, just before his uncle's first line to him; this made his first aside a little unconvincing, to say the least of it, and, as he was also accompanied by a burst of limelight, he evidently thought differently from Irving.

In the Barrymore-Arthur Hopkins production the curtain rose in darkness, and sibilant whispering and laughter opened the scene, until the court was discovered lolling in amorous groups on a stage built up in masses of steps and at the top of them a great curtained arch. This first effect was most imposing, but the setting remained unchanged through-out the play, and the steps and arch became monotonous when used in many scenes. Harcourt Williams, in his Old Vic production (1929) had the Queen and her ladies sewing and the King entering in cloak and gloves, as if from hunting. This was original, as well as being alive and vigorous.

The design of Gordon Craig for his Moscow production with Stanis-lavsky in 1911 has been often reproduced, and I have always been greatly impressed by it. Hamlet is sitting wearily in the foreground by a dark pillar. He is separated from the court by a barrier of mysterious shadow which cuts across the front of the stage, embracing the slight figure of the Prince. Beyond rises a brilliant pyramidal group of heads growing to a peak formed by the figures of the King and Queen, wearing huge cloaks, the folds of which seem to envelop the whole court. Actually at Moscow I believe the actors representing the courtiers put their heads through holes in the cloak (Komisarjevsky employed a slightly similar device recently in the trial scene of his Stratford production of *The Merchant of Venice*). How the exit was managed as the scene progressed and the cue was reached I have never been able to discover. The drawing is extraordinarily dramatic and right in feeling, but it seems to me rather an idea than an actual practical stage arrangement. What attracts me most in it is the placing of Hamlet, the contrast of light and shade, and the focusing of attention on the King and Queen at the rise of the curtain.

I followed this scheme of grouping in my own production in 1934, but at an angle to the audience instead of straight, with courtiers ranged in a semi-circle before the thrones and hiding Hamlet from his mother and uncle. The exit of Laertes caused a slight change in the positions of some of the courtiers and opened a space through which Claudius became suddenly aware of the presence of Hamlet. Then as Hamlet spoke his first lines the courtiers naturally turned to look at him, and the scene con-tinued as the Queen came down from her throne to speak to her son, turning the whole focus of grouping and attention at the right moment in the scene (and not before) to the other side of the stage and to Hamlet himself.

Guthrie McClintic (in New York in 1936) placed the scene in a council chamber, and the King and Queen were seated behind a table. The court left the stage before the King addressed Hamlet, and the scene thus became a domestic argument between the three principal characters. This had a certain effect of concentrated development of the story, but I cannot help feeling that the formality of address used by Hamlet and the flowery tone, half rebuking, half avuncular, of Claudius' speeches have greater point and effect when uttered for the benefit of his admiring and sycophantic courtiers. There is also a legitimate stage effect in a 'grand exit' at the departure of the King and Queen (and perhaps entrance, too, as the scene begins). They can sweep from the stage to music and trumpets, the courtiers bowing and curtseying before they follow, until the solitary figure of Hamlet is left alone on the big empty stage looking bitterly after them as he begins his first soliloquy. I think, however, that the privy council treatment, done more elaborately, with other councillors, like Polonius, sitting around the table, might be very admirable.

First soliloquy. I find this the most exciting of the soliloquies[1] to speak, partly because it seems to set the character once and for all in the actor's and the audience's minds, and partly for its extraordinary, forthright presentation of information as to the whole plot, matched unerringly in the march of the words and the punctuation of the sentences. Executed correctly, it has no possible pauses except at the natural places marked for taking breath or when there are full stops. A short break seems to be demanded before 'Frailty, thy name is woman!', and another more definite one before the last two lines which sum up the whole speech. Otherwise thoughts and exclamations succeed each other in the most vivid and natural manner, so that it is impossible to falter either in speaking or thinking. One is driven on at a naturally steady pace—in spite of a certain intensity of feeling which at first makes one tend to dwell upon some of the lines at greater length than others.

The following scene in which the soldiers come with Horatio to tell Hamlet of the Ghost has always been my favourite in the whole play, and I knew every word of it by heart long before I ever dreamt I should have the chance of playing the part. I also knew by heart the vivid description in Ellen Terry's memoirs of how Irving played it, and tried to follow him in every detail from the first. It may seem lazy for an actor to copy 'business' or readings from other actors, but I do not believe that one should ever discard tradition without first examining its purposes and inspiration. Quite recently, in London, I saw a production of *Julius Caesar* in which the murder scene was 'improved' by a curtain in which Calpurnia was discovered kneeling in heavy mourning (which she must have ordered very

---

[1] In this speech I very much wished to use the word 'sullied' for 'solid.' It is now agreed upon by most of the commentators as the correct reading, but fearing I should be accused either of altering the line because I am thin, or else of pronouncing 'solid' with an Oxford accent, I gave up the idea. 'Faint and scant of breath' in the last scene has also luckily been blessed with academic warrant as well as physical appropriateness in my own case.

quickly) at the side of her husband's corpse! This business had been invented by Tree, who was famous for such touches of originality. (At the first rehearsal of his *Othello* he is supposed to have said to Roderigo— Ernest Thesiger—'We enter at the back in a gondola—and I thought it would be effective if you were hauling down the sail!')

Unfortunately, audiences love striking pieces of business and show-manship, and remember them long after they have forgotten the play in which they occurred. In Shakespeare, when they are pictorial, attractive to the audience and make a personal effect for the actor too, they are difficult to resist. Irving was a great actor, and people who saw him will tell you that he was a genius at this kind of thing, and used it sincerely, originally, to the best advantage, but all the stars who followed him, par-ticularly Tree, tried to outdo him in their lavishness and inventiveness.

Irving's famous invention of Shylock's return over the bridge after the flight of Jessica—Irving, I believe, never actually reached the door before the curtain fell—has been copied and elaborated out of all recog-nition. Shylocks have knocked once, twice, ten times, rushed in, rushed out again, cried out, called through the house, rushed off down the street in pursuit. Tree topped them all by finding a handy pile of ashes on the doorstep and pouring them on his head. Nowadays, if the Jew does not return at all, people ask why the great moment has been cut. It became the 'star' episode of the part because it was conceived by a fine star actor —and Shakespeare never meant it to occur at all!

Invented business such as this is obviously an interpolation. Audiences love it, but it is a bad concession to the picture stage and falling curtain, which Shakespeare never imagined, and underlines and elaborates a situa-tion which the dramatist purposely touched on very lightly—and to us it smacks of the 'problem picture' so popular in the Royal Academy Exhibi-tions of twenty years ago. Therefore there is little or no excuse for borrow-ing it or for inventing similar business at the same point in the text, though I am sure if I had seen it when Irving himself did it for the first time, I should have admired it as part of his invention, and, magnificently carried out, it must certainly have contributed to the brilliance of his performance as Shylock.

But when I read how, as Hamlet, Irving greeted Horatio, warmly but still abstractedly, still in his dream when he said 'My father, methinks I see my father—' how he half heard Horatio's line 'My lord, I think I saw him yesternight—,' the dawning of intelligence on 'Saw. Who?' breaking into flashing realization as his face blazed with intelligence from 'For God's love, let me hear!'—on to the quick doubts and suspicions in his questions and his touching appreciation of loyalty in saying farewell to his friends—then I find a guide to the playing of the scene which seems to me still so perfect that I have never veered a step from it ever since I first rehearsed the part.

Ellen Terry says that at the last couplet of the scene,

> . . . *foul deeds will rise,*
> *Though all the earth o'erwhelm them, to men's eyes.*

Irving's acting appalled by its implication of rising rage and horror, and this description, too, helped me to realize how those few short words bind the end of the scene together. The understatement of the court scene, the dull bitterness of the soliloquy, the rising excitement of the scene with the men, all of this is caught together in these words and leads the actors and audience unerringly towards the subsequent revelation of the Ghost and the setting in motion of the whole machinery of the play's action.

I am always glad that we have few actual records, in films or gramophones, of the great ones of the past, though this feeling may seem to run contrary to what I have just been saying of the inspiration given me by the description of Irving's performance. I cannot help thinking that the greatness of all fine acting lies to some extent in its momentary creation before an audience, that the inspiration (and the 'copy' of the inspiration which in many consecutive performances actors give by means of what we call technique) is partly contributed and guided by the audience present at any particular performance. The effect of an acting moment may be one of unforgettable vividness, but it passes immediately and merges into another, which the actor has carefully prepared and arranged so that his performance may proceed harmoniously and in a certain line with his development of the character and the progress of the play's action. Afterwards the spectator may remember and record certain vivid impressions, but probably if he goes again to see the same performance—indeed, even if he sees rehearsals and watches a performance every night—he will never again receive exactly the same impression. The temperament of the actor must vary, to a greater or less extent, according to his own mood and the mood of the other actors and of the audience.

But, just as a great teacher trains his pupils to adopt a correct method of study, and leads them towards the most sincere approach to an appreciation of style, so, it seems to me, an aspiring actor should be able to study these essentials from watching his masters in the craft. It is not from a great actor's mannerisms, or some brilliant but fundamentally personal expression of voice, gait, or carriage that he will learn, but from the

master's approach to character, and from every moment in his performance in which he reveals or clarifies the text. These moments, I am sure,
are only evident to one who has actually seen a stage performance. A great
actor, even if he is not playing his best, is more interesting to me 'in the
flesh' than his shadow, however well made up and lighted, and his voice,
however husky, or even bored, has more life in it than a reproduction, no
matter how cunningly reproduced by machinery. The mechanics of cinema
and gramophone advance too quickly. The films and records of Bernhardt
and Ellen Terry are ridiculous and inadequate curiosities today—and who
knows that future generations will not laugh at the records of Caruso and
Chaliapin and the plangent masks of Garbo, Dietrich and Gable. Some
idea of an actor's performance may be conveyed to a third person by a
brilliant and expert description or critique, written or told by an eye-
witness, but I do not believe that any mechanical reproduction can recreate
an acting performance that one has never seen (though it may be an
interesting reminder or a valuable curiosity) whereas a description may
suggest it most vividly and encourage those who come after to use it
creatively without any spirit of imitation.

Hamlet is, of course, the greatest play of tradition in our language.
Nearly all the great players (and many not great at all) have attempted
to make history in it by touches of originality—from Garrick overturning
the chair in the closet scene to Edmund Kean kissing Ophelia's hair, from
the deathshield of Forbes-Robertson to the plus-fours of Sir Barry Jackson's production in modern dress. I see no possible harm in reading about
all these traditional or sensational innovations, and borrowing or discard-
ing them as they seem to fit the character, the play, and the meaning of
the text, as long as one does this sincerely and without losing sight of
one's own original study and characterization. It is curious to find, however, that the fuller the text used the less is it necessary to waste time
resorting to business to illustrate the meaning or clarify the effect upon the
stage. On the other hand business has often to be invented by actors to
cover the gap in thought made by a bad cut; often it takes no longer to
speak the cut line than to carry out the business or to make the pause
that replaces it.

Tree, in trying to rival Irving's method without such good taste, and
rearranging the text to allow of sumptuous tableaux and pageantry, found
it necessary to cut extensively. The Victorian editors had already done
their worst by publishing versions of the play ridiculously bowdlerized,
and with long and inaccurate descriptions of scenery of which Shakespeare
never dreamt. Tree was an eccentric character actor, and relied on brilliant

makeups and stage effects far more than on any real interpretation of Shakespeare. He and others started a fashion for hearty laughter, back-slapping, worked up entrances and effective curtains, which substituted pictorial show for real dramatic speed and the marvellously dramatic contrast of scene against scene, which lasted until the Granville-Barker productions just before the war.

Remnants of this style of Shakespearian acting have survived with some actors right up to the present day. The picture stage with its curtain, the successful use of elaborate scenery, lighting, and incidental music went to the heads of the Victorian and Edwardian theatre managers, and their audiences revelled in them too. They responded gladly to the 'inexplicable dumbshows and noise' which Shakespeare knew they loved so well. Today we have much to be grateful for. The circus and cinema can always be relied upon to out-herod Herod and we are forced back, in the theatre, to the realization that nobody looks at the scenery, however fine, after the first minute or two, but that acting—voice, characterization, movement—interpreting a fine play correctly will still hold an audience enthralled for hours on end. More time and hard work at rehearsals are of greater use than masses of money spent on scenery and costumes, and a producer who can handle actors is more valuable than a pageant master. Granville-Barker, Robert Atkins, Sir Philip Ben Greet, William Poel, and others like them have done immeasurable service in rescuing the text from the ravages of the star actor-managers, and proving in performance how amazingly Shakespeare catered for his stage with its limited means of presentation and for nearly every actor in his plays, even in the small parts, if they are given their proper importance by the director and acted correctly by the performers.

SCENE 3

Polonius' House. Ophelia, Laertes and Polonius / (Act I, Scene III)

Ophelia, as Ellen Terry has observed, only 'pervades' her early scenes, and they are therefore notoriously difficult both for actress and producer. Compare her first appearance with that of Desdemona, who is talked of long before she appears, so that the audience is impatient to see her, and whose strikingly gracious entrance onto a stage full of men is such a beautiful moment in the Senate scene. Cordelia, too, is a lonely and unforgettable figure—almost like Hamlet—in the great scene at the opening of Lear, and when she speaks for the first time the whole interest concentrates upon her immediately.

But not so with Ophelia. Too much else has to be set forth in the first scenes of *Hamlet*. Though we meet her father and brother in the court scene, and they are marked for us in two or three telling little speeches, there is no slightest mention of Ophelia until we see her in a first scene which gives her little opportunity to be anything but a charming sister and an obedient daughter. But her first two appearances follow scenes of great dramatic power and emotion, and hers are apt to suffer by contrast. The audience is inclined to relax rather than stiffen in attention, especially as she usually finds herself in the modern theatre before curtains or a drop. It always seems to me that the audience reacts to such scenes very much as children do. They attend with difficulty to what is going on in a front scene, knowing that something splendid is being prepared behind the curtain, and subconsciously longing to see what it will be. In spite of this handicap Ophelia's first scene is a justly famous and beautiful one, and makes a brilliant pendant, in its triangle of father, son and daughter, to that of the uncle, son and mother in the preceding scene.

Polonius is a grateful and rewarding part for a good actor, and has been conspicuously successful with audiences, particularly since the brilliant performance of A. Bromley Davenport in the modern dress *Hamlet* of Sir Barry Jackson in 1925. Before this the part was usually cut extensively, and the admittedly difficult combination of wisdom and sententiousness was not appreciated or properly characterized. People are still confused by the speech of advice to Laertes with its worldly wisdom and the moral precepts put into the mouth of the 'tedious old fool' and 'foolish, prating knave' of the later scenes. Davenport was the first to combine the elegance and admirably diplomatic manner of the court official with the selfish but strict attitude of a loving parent. This was his outward appearance. He used it to conceal his true character which revealed itself as that of an inquisitive, pompous, spying old fox, who had surely bought his position with the new king by tactfully forgetting his allegiance to the old.

There has always been much speculation, particularly among actors, as to whether Hamlet and Ophelia were lovers before the opening of the play. Mr. Granville-Barker has remarked on how useless it is to imagine that Shakespeare characters have lives apart from those they lead in the play. Though it is certainly true that we gain little by day-dreaming about the mothers of Desdemona or Cordelia, the question of Hamlet's relationship to Ophelia is very important to the actress who attempts to portray her—especially as Hamlet is too busy to mention the poor girl (even to Horatio) except in the scenes when he is actually confronting her. He makes sly digs about her to Polonius, and rants at her graveside, but in the soliloquies and sane moments, to his mother even, not a word.

The lines about conception and the fishmonger and the bawdy songs in the mad scene are the main reasons for supposing that Hamlet has been Ophelia's lover, but Dr. Dover Wilson has explained the first, to my satisfaction at any rate, in his remarks on the entrance of Hamlet in his first 'mad' scene of which I shall speak later. Mr. Granville-Barker, however, does not take this view of the fishmonger scene, though he does not hold any brief for the lover theory. All we know for certain is that Ophelia says 'he hath importun'd me with love in honourable fashion' and further that he had 'given countenance to his speech . . . with almost all the holy vows of heaven.'

In the nunnery scene, Hamlet exclaims: 'I did love you once' and 'I loved you not,' 'you should not have believed me.' Then he proceeds to rail at her as though she were a harlot, but it does not seem justifiable to make her one. If Ophelia is lying to her father in her first scene the effect of her lying to Hamlet in the nunnery scene would be lost, and her innocence and purity as the thwarted ideal of his love spoilt entirely in its place in the play. As to the bawdy songs, psychoanalysis would nowadays seem to be so generally understood that any modern audience accepts them as the result of repression or wish fulfillment rather than reminiscence. We are told that the purest women often use bad language under anaesthetic. The Victorians and Edwardians, who might have taken another view of the meaning of Ophelia's songs because of their stricter upbringing, naturally never heard the lines, as they were always cut on the stage and often not even published in the books. Above all, for the purposes of acting and production, an Ophelia guilty of a concealed love affair is even more difficult for the actress to suggest than an Ophelia innocent of anything but the best intentions. The actress has a difficult task in any case, and nothing she has to do or say in this short scene, or indeed in any other, is clarified or explained by an interpretation based on her guilt.

SCENE 4

The Sentinel's Platform. The Ghost Scene / (Act I, Scenes IV and V)

The two scenes on the platform should, I believe, be played together as they were in our New York production. The dropping of the curtain between them is most harmful to the continuity, and though the applause may be tempting, the difficulty of, starting the following scene after the break soon dispels the charm of that. In the old days much play was made by the scene painters with a more remote part of the platform for the second part of the scene—cairns, gnarled trees, and Horatio's 'dreadful summit of the cliff that beetles o'er his base into the sea,' were painted and built in detail. Leslie Howard played the scene in a crypt and Moissi by a large cross in a churchyard which the Ghost leant on, looking like a very large turnip on top of a nightshirt (but rather terrifying all the same) growling out revengefully, while Hamlet sat on a step below, and jumped like a jack-in-the-box at the word 'murder!'

The difficulties in the acting and production of these scenes are manifold. The Ghost must be unearthly yet revengeful, sad and yet inspiring, not too sorry for himself, nor yet too human in his resentment. I was not myself impressed by the much praised Ghost of Courtenay Thorpe, with Barrymore, nor have I ever seen the part played altogether to my satisfaction. In spite of the elaborate care with which he is described in the text, he is never dressed in full armour, and his vanishing is usually poorly contrived in a blackout. (But perhaps a too successful effect by Mr. Maskelyne might be too distracting and sensational. One never knows.) I imagine that his disappearance down a trap—which would, I suppose, be laughed at by a modern audience—gave point, long lost today, to the lines about the 'cellerage' and 'old mole.'

In our American production, the voice was done with a microphone and loudspeakers, the actor being of course behind the scenes and another silent one walking on the stage. Though this was most effective for the first 'Mark me' and the 'Swears' under the stage (which often used to make the audience laugh in London, but were very impressive in New York) the house was quickly aware of the microphone device. It was impossible to hold the audience with it for long speeches, so later it was cut out and the lines spoken ordinarily from the wings. Even this was not as effective, to my mind, as a real actor would have been. He should, also, I think, be lit clearly and not over-disguised facially, as an audience cannot be interested in a mask-like face for very long.

Hamlet has a terribly difficult task in this scene, made twice as difficult by familiarity with the story, which robs the whole scene, with its purposely delayed climax, of half its effectiveness for actors and audience alike. The long speech on seeing the Ghost, which I have always spoken kneeling, is very difficult to build up with correct breathing, pace and emphasis in the right places. It needs a good deal of voice yet must be at any rate begun and finished with awe—and yet too much whispering in the dark hereabouts in the play gets on the audience's nerves. The line, by the way, that got a safe laugh every night in the tryout in America was 'something is rotten in the state of Denmark.' This did not seem very helpful for the scene, and so we cut it out. It is evidently a comic phrase to Americans!

I do not know how the tradition started of Hamlet saying 'O, horrible! O, horrible! Most horrible!' It belongs of course to the Ghost, and though I have taken it, thinking to do something very effective with it, I have always regretted it afterwards, and would like to play with a Ghost who could utter it as it ought to be uttered. Irving is said to have made a great effect with it as Hamlet, and could no doubt have made an equally great one if he had said it as the Ghost.

I think the main difficulty of the Ghost is the timbre of voice needed for the part. The scene is not usually rehearsed or played sufficiently in cooperation between the two actors. A director might, I think, get an extraordinary result by sound alone, but it is an impossible scene to play in and direct as well. It may be that I seldom please myself in it, and so I think it more ineffective because it is technically so difficult. I should like to see and hear Leon Quartermaine play the Ghost; he has to my mind the perfect voice for the part, combining dignity and sweetness with emotion and authority, as well as a spiritual remoteness.

I have also an idea that it might be good to double the Ghost and Claudius—very effective, their physical likeness, from my point of view as Hamlet—but the qualities of voice and character needed for the two parts are so different that it would need a superb actor to differentiate between them without confusing the audience. Malcolm Keen read the Ghost's lines in New York and also played Claudius—but as he did not appear on the stage as the Ghost this was not quite the same thing.

I do not know whether I invented or acquired from someone else the business of seeing the Ghost from the expression of Horatio's face and then turning slowly and looking at it before 'Angels and ministers of grace' but I do know that this came off very well in London. For some reason I could not make it so convincing in New York. I have never written on the tablets, because I could not manage them and a pencil and a sword all at the same time. I have always used 'the table of my memory' and banged my head at 'So, uncle, there you are.' School-children always thought this funny, and I have to cut it (or do it very quietly) at matinees!

I copied from H. B. Irving—not that I remember it myself, but read it in a criticism—the putting of my cloak around Horatio at the end. I added to it by leaving my own cloak when I rush from the men in the beginning of the scene (how actors have chosen to play such an emotional scene in a cloak throughout baffles me completely) and having Horatio put his around my shoulders because I was shivering. This is effective and not as elaborate as it seems in describing it, though possibly it falsely emphasizes the 'curtain' when Shakespeare intended a quick exit, and then the next scene following immediately. Effects of this kind, if not too complicated, are to some extent, I think, demanded by a picture stage and descending curtain, though I fear we actors like them particularly because they bring applause more surely than a simple exit. When I directed a production of *Romeo and Juliet* in which the front curtain came down only once, and one scene followed another in a different part of the stage —with even blackouts reduced to a minimum—I found it far less necessary to build up the ends of scenes with any device to encourage applause. Sometimes, indeed, several scenes would pass without any, and this certainly did no harm to the play, though unfortunately it always depresses the actors.

SCENE 6

The Council Chamber in the Castle. Hamlet and Polonius; the arrival of the Players; the Hecuba soliloquy / (Act II, Scene II)

When one studies and considers *Hamlet* through a great number of consecutive rehearsals and performances one realizes perhaps some of the things which account for its perennial popularity with actors and audiences alike. The scenes themselves are audience-proof. By this I mean that if they are played theatrically for all they are worth they will always hold the house. But audiences at this play are apt to be composed either of people who know nothing of Shakespeare or *Hamlet* except what their parents and schoolteachers have told them, or else of students, scholars and 'Hamletomanes' for whom every moment in the play is important not only for its own sake but for its significance with regard to the rest of the action and the psychological relation and development of the characters.

People who love the play and have studied it closely can frequently interpret motives in an actor's performance of a part of which he never dreamt himself. Conversely, with such a complicated character as Hamlet, the actor may try his utmost to convey a certain meaning and yet never be sure that he has conveyed it clearly to the people in the audience, some of whom are admiring the poetry, some watching a pet theory of their own, some comparing the performance with others they have seen, some not attending at all.

The director, therefore, or so it seems to me, must take a very firm hand and do his best to help the actor to give and the audience to receive the same meaning at the important moments in the play. Perhaps this is to under-estimate the average intelligence of the average audience, but all theatrical representation suffers when actors and audience are not properly fused; and in this particular play the fact already mentioned—that the scenes themselves are audience-proof—often makes it appear that this fusion has come about when really there is little except ordinary theatrical contact.

To develop this argument a little in relation to Hamlet's first appearance when he is feigning madness: the lines with Polonius about the fishmonger and conception are archaic and to a modern audience vaguely connote rudeness, bawdry, suggestiveness, etc. But they will always be funny when spoken in the theatre (by which I mean they will get laughs and 'go' with an audience because the actors instinctively say them rightly, even if they do not completely understand them). Yet at rehearsals, actors and directors always try to reason out this scene. Dr. Dover Wilson has evolved a clever theory that Hamlet's entrance should take place some lines earlier than when the Queen's 'but look where sadly the poor wretch comes reading' heralds his appearance. Both in my own production and in Mr. McClintic's I have tried different cues for the entrance in the hope that Hamlet's overhearing the last lines of Polonius to the King and Queen would make clearer the lines in his scene with Polonius as well as his subsequent treatment of Ophelia in the nunnery scene.

One or two people have noticed this treatment, but on the whole I do not think it clarified the meaning sufficiently to warrant the trouble we took with it at rehearsals. I was also afraid that the audience might mistake my meaning or wonder what was happening (whether one had made a mistake and come on too early) and, while they were speculating thus, miss what followed. I was continually struck with the feeling when playing this scene that if Shakespeare had meant Hamlet to overhear something, he would surely have made it clear in the text. The play has much spying in it, and two or three of the most vital moments in subsequent scenes are built around this device, but in each case it is Hamlet who is spied upon. I think it unlikely that Shakespeare would weaken this characteristic feature of his play by making Hamlet spy on, or overhear, any other character before the more important point of his enemies' spying on him had been definitely registered with the audience.

Mr. Granville-Barker draws attention to the long stretch in this part of the play in which the actual plot is not touched on at all. From the entrance of Hamlet until he says to the Player: 'Can you play The Murder of Gonzago?' the plot does not move forward at all. The variety of the dialogue and wealth of theatrical invention is so extraordinary that I had never noticed this important point either in acting or producing the play.

Reading Mr. Granville-Barker's stimulating essay I was greatly helped by his remarks, forcing myself to decide on certain definite moments in the scene in which Hamlet must remember his mission of vengeance and is shocked to find how easily he has been forgetting it. Yet, though I tried to make these moments clear in my by-play, for an audience seeing the scene there is so much else for them to watch and to listen to—so much beauty and wit, action and counteraction—that this point, so very important to the actor playing Hamlet, does not really matter greatly to the spectator.

I cannot quite decide in my own mind whether Hamlet asks the Player emphatically for a passionate speech, thinking at that moment of his own lack of passion, or whether Shakespeare is simply writing towards his climax with unerring instinct, suggesting it in advance, as a composer might use a warning note before introducing a great theme in a symphony. I have been struck later in the play by the lines:

> . . . *bless'd are those*
> *Whose blood and judgment are so well co-mingled*
> *That they are not a pipe for fortune's finger*
> *To sound what stop she please.*

coming only a little while before the scene with the recorder. This seems to me something of the same kind. At any rate, Mr. Granville-Barker has led me to much greater ease during the recital of the Player's speech by his remarks on the subject. 'The unnerved father falls' would surely strike Hamlet as a vivid reminder of his own forgetfulness; and 'Aroused vengeance sets him new a-work' serves finely as the first point of his determination to clear the room and unburden himself to the culminating 'O! Vengeance.'

I shall never forget the tremendous effect of this scene in the Moissi *Hamlet,* of which I have spoken before. The First Player was, perhaps, the finest actor in the company—an enormously tall man, over six feet, with deep-set eyes and black hair and beard. He played the part as high tragedy and at the end of the speech on Hecuba he veiled his face with his cloak thrown over his forearm and fell headlong on the stage. This was extraordinarily moving, and beautifully carried out. It showed, as usual, what can be made of the smaller parts of Shakespeare and how greatly it helps the central character when they are played, as they so seldom are, to the full extent of their possibilities.

If the Player has done his work well, Hamlet's comments need only echo the audience's thoughts, and how much more moderately and easily expressed than if Hamlet must 'tear a passion to tatters' to convince himself and the audience of something they have not really seen. In Moissi's production also, Hamlet left the stage at the end of the Hecuba soliloquy, and, as far as I remember, received just as much applause at this point as any other Hamlet. For some reason I have never been able to bring myself to do this, though of course it is what Shakespeare intended. I suppose I was hypnotized by the famous business of Irving, when, as the curtain falls, he is seen writing madly on his tablets. One cannot help feeling that

> *the play's the thing*
> *Wherein I'll catch the conscience of the king*

should be the signal for the greatest applause in the play. When I have played the part on first nights I have never been able to believe that I could succeed in it until this applause has come. At later performances, however, I have been and still am, irritated by my actor's desire to make such a 'curtain' of it. If we could bury the play for twenty years we might perhaps feel it mattered less how certain parts of it would be received than whether the great speeches would be correctly interpreted in their own place in the play.

I have spoken a great deal in these notes about stage business and the Victorian and Edwardian traditions of Shakespeare which I deplore in the theatre. At the same time I know only too well that my own performance has been cluttered with these things. I have never been either sufficiently experienced or sufficiently original to dare to direct or play *Hamlet* without including a great deal of this kind of theatricalism for fear of being unable to hold the interest of the audience by a more classical and simple statement of the written text. As in music, it needs the greatest artist to perform most simply and perfectly the greatest composition.

SCENE 7

The Great Hall in the Castle. 'To be, or not to be'; the Nunnery
Scene / (Act III, Scene I)

I remember in the Moissi production, the German text of which I could not follow, that I was surprised by 'To be, or not to be' coming so quickly on top of 'O! what a rogue and peasant slave am I.' This contrast had never struck me before, because there had always been an act wait between these two scenes, and then another before the play scene. When we first rehearsed the play at the Old Vic it seemed obvious that the best

place to have the only interval was after the nunnery scene rather than
before it. Apart from the time lapse which is suggested in the text there
is also the practical consideration of preventing people coming in late and
slamming down their seats during 'To be, or not to be,' whereas if they
miss the whole of the advice to the players (which, however, is hellishly
difficult to play under such circumstances) they will have lost nothing of
the main progress of the plot.

Apart from this, I realize now that the effect of despondency in 'To
be, or not to be' is a natural and brilliant psychological reaction from the
violent and hopeless rage of the earlier speech. If it were not such a
famous purple patch which everybody in the audience waits for all evening, it would seem perhaps more perfectly placed for the character than
it does. I imagined I created a great innovation by walking about in this
speech and was extremely proud of the way I slipped in the opening
words, trying to make not too long a pause before them and to get under-
way before the audience was quite sure it really was the big speech. But
of course this defeated its own ends in time. When I did the play in New
York I became self-conscious in the walking and after a few nights Mrs.
Patrick Campbell, who came to see the play, implored me to cut it out as
she said that watching the movements distracted from the words and
destroyed the essential sense of composure necessary for the full effect
of the lines.

The familiarity of this scene is an utter curse. Several times a week
one is distracted by the knowledge that the audience is repeating one's
lines after one—frequently one can hear words and phrases being whispered by people in the front rows, just before one is going to speak
them—indeed, Leica cameras and the quoting of famous passages aloud
are two of my worst phobias in a performance of *Hamlet*. This particular
speech in itself is such a perfect thing that if you have executed it correctly you are apt to feel complete and satisfied at the end of it, but not
ready to go straight into the rest of the scene. Like so many other great
speeches in this play, it has to be studied, spoken, re-studied and re-
spoken, until one can combine in it a perfect and complete form of poetry
and spontaneous thought and at the same time use it only as a part of
the action. The character and the value of the speech lie in the fact that
it leads on to the next part of the scene, just as it must grow out of the
previous action. Of course, the better one speaks it and the more completely one can win the audience by a good delivery of it, the more difficult it is to join it to the subsequent conversation and interplay with
the other characters.

The scene with Ophelia has never really been explained to my satisfaction in any book I have read or performance I have seen. I have certainly never been able to decide positively for myself its general meaning or the particular meaning of many of the lines. I cannot be convinced by the traditional business of Hamlet seeing the King and Polonius before saying 'Where's your father?' nor am I sure when Hamlet says 'I loved you not' that he should immediately belie his words with affectionate byplay behind Ophelia's back. This is another of Irving's legacies which I inherited at an early age. (Moissi, by the way, took out a big white handkerchief to cry in before Ophelia even came on the stage.) It seems to me reasonable to suppose that Hamlet suspects from the very first that Ophelia has been set on to spy upon him. 'Are you honest? . . .' That is why I have been inclined to favour Dr. Dover Wilson's theory of overhearing Polonius' 'I'll loose my daughter to him' in the other scene, though against this I feel that so much time has elapsed between the two occasions that I doubt if an ordinary audience seeing the play for the first time would notice the connection.

'Why wouldst thou be a breeder of sinners?' has led some commentators to suppose that Ophelia might be pregnant, and bolsters the theory already discussed that Hamlet and she had been lovers. The prevalent opinion seems to be, however, that the idea refers to his mother. This applies also to the later references to women painting their faces. The lines in which Hamlet accuses himself seem to me most poignant if they are spoken as if pleading with Ophelia to admit that she is not telling the truth. He is giving her every chance to speak out by showing her that he has just the same weaknesses as she. The scene is such an extraordinary mixture of realism and poetry that it needs elucidation. It maddens me to think that the author, were he here today, could so easily enlighten us as to the way it should be acted. The fact that like the other great scenes in *Hamlet* it is full of theatrical effect and is sure-fire with the audience does not make it any less of a problem for both the actor and the director.

ACT II—SCENE 8

The Great Hall in the Castle. The Advice to the Players; the Play Scene / (Act III, Scene II)

The advice to the players is always slightly embarrassing for the actor because he feels the audience is only waiting to catch him doing all the things he has told the players not to do. One of the most curious and amusing things about *Hamlet* is Shakespeare's mania for what one might call double suggestion. For instance, he invites an audience to watch an actor pretending to be a Prince apparently weeping real tears for his father, and a few scenes later he shows them the same actor being impressed by the mimic tears of another actor weeping for Priam's slaughter. He invites them to watch the actor who is playing the Prince discourse on acting and to see a play acted within a play. He asks them to mock at the damnable faces of Lucianus and the next instant to be thrilled by the terror of the King; to grieve with Laertes at his sister's grave, and yet to sneer a few moments later at the violent ranting of the two young men. The effect of contrast is echoed in the characters themselves—in the two sons avenging their fathers, the two princes waiting for their kingdoms, the two brothers, poisoner and poisoned, and the two women, shallow, weak, victims of circumstances and tools of men stronger than themselves.

The question of the dumb-show and the whole content of the play scene has been most exhaustively discussed by Dr. Dover Wilson. His views are fascinating, but I do not think that in carrying them out to the letter the conduct of the scene itself would gain, particularly for the average spectator. Well or badly played, well or badly cut, this scene has been and always will be one of the most exciting ever invented, although the great climax 'Give me some lights. Away!' has never been staged with any great invention.

Presumably, in the Elizabethan theatre, the King and his Court were brought on by attendants with torches. These retired during the action of the play, and at the King's cry they re-entered and the Court left the stage, surrounded by this blaze of light, leaving Hamlet and Horatio alone. It is difficult to imagine that this was effective without artificial light, but perhaps torches flickering on the inner stage, which was out of the full sunlight, may have provided some illusion. Today fire regulations are so strict that it is extremely difficult to devise anything really effective with naked lights on the stage. They are not allowed either in London or in New York and a sore problem is added to the trials of the modern producer of classical plays.

Sarah Bernhardt is supposed to have snatched a torch from an attendant and held it to the King's face on 'What! frighted with false fire?' and Moissi did much the same with a large candelabra. Shakespeare, however, said 'Suit the action to the word, the word to the action,' and as such fire is hardly false it seems a paradoxical gesture, though no doubt theatrically telling. Irving, I believe, created the business of lying on the floor with the manuscript in his hand and of squirming on his stomach across the stage. He also played with a fan of peacock's feathers which

Ophelia let drop, and which he tore to pieces as he lay exhausted on the throne, and flung away on the words 'A very, very—pajock.' I do not know where the tradition originated of tearing up the manuscript—this has often been followed.

Macready, in this scene, waved a white handkerchief two or three times at the entrance of the King and the Court. I have never been able to discover on what particular line he did it, but apparently it was a signal for applause from the audience in the same way as was the famous business of Edmund Kean in the nunnery scene when, having left the stage, he electrified the house by returning, tiptoeing across the stage, and kissing Ophelia's hair. I always wonder how he accomplished this without her noticing it, and what she was doing while it was happening. At any rate, it brought down the house. And so did the handkerchief business of Macready, until the American actor Edwin Forrest attended the performance one night, and hissed at this particular piece of business. Macready's diary is full of the incident and the rows and taking of sides which ensued on the subject, both in England and America.

The recorders scene was one of Irving's great triumphs, but many subsequent Hamlets cut it out. Personally, I would rather sacrifice almost anything else in the play, while admitting frankly that the breaking of the recorder at the end of it—taken also, I think, from Irving, though I am not sure—is pure theatrical business and not justified by the text. Unfortunately, I succumbed to it at the Queen's Theatre—not having done it originally at the Old Vic—and found the resulting applause, and chance of cutting several seconds playing time in a version that was inclined to run too long, too strong a combination to resist. When I played the soliloquy that followed, 'Tis now the very witching time of night,' the scene would pass entirely without applause. This soliloquy, with its curious references to Nero and Hamlet's thought of matricide (never touched on anywhere else in the play), is one that does not go with an audience—at any rate, when I have played it—any more than the following one of the King at prayers. Perhaps the speeches are too frankly Elizabethan in feeling, or it may be that they have less poetic appeal than others. In any case they are very difficult to deliver and unrewarding to play. Sir Philip Ben Greet wrote me that it was impossible to break a recorder, as it was then made in one piece, not screwed together like a modern flute. I replied, undaunted, that it was the most effective piece of business in the play and that people always liked it. I fear I am an inveterate ham, and shall never be the conscientious interpreter of Shakespeare that I should like to be.

In the Harcourt Williams production at the Vic Polonius came with a candle, which I took from him, pointing with it to the cloud, which made these lines frankly fantastic. I carried the candle through the rest of the scene, on into the King's room, and finally into the Queen's closet, where I set it down on a table. This gave a certain sense of continuity which I liked, but it did not fit into the stage management of subsequent productions.

Both Rosencrantz and Guildenstern, as well as Polonius, are frightened by Hamlet's behaviour at the play and anxious to get him to his mother as quickly as possible. I am sure it is this feeling of being hustled that makes Hamlet delight in ridiculing them and in forcing them to leave him to come in his own time. This situation is a sort of pendant to the early part of the scene when they had announced that the King would see the play and Hamlet had hurried them off to summon the players. It could easily be stage-managed so that the audience would notice this excellent parallel stage effect.

I wonder, by the way, why the court of Claudius and Gertrude is always portrayed by actors representing young men and women. Gertrude must be nearly fifty, and in spite of the vanity of Queen Elizabeth, who certainly liked young people about her, it is surely more probable that a corrupt court under the influence of a king such as Claudius would include a great many older people. If I ever direct the play again I should like to have supers representing old councillors and ladies-in-waiting of about the Queen's age. The appearance of these in all the court scenes would suggest the complacent stupidity and mature decadence of Claudius' entourage. Hamlet, Horatio, Ophelia, Laertes, Rosencrantz and Guildenstern would stand out by contrast as the rebellious young people of the play. It would also be a change to indicate that Polonius did not run the entire affairs of Denmark single-handed. On the other hand, the modern custom of casting a younger woman for Gertrude greatly enhances the effect of the part and the meaning of the story. In the old days, the part of Hamlet being usually played by older men, his mother naturally became the property of the 'heavy' actress in the company, and the result was not advantageous to the play.

SCENE 9

A Room in the Castle. The King at Prayers / (Act III, Scene III)

Mr. Granville-Barker points out that the effect of this scene lies in the fact that the audience knows that Claudius cannot pray. Therefore, if Hamlet had known that the King was not in a state of grace he would have killed him. Of course this is brilliantly true. But how can it be shown to an audience and how can the scene be arranged so that Hamlet's long speech may seem natural and yet audible? I should like to try an effect which I venture to think may have been the one achieved in the Elizabethan theatre. Kneeling on the stage is a conventional symbol for prayer, but kneeling at a prie-dieu immediately suggests prayer itself. It seems to me that if the King knelt at the front of the stage on the floor and not at a prie-dieu or altar, and Hamlet appeared above (the upper stage of the Elizabethan theatre—a balcony or rostrum would serve the same purpose in ours) the kneeling figure would convey to Hamlet the idea that the King was praying, but the King's face, which the audience could see clearly, would belie the attitude of his figure. Hamlet could not actually reach Claudius without coming down onto the stage. His pause and his subsequent speech would seem naturally to check him from doing this. He could then pass on along the upper stage, the King would rise and speak his final lines, leaving by a side door. The inner curtains could then open to disclose Polonius with the Queen, and Hamlet would enter as if he had traversed a passage and descended a staircase—as he would actually have to do—behind the scenes.

Played as it usually is today before a drop curtain, the scene with Claudius is extremely difficult for the actor. He is so close to the King that, even when the words are whispered, the audience is aware of the falseness of the convention and thinks it very odd that Claudius does not hear. The sentiments of the speech are intensely Elizabethan and therefore do not appeal much to a modern audience. As Mr. Granville-Barker says, the play is much more deeply concerned with what will happen to the individual after death than with any question of the momentary pain and violence of the act of dying. Today a lingering illness and the ugly attributes of the deathbed are what many of us fear the most, whereas the physical fact of sudden death must have been so continually present to the Elizabethans that they were inclined to consider the matter with greater philosophy than we do.

I am proud of a piece of business I invented in this scene—the only one I think that I can call entirely my own. I did not want to wear a sword in the play scene, as it is an impossible appendage to violent movement, but it is essential in the killing of Polonius in the scene with the Queen. In London the sword was carried before the King in the play scene, and at the beginning of the following one he was seen taking off his crown and robe but keeping the sword by him as if afraid to be left alone without it. Hamlet finds the sword lying on the chair, picks it up to kill the

King, and at the end of the speech goes off with it in his hand to his mother. The King rises from his knees, finds the sword gone, and the discovery of its loss ends the scene on a legitimate note of excitement, and softens, to a certain degree, the rather trite-sounding rhyming couplet with which it closes.

Many critics believe that this scene is really the crux and climax of the entire play, but perhaps because I have never felt that I played it effectively, or that it was staged to the best advantage either in my own or other productions, I have not been able to agree with them. The following scene and the killing of Polonius is to me, as an actor, the climax of Hamlet's long inaction. The whole of the subsequent tragedy springs from this later moment. Besides, it is this physical act that seems to break the spell of doubt in Hamlet's mind and unloose his stream of repressed anguish and revenge.

SCENE 10
The Closet Scene / (*Act III, Scene IV*)

It is a terrific strain to open this scene at the pitch which the text demands, but it is essential to carry the mood of the play scene through the four or five scenes that follow it and maintain the feeling of a consecutive time-lapse. I realized from a description of Bernhardt's cry 'Is it the king?' when her sword was held above her head making her whole figure into a great interrogation mark (as, I think, Maurice Baring has described it) the tremendous theatrical effect of the killing of Polonius. The lines which follow have to be most carefully presented by the actors so that the audience may not miss the significance of both characters at this point. The Queen's line 'As kill a king!' has to convey to the audience not only her horror at what Hamlet has just tried to do but her dawning knowledge of what he implies Claudius has done. Hamlet has to understand in a very few seconds, and convey clearly to the audience (1) that he realizes his mother did not know Claudius was a murderer, (2) that she set someone to spy on him behind the arras, and (3) that it is evident from her cry that it is not, as he imagined, Claudius whom he has killed.

I am constantly receiving letters asking me whether the Queen was an accomplice of her husband's murder. This is, I suppose, because the actresses who have played the part recently—Martita Hunt and Laura Cowie in London, and Judith Anderson in New York—have played her with real fire and sensuality, whereas in the old days as I have said she was played as the heavy woman—nothing more. It seems obvious to me, and I

should have thought to everyone else (but one is never done with speculation in *Hamlet*), that Shakespeare meant her to be an adulteress, shallow,
handsome, but not in the least wicked in the sense of being a murderess.
Mrs. Campbell said to me, 'The point about Gertrude in the closet scene is
not that she didn't know Claudius was a murderer, but that she doted on
him so much that she wouldn't have minded if he had been.' This seems to
me feminine and shrewd.

The business of the pictures, which to judge from old prints was done
at one period with portraits on the wall and later with miniatures around
the necks of the characters, is another vexed point of theatrical tradition.
Many recent Hamlets, myself included, have dispensed with both. But
Mr. Granville-Barker, to my surprise, advocates the miniatures. I suppose
they are really warranted by the text, but I never dared to use them for fear
that they would lead me inevitably to the elaborate business of dashing
down Claudius' picture and stamping on it at the line 'A king of shreds
and patches!' This, I imagine, was the point at which Garrick knocked over
the chair, which was supposed to be very effective. This is the point, also,
where, it seems to me, the Ghost should appear in ordinary dress and not
in armour.

The arrangement in New York was criticized in one case because
Hamlet was between the Ghost and his mother The Queen should be in
the middle, it was said, to get the full effect of her inability to see the
Ghost. On the other hand, if Hamlet is in the middle, there is a fine effect
when the Ghost bids him speak to her and he addresses her over his
shoulder with a movement of his arm, but still not looking around, his
eyes fixed on his father.

The text seems to warrant a chair in this scene for the Queen to sit on,
but I have always thought there should be a bed as well. In London we
used curtains which hung in the middle of the stage, suggesting a bed.
One half of the stage represented the King's room and the other the
Queen's. The King knelt in prayer at one end of the bed and the Queen
was discovered kneeling at the other. This gave a sense of atmosphere, but
without too definite localization. In New York we had a real bed and no
chair. I imagine it was very effective when I leaped on the bed and stabbed
Polonius through the hangings, but on the other hand it was necessary for
the Queen to sit on it and as somebody said, a Queen would never sit on a
bed—it makes her look like a housemaid! Another difficulty is that later
when the Queen is going out of the room and Hamlet begs her not to go
to his uncle's bed, a real bed on the stage may encourage the audience to
indulge in speculation as to the sleeping accommodations of the palace.
This scene and the scenes that follow could probably still be played best on

an Elizabethan stage, with the inner stage arranged with hangings for the killing of Polonius. The action in the scenes before and after could then continue on the forestage, backstage, and above, in quick succession.

SCENE 13

A Plain in Denmark; the Fortinbras Soliloquy / (Act IV, Scene IV)

The scene with Fortinbras and his army seems certainly to require a change of scene, yet the modern picture stage fails as usual, just at the moment when it should be most useful. A really striking setting might be possible with a revolving stage, but though we planned in London to use the entire extent of the permanent set for this one scene, lighted and angled at a different point from any other, we found when we came to the dress rehearsal that this particular arrangement was not good. We had to fall back on curtains as we did also in New York. Of course the soliloquy is most easily spoken close to the footlights, but it would also be of enormous value to suggest space, open air, and nature in the background after the madness and scurryings of the dark scenes in the palace.

I did not see Chaney's Viking ship in Howard's production, which I am told was a fine innovation for this scene, but there is a drawing in Craig's *Toward a New Theatre* called 'Enter the Army' which I should love to see carried out in the theatre. If the audience could be somehow persuaded that they could see an army marching as clearly as Hamlet does, it would be an excellent cross-current in the action of the play. But when one's mind begins to dwell on masses of soldiers and banners, one knows at once the danger of turning a production of the play into the kind of pageant that no doubt the pageant-master producers and Hollywood would be glad to make of it. If Hamlet is forced to conjure up in his imagination an army on the march, and succeeds in doing so, the audience may be readier to believe in its existence than if it were really there. I am told that Tyrone Guthrie arranged the scene brilliantly in his recent production at the Old Vic with Fortinbras above on an eminence, in shadow, while Hamlet spoke on the stage below—and that Herbert Menges devised a brilliant effect with music to heighten the mood as the scene closed.

SCENES 14 AND 16

The Great Hall of the Castle, and the Council Chamber. Ophelia's Mad Scene / (Act IV, Scenes V and VII)

This is the point in the play where Hamlet at last gets ten minutes in his dressing room, so perhaps I am not very well fitted to discuss it in detail. Once Ophelia has done her two showy pieces the house becomes inclined to polite indifference until the gravediggers appear. But the King and Laertes have a difficult scene to play here which never seems to be very effective and is always severely cut, which probably does not make it any easier. And perhaps it is not possible in any play of Shakespeare's to avoid two or three stretches, usually in the forth act of the standard editions, that are less interesting than others.

The Victorians often set this scene in a garden or exterior of some sort, presumably to help the idea of Ophelia's flowers and the Queen's description of her drowning. Needless to say, pastoral scenery is of little avail in illustrating Shakespeare's text. The entrance of Laertes with the mob is obviously more effective played indoors, and I am told it was one of the great successes of lighting and stage management in the Norman Bel Geddes production of *Hamlet,* in which Raymond Massey played.

Technically, the most difficult part of the scene is the entrance of the Queen to tell of Ophelia's death. Laertes' 'Drown'd! O, where?' has defeated many actors, and if the Queen is a good character actress she finds it difficult to fit the willow speech (as it is called by actors), which is a sort of cadenza, into the rest of her performance, to which it seems to have no particular relation. Here, I think, there is no doubt that a bit of the old grand manner is required. The actress must be given the stage and know how to take it and not attempt to make a realistic effect with her lines. After all, if one examines it carefully, the whole situation is absurd, for if the Queen or anybody else had seen the drowning in such detail, obviously something would have been done to prevent it. Shakespeare merely uses the Greek messenger method of describing an important incident happening off-stage, and no producer can hope to make the incident more convincing by arranging it realistically for the actress.

SCENE 15
Hamlet's Letter / (Act IV, Scene VI)

I have always retained the letter scene with Horatio as it gives some sense of continuity. The actor has a difficult time at about this point in the play for after being in attendance on Ophelia, we see him receiving Hamlet's letter and then when we next meet him he is with Hamlet in the graveyard knowing nothing of Ophelia's death. Here again it is no good trying to build the character too realistically in sequence. Shakespeare uses him all through the play in whatever way he wills, as a foil to Hamlet and the other characters, but he is so tactfully and rightly put in the foreground when Shakespeare needs him that the audience accepts him exactly as is intended and believes all that he stands for in Hamlet's eyes.

SCENE 17

A Churchyard. Hamlet's Return; Ophelia's Funeral / (*Act V, Scene I*)

Here a serious technical problem is presented to the scene designer. There is no time for an interval before or after—yet he must have a practical set, a grave, a glint of sky, besides some other suggestion of an exterior. Beerbohm Tree indulged in a spring landscape with blossoms, sheep scattered on the hills, and flowers which he picked for Ophelia's grave. In the Reinhardt-Moissi production the scene was played at night by torchlight and Ophelia was carried on in white robes on an open bier. This was all very well. Unfortunately there was no trap, and having set the bier above the grave, the men fought over her, were parted, the Court retired, and poor Ophelia was left out all night for the daws to peck at, which seemed a little unchristian, to say the least of it.

A most impressive version of this scene was given in the modern dress *Hamlet,* for I suppose all of us (unless we are Irish) have a rooted aversion to modern funerals. The black, brass-handled coffin, wreaths, boots and mourning veils lent a sordid reality to the scene which I found quite unbearable. The gravedigger was, in this production, played by Sir Cedric Hardwicke and he gave a brilliant performance on the lines of his old countryman in *The Farmer's Wife.* Ralph Richardson in another Old Vic performance also gave a memorable reading. The part does not seem to amuse an audience very much as a rule, but children love it and roar at the jokes and the business of the skulls, which seems rather surprising. George Nash, who was the clown in our American production, is certainly the best gravedigger I have ever played with. Without resorting to ten waistcoats or any of the old business, and with a very cut version of his lines, he contrived, it seemed to me, to present a most Shakespearian and delightful rendering of the old fellow.

Hamlet and Laertes should surely not fight in the grave, for the moment they disappear from view it is impossible to see clearly what is happening and the effect on the stage is bound to be ridiculous when they are separated and have to climb sheepishly out again. The lines do not really demand it anyway.

SCENE 18

A Corridor. Hamlet and Osric; the Challenge / (*Act V, Scene II*)

Martin-Harvey, who played Osric at the Lyceum, says that Irving seemed to be surrounded by an aura of death in this scene. It is a very difficult passage to play, especially when the audience is flagging, and the

...the rant in the graveyard which immediately pre-
...y cuts always make one feel as if something had been
...played in full there is an abrupt transition of mood and
...e necessary front scene demanded for the striking of the
...d the setting of the final scene cramps the actors for space
...e audience, who begin to cough and look at their watches. The
...on of the pirate ship and the changing of the letters comes too late
for the audience to be interested in it and the actors always feel, however
the scene is cut, that it is difficult to settle the house so that it will be attentive for the last stretch of the play.

A good Osric does much to remedy this, and I have been very lucky
in those who played the part with me—Alex Guinness in London and
Morgan Farley in New York. Mr. Granville-Barker has an interesting
theory about Hamlet's attitude in this last part of the play, and I think
there is much to be said for his suggestion that he should be keen, ruthless,
his mind made up. But with this must be weighed the half affectionate, half
philosophical mood of the scene with the gravedigger, of his words about
Yorick, and his touching farewell to Horatio. These moments win such
obvious sympathy from the audience that no doubt this is apt to encourage
the actor at the end of a long part to play for pathos and sentiment more
than he should.

The fatalistic vein in which he speaks 'It is no matter . . . A man's
life's no more than to say "One!" . . . If it be not to come, it will be now
. . .' these are simple moments which, when spoken sincerely, will move
almost any audience. But the general attitude of the character all through
these last three scenes is extremely difficult to reconcile with the violent
and often more showy passages in the earlier scenes and the actor has to
take the line which he feels is most justified by his reading of the text and
his whole conception of the character.

SCENE 19

The Great Hall. The Duel; the Death Scene / (Act V, Scene II)

The final scene is apt to be a little ridiculous unless everybody concerned is very careful. Irving made his one really ill-judged cut in this play
here, and left out Fortinbras altogether. The rest of his acting version is
well arranged and compares favourably with his other Shakespearian texts,
which were maltreated and bowdlerized to a shameless degree. Recent productions have made the fight tremendously pictorial and built the whole
scene around it, especially in the productions in which Raymond Massey

and Laurence Olivier played. As I am not a good swordsman I have never myself attempted more than is absolutely necessary. Frankly, also, I haven't the energy for it at the end of such a long and exhausting part. But the better the fight is done, of course, the better for the scene, and if the stage can be arranged for different levels to be used for the duelling the effect is proportionately greater.

I have always fought with rapier and dagger as the text seems to demand. Moissi, to my amazement, after an elaborate but quite anachronistic eighteenth century fight with foils (in a Gothic production) took the poisoned sword by the blade with both hands, and stabbed the King in the back! The guards, in diagonally striped cloaks, then closed in in three groups covering the bodies of the King and Queen and Laertes, making a background for Hamlet himself to die against. This was too much of a stunt and I prefer my own arrangement of the scene, in which the Queen and Laertes died on big thrones, one on each side of the stage close to the footlights, and the King in a big cloak and crown was pursued up to a centre platform where he fell in a swirl of red folds. There were still steps below for Hamlet and Horatio to play their final scene, and Fortinbras and his army in grey cloaks and banners came from above over a kind of battlement and dipped their flags at the final curtain.

Forbes-Robertson died sitting on the throne with the King's crown set on his lap, and was then borne off on locked shields. Leslie Howard also, I believe, was carried off in a great procession to end the play. The poisoning of the Queen is difficult to manage and Mr. Granville-Barker has a fine idea that she should really play her death scene on the ground like the pictures of the death of Queen Elizabeth, suffering and moaning in her ladies' arms, and not die until Hamlet says 'Wretched queen, adieu!' I had never noticed what he so brilliantly points out—that the King, being a professional poisoner, was unable to resist using a device a second time, as so many great criminals have done. It is indeed ironic for Hamlet to realize at this moment that his mother has died just as his father did, and undoubtedly the King should have poison in a ring and the audience should see him pour it into the cup. In Tyrone Guthrie's production the scene was produced for violent melodrama, and the Queen fell from a six-foot platform into the arms of the attendants.

The supers in the scene are an added problem, for one cannot think of actions which appear violent enough to express their horror at these tragic happenings without distracting from the main characters and the dialogue and action of the scene that follows. In London I had soldiers holding the people back, but in New York the courtiers left the stage altogether just before the King was killed. There is reason, however, to keep them on the scene in order that they should be in contrast to the corpses and also so that Hamlet may have someone to whom to address his 'You that look pale and tremble at this chance.' I should like, another time, to use the old councillors and ladies-in-waiting of whom I spoke in the play scene, for it would give point to Hamlet's lines if he could indicate this group of important people in the kingdom as those to whom Horatio would afterwards justify all that Hamlet has done.

Mr. McClintic invented for me the device of standing until the very end. I have never seen this done by anyone in the part and rebelled against trying it at first. It proved an admirable departure from tradition, for there are three recumbent figures on the stage already, and Hamlet in Horatio's arms is always faintly reminiscent of 'Kiss me, Hardy' at the death of Nelson. The standing figure holds the audience's attention just as they are on the verge of reaching for their hats, and 'The rest is silence,' spoken standing, appears to gain greater simplicity and significance if the actor can still command the audience with his full height.

BIBLIOGRAPHY ENTRY FOR RESEARCH PAPERS:

Gielgud, John. "The Hamlet Tradition—Some Notes on Costume, Scenery, and Stage Business." From Rosamond Gilder, *John Gielgud's Hamlet*. New York, 1937. In *Interpreting Hamlet*, ed. Russell E. Leavenworth. San Francisco, 1960.

FIRST FOOTNOTE:

* John Gielgud, "The Hamlet Tradition," from Rosamond Gilder, *John Gielgud's Hamlet* (New York, 1937), in *Interpreting Hamlet*, ed. Russell E. Leavenworth (San Francisco, 1960), pp. 138-172.

SUBSEQUENT FOOTNOTES:

* Gielgud, *op. cit.*, IH, p. ■■.
* Gielgud, "The Hamlet Tradition," *IH*, p. ■■.
* Gielgud, *IH*, p. ■■.

In place of *"IH,"* "ed. Leavenworth" may be used in these subsequent-footnote forms.

ERNEST JONES

ON

the Meaning of Hamlet

Dr. Ernest Jones (1879–1958), the biographer of Freud and author of hundreds of medical and psychological works, was writing his first essay on Hamlet *in 1909. Forty years later appeared the more detailed* Hamlet and Oedipus *(London, 1949). The following essay composed the introduction to* Hamlet, Prince of Denmark, *by William Shakespeare, with a psycho-analytical study by Ernest Jones, M.D. (London, 1947). By permission of Vision Press, Ltd.*

THE PROBLEM OF HAMLET AND THE OEDIPUS-COMPLEX

IT HAS BEEN found that with poetic creations the critical procedure cannot halt at the work of art itself; to isolate this from its creator is to impose artificial limits to our understanding of it. A work of art is too often regarded as a finished thing-in-itself, something almost independent of the creator's personality, so that little would be learned about the one or the other by connecting the two studies. Informed criticism, however, shews that a correlated study of two sheds light in both directions, on the inner nature of the composition and on the mentality of its author. The two can be separated only at the expense of diminished appreciation, whereas to increase our knowledge of either automatically deepens our understanding of the other. Masson well says: 'What a man shall or can imagine, equally with what he shall or can desire, depends ultimately on his own nature, and so even on his acquisitions and experiences . . . Imagination is not, after all, creation out of nothing, but only re-combination, at the bidding of moods and of conscious purposes, out of the materials furnished by memory, reading and experience; which materials vary with the individual cases.' In asserting this deterministic point of view, one characteristic also of modern clinical psychology, Masson gives us a hint of one of the difficulties that psychological analysis has to overcome—namely the preference for the belief that poetic ideas arise in their finished form, perhaps from one quasi-divine source, rather than as elaborations of simple and familiar elements devoid in themselves of glamour or aesthetic beauty.

This attitude becomes still more comprehensible when one realises that the deeper, unconscious mind, which is doubtless the actual source of such ideas, as of all abstract ideas, is comprised of mental material discarded or rejected by the conscious mind as being incompatible with its standards: material which has to be extensively transformed and purified before it can be presented to consciousness. The attitude, in short, is one more illustration of the constant resistance that man displays against any danger he may be in of apprehending his inner nature. The artist himself has always avoided a closely analytic attitude towards his work, evidently for the same reason as the ordinary man. He usually dissociates the impelling motive force from his conscious will, and sometimes ascribes it to an actual external agency, divine or demonic. D'Annunzio, for example, in his *Flame of Life* makes his artist-hero think of 'the extraordinary moments in which his hand had written an immortal verse that had seemed to him not born of his brain, but dictated by an impetuous deity to which his unconscious organ had obeyed like a blind instrument.' Nowhere is the irresistible impetuosity of artistic creation more perfectly portrayed than in the memorable passage in *Ecce Homo* where Nietzsche describes the birth of *Thus Spake Zarathustra,* and its involuntary character has been plainly indicated by most great writers, from Socrates to Goethe.

The particular problem of Hamlet, with which we are here concerned, is intimately related to some of the most frequently recurring problems that are presented in the course of psycho-analytic work, and it has thus seemed possible to secure a fresh point of view from which an answer might be proffered to questions that have baffled attempts made along purely literary and non-analytical lines. Some of the most competent literary authorities have freely acknowledged the inadequacy of all the solutions of the problem that have hitherto been suggested, and when judged by psychological standards their inadequacy is still more evident. The problem

presented by the tragedy of *Hamlet* is one of peculiar interest in at least
two respects. In the first place, the play is almost universally considered to
be the chief masterpiece of one of the greatest minds the world has known.
It probably expresses the core of Shakespeare's psychical personality and
outlook on life as no other work of his does. It may be expected, therefore,
that anything which will give us the key to the inner meaning of the play
will necessarily provide a clue to much of the deeper workings of Shakespeare's mind. In the second place, the intrinsic interest of the play itself is
exceedingly great. The central mystery in it—namely, the cause of Hamlet's
hesitancy in seeking to obtain revenge for his father's murder—has well
been called the Sphinx of modern Literature.

The cause of Hamlet's vacillation lies in some special feature of the
task which renders it peculiarly difficult or repugnant to him. He suffers
from an inhibition of the power to will in the particular direction of
avenging his father's death. This conclusion, that Hamlet at heart does
not want to carry out the task, seems so obvious that it is hard to see how
any open-minded reader of the play could avoid making it. The whole
picture presented by Hamlet, his deep depression, the hopeless note in his
attitude towards the world and towards the value of life, his dread of
death that is a dread of the unresolved and seething darkness within, his
fear of dying into eternal conflict because, not conscious of what constitutes the burden of his repression, he can never reach redemption either in
life or in the grave, his repeated reference to bad dreams, his self-accusa-
tions, his desperate efforts to get away from the thoughts of his duty, and
his vain attempts to find an excuse for his procrastination; all this unequivocally points to a tortured conscience, to some hidden ground for
shirking his task, a ground which he dare not or cannot avow to himself.
We have, therefore, to seek for some evidence that may serve to bring to
light the hidden counter-motive.

The extensive experience of the psycho-analytic researches carried out
by Freud has amply demonstrated that certain kinds of mental processes
shew a greater tendency to be inaccessible to consciousness, to be 'repressed,'
than others. In order therefore to gain a proper perspective it is necessary
briefly to inquire into the relative frequency with which various sets of
mental processes are repressed. Experience shews that this can be correlated with the relation between these various sets and their degree of com-
patibility with the ideals and standards accepted by the conscious ego; the
less compatible they are with these the more likely are they to be repressed.
As the standards acceptable to consciousness are in a considerable measure
derived from the immediate environment, one may formulate the following

generalisation: those processes are most likely to be repressed by the individual which are most disapproved of by the particular circle of society to whose influence he has chiefly been subjected during the period when his character was being formed. Biologically stated, this law would run: 'That which is unacceptable to the herd becomes unacceptable to the individual member', it being understood that the term herd is intended here in the sense of the particular circle defined above, which is by no means necessarily the community at large. It is for this reason that moral, social, ethical or religious tendencies are hardly ever repressed, for, since the individual originally received them from his herd, they can hardly ever come into conflict with the dicta of the latter. By the term 'repression' we denote an active dynamic process. Thoughts that are repressed are actively kept from consciousness by a definite force and with the expenditure of more or less mental effort, though the person concerned is seldom aware of this. Further, what is thus kept from consciousness typically possesses an energy of its own. A little consideration of the genetic aspects of the matter will make it comprehensible that the trends most likely to be repressed are those belonging to what are called the natural instincts. As the herd unquestionably selects from the natural instincts the sexual one on which to lay its heaviest ban, so it is the various psycho-sexual trends that are most often repressed by the individual. We have here the explanation of the clinical experience that the more intense and the more obscure is a given case of deep mental conflict the more certainly will it be found on adequate analysis to centre about some sexual problem. On the surface, of course, this does not appear so, since, by means of various psychological defensive mechanisms, the depression, doubt, despair and other manifestations of the conflict are transferred on to more tolerable and permissible topics, such as anxiety about worldly success or failure, about immortality and the salvation of the soul, philosophical considerations about the value of life, the future of the world, and so on.

Bearing these considerations in mind, let us return to Hamlet. It should now be evident that the conflict hypotheses which see Hamlet's conscious impulse towards revenge inhibited by an unconscious misgiving of a highly ethical kind, are based on ignorance of what actually happens in real life, for misgivings of this order belong in fact to the more conscious layers of the mind rather than to the deeper, unconscious ones. Hamlet's intense self-study would speedily have made him aware of any such misgivings and, although he might subsequently have ignored them, it would almost certainly have been by the aid of some process of rationalisation which would have enabled him to deceive himself into believing that they were ill-founded; he would in any case have remained conscious of the nature of them. We have therefore to invert these hypotheses and realise that the positive striving for vengeance, the pious task laid on him by his father, was to him the moral and social one, the one approved by his consciousness, and that the repressed inhibiting striving against the act of vengeance arose in some hidden source connected with his more personal, instinctive life. The former striving is manifest in every speech in which Hamlet debates the matter; the second is, from its nature, more obscure and has to be investigated. This is perhaps most easily done by inquiring more intently into Hamlet's precise attitude towards the object of his vengeance, Claudius, and towards the crimes that have to be avenged. These are two: Claudius' incest with the Queen, and the murder of his brother. It is of great importance to note the profound difference in Hamlet's attitude towards both these crimes. Intellectually of course he abhors both, but there can be no question about which arouses in him the deeper loathing. Whereas the murder of his father evokes in him indignation and a plain recognition of his obvious duty to avenge it, his mother's guilty conduct awakes in him the intensest horror. Now, in trying to define Hamlet's attitude towards his uncle we have to guard against assuming off-hand that this is a simple one of mere execration, for there is a possibility of complexity arising in the following way: The uncle has not merely committed *each* crime, he has committed *both* crimes, a distinction of considerable importance, for the *combination* of crimes allows the admittance of a new factor, produced by the possible inter-relation of the two, which prevents the result from being simply one of summation. In addition it has to be borne in mind that the perpetrator of the crimes is a relative, and an exceedingly near relative. The possible inter-relationship of the crimes, and the fact that the author of them is an actual member of the family, gives scope for a confusion in their influence on Hamlet's mind which may be the cause of the very obscurity we are seeking to clarify.

Let us first pursue further the effect on Hamlet of his mother's misconduct. Before he even knows that his father has been murdered he is in deepest depression, and evidently on account of this misconduct. The connection between the two is unmistakable in the monologue in Act 1, Scene 2, in reference to which Furnivall writes: 'One must insist on this, that before any revelation of his father's murder is made to Hamlet, before any burden of revenging that murder is laid upon him, he thinks of suicide as a welcome means of escape from this fair world of God's, made abominable to his diseased and weak imagination by his mother's lust and the dishonour done by her to his father's memory'. But we can rest satisfied with this seemingly adequate explanation of Hamlet's weariness of life only if we accept unquestioningly the conventional standards of the causes of deep emotion. Many years ago Connolly, a well-known psychiatrist, pointed out the disproportion here existing between cause and effect and gave as his opinion that Hamlet's reaction to his mother's marriage indicated in itself a mental instability, 'a predisposition to actual unsoundness'; he writes: 'The circumstances are not such as would at once turn a healthy mind to the contemplation of suicide, the last resource of those whose reason has been overwhelmed by calamity and despair.' We have unveiled, therefore, only the exciting cause, not the predisposing cause. The very fact that Hamlet is content with the explanation arouses our grave suspicions, since, as will presently be expounded, from the very nature of the emotion he cannot be aware of the true cause of it. If we ask, not what ought to produce such soul-paralysing grief and distaste for life, but what in actual fact does produce it, we are compelled to go beyond this explanation and seek for some deeper cause. In real life speedy second marriages occur commonly enough without leading to any such result as is here depicted, and when we see them followed by this result we invariably find that there is some other and more hidden reason why the event is followed by this inordinately great effect. The reason always is that the event has awakened to increased activity mental processes that have been repressed from the subject's consciousness. The person's mind has been specially prepared for the catastrophe by previous mental processes with which those directly resulting from the event have entered into association. This is perhaps what Furnivall means when he speaks of the world being made abominable to Hamlet's 'diseased imagination'. In short, the special nature of the reaction presupposes some special feature in the mental predisposition. Analysis of such states always reveals the operative activity of some buried group of mental processes. Hamlet's state of mind, as Freud has pointed out, corresponds with that characteristic of a certain form of hysteria. Therefore if Hamlet has been plunged into this abnormal state by the news of his mother's second marriage it must be because the news has awakened into activity some slumbering memory of an associated kind, which is so painful that it may not become conscious. For some deep-seated reason, which is to him unacceptable, Hamlet is plunged into anguish at the thought of his father being replaced in his mother's affections by someone else. It is as though his devotion to his mother had made him so jealous for her affection that he had found it hard enough to share this even with his father and could not endure to share it with still another man. Against this thought, however, suggestive as it is, may be urged three objections. First, if it were in itself a full statement of the matter, Hamlet would have been aware of the jealousy, whereas we have concluded that the mental process we are seeking is hidden from him. Secondly, we see in it no evidence of the arousing of an old and forgotten memory. And, thirdly, Hamlet is being deprived by Claudius of no greater share in the Queen's affection than he had been by his own father, for the two brothers made exactly similar claims in this respect—namely, those of a loved husband. The last-named objection, however, leads us to the heart of the situation. How if, in fact, Hamlet had in years gone by, as a child, bitterly resented having had to share his mother's affection even with his own father, had regarded him as a rival, and had secretly wished him out of the way so that he might enjoy undisputed and undisturbed the monopoly of that affection? If such thoughts had been present in his mind in childhood days they evidently would have been repressed, and all traces of them obliterated by filial piety and other educative influences. The actual realisation of his early wish in the death of his father at the hands of a jealous rival would have produced, in the form of depression and aggression, guilt and sadism, an obscure aftermath of his childhood's conflict. Furthermore, it is typical that the feelings of tenderness are directed only towards the dead father, the father who is no longer a rival, and are totally withheld from the uncle, the living father-imago. This is at all events the mechanism of the Oedipus-complex that is actually found in the real Hamlets who are investigated psychologically.

In order that the point of view put forward above may be better apprehended I feel constrained to interpolate a few considerations on two matters that are not at all commonly appreciated at their true importance —namely a child's feeling of jealousy and his ideas on the subject of death. It was reserved for the genetic studies of psycho-analytic research to demonstrate the lasting and profound influence that infantile jealousies may have upon later character reactions and upon the whole course of a person's life.

The close relation between adult jealousy and the desire for the removal of the rival by the most effective means, that of death, and also the common process of suppression of such feelings, is clearly illustrated in a remark of Stanley Hall's to the effect that 'Many a noble and even great man has confessed that mingled with profound grief for the death and misfortune of their best friends, they were often appalled to find a vein of secret joy and satisfaction, as if their own sphere were larger or better.' He has doubtless in mind such passages as the following from La Rochefoucauld: 'Dans l'adversité de nos meilleurs amis, il y a quelque chose qui ne nous déplaît pas.' A similar thought is more openly expressed by Bernard Shaw when he makes Don Juan, in the Hell Scene, remark: "You may remember that on earth—though of course we never confessed it—the death of any one we knew, even those we liked best, was always mingled with a certain satisfaction at being finally done with them.' Such cynicism in the adult is exceeded to an incomparable extent by that of the child, with its notorious, and to the parents often heartbreaking, egotism, with its undeveloped social instincts, and with its ignorance of the dread significance of death. A child very often unreasoningly interprets the various encroachments on its privileges, and the obstacles interposed to the immediate gratification of its desires, as meaningless cruelty, and the more imperative is the desire that has been thwarted the more pronounced is the hostility towards the agent of this supposed cruelty, most often of course a parent. The most important encroachment, and the most frequent, is that made on the child's desire for affection. The resulting hostility is very often seen on the occasion of the birth of a subsequent child, and is usually regarded with amusement as an added contribution to the general gaiety called forth by the happy event. When a child, on being told that the doctor has brought him another playfellow, responds with the cry 'Tell him to take it away again', he intends this, however, not, as is commonly believed, as a joke for the entertainment of his elders, but as an earnest expression of his intuition that in future he will have to renounce his previously unquestioned pre-eminence in the family circle, a matter that to him is serious enough.

The second point, on which there is also much misunderstanding, is that of the child's attitude towards the subject of death, it being commonly assumed that this is necessarily the same as that of an adult. When a child first hears of anyone's death, the only part of its meaning that he realises is that the person is *no longer there,* a consummation which time and again he has fervently desired when being interfered with by the persons around him. It is only gradually that the grimmer implications of the phenomenon are borne in upon him. When, therefore, a child expresses the wish that a given person, even a near relative, would die, our feelings would not be so shocked as they sometimes are, were we to interpret the wish from the point of view of the child. The same remark applies to the dreams of adults in which the death of a near and dear relative takes place, dreams in which the underlying repressed wish is usually concealed by an emotion of grief. But on the other hand the significance of these death-wishes is not to be under-estimated, either, for the later conflicts they may give rise to can be of the utmost importance for the person's mental welfare, and this in spite of the fact that in the vast majority of cases they remain merely wishes. Not that they always remain wishes, even in children. The recent case in which a group of schoolboys sought to murder their headmaster (the father-imago) comes at once to mind.

Of the infantile jealousies the most important, and the one with which we are here occupied, is that experienced by a boy towards his father. The precise form of early relationship between child and father is in general a matter of vast importance in both sexes and plays a predominating part in the future development of the child's character. The only aspect that at present concerns us is the resentment felt by a boy towards his father when the latter disturbs, as he necessarily must, his enjoyment of his mother's exclusive affection. This feeling is the deepest source of the world-old conflict between father and son, between the younger and the older generation, the favourite theme of so many poets and writers, the central *motif* of most mythologies and religions. The fundamental importance that this conflict, and the accompanying breaking away of the child from the authority of his parents, has both for the individual and for society is clearly stated in the following passage of Freud's: 'The detachment of the growing individual from the authority of the parents is one of the most necessary, but also one of the most painful, achievements of development. It is absolutely necessary for it to be carried out, and we may assume that every normal human being has to a certain extent managed to achieve it. Indeed, the progress of society depends in general on this opposition of the two generations.'

It was Freud who first demonstrated, when dealing with the subject of the earliest manifestations of the sexual instinct in children, that the conflict rests in the last resort on sexual grounds. He has shewn that this instinct does not, as is generally supposed, differ from other biological functions by suddenly leaping into being at the age of puberty in all its full and developed activity, but that like other functions it undergoes a gradual evolution and only slowly attains the particular form in which we know it in the adult.

It must be mentioned how frequently these earliest dim awakenings are evoked by the intimate physical relations existing between the child and the persons of his immediate environment, above all, therefore, his mother. There is a considerable variability in both the date and the intensity of these early sexual impressions, this depending partly on the boy's constitution and partly on the mother's. When the attraction exercised by the mother is excessive it may exert a controlling influence over the boy's later destiny; a mass of evidence in demonstration of this, too extensive to refer to in detail, has been published in the psycho-analytical literature. Of the various results that may be caused by the complicated interaction between this influence and others only one or two need be mentioned. If the awakened passion undergoes an insufficient repression—an event most frequent when the mother is a widow—then the boy may remain throughout life abnormally attached to his mother and unable to love any other woman, a not uncommon cause of bachelorhood. He may be gradually weaned from the attachment if it is less strong, though it often happens that the weaning is incomplete so that he is able to fall in love only with women who in some way resemble the mother; the latter occurrence is a frequent cause of marriage between relatives, as has been interestingly pointed out by Abraham. The maternal influence may also manifest itself by imparting a strikingly tender feminine side to the later character. The trait in Hamlet's character has often been the subject of comment. Vining even suggests that Hamlet really was a woman. That the same trait was a prominent one of Shakespeare's himself is well known, a fact which the appellation of 'Gentle Will' sufficiently recalls; Harris even writes: 'Whenever we get under the skin, it is Shakespeare's femininity which startles us.' The relationship with Ophelia never flowers because Hamlet's unconscious only partly desires her; in part Ophelia is felt to be a permitted substitute for the desired relationship with Laertes.

When the aroused feeling is intensely repressed and associated with shame, guilt, and similar reactions the submergence may be so complete as to render the person incapable of experiencing any feeling at all of attraction for the opposite sex; to him all women are as forbidden as his mother. This may declare itself in pronounced misogyny or even, when combined with other factors, in actual homosexuality.

The attitude towards the successful rival, namely the father, also varies with—among other factors—the extent to which the aroused feelings have been repressed. If this is only slight, then the natural resentment against the father may be more or less openly manifested later on, a rebellion which occurs commonly enough, though the true meaning of it is not recognised. To this source many social revolutionaries—perhaps all—owe the original impetus of their rebelliousness against authority, as can often be plainly traced—for instance, with Shelley and Mirabeau. The unimpeded train of thought in the unconscious logically culminates in the idea, or rather the wish, that the father (or his substitute) may disappear from the scene, i.e. that he may die. Shakespeare himself provides a good example of this (King Henry IV, Part II) in the scene between the dying king and his son:

Prince Henry. *I never thought to hear you speak again.*
King Henry. *Thy wish was father, Harry, to that thought.*

If, on the other hand, the repression is considerable, then the hostility towards the father will be correspondingly concealed from consciousness; this is often accompanied by the development of the opposite sentiment, namely of an exaggerated regard and respect for him, identification with his temperament and social aims, and a morbid solicitude for his welfare, which completely cover the underlying attitude. The complete expression of the repressed wish is not only that the father should die, but that the son, taking over the sexual role of the father, should then espouse the mother. The son, who so often inherits the character-formation of the father, is merely a repressed father-image. As soon as the father is out of the way the repressed identification with him returns to the surface and the son endeavours to outdo the father in the practising of father-hood. Hamlet has all the makings of as great a criminal as was Claudius. The desire to espouse the mother was openly expressed by Diderot in speaking of boys: 'If we were left to ourselves and if our bodily strength only came up to that of our phantasy we would wring our fathers' necks and sleep with our mothers.' The attitude of son to parents is so tran-spicuously illustrated in the Oedipus legend, as developed for instance in Sophocles' tragedy, that the group of mental processes in question is generally known under the name of the Oedipus-complex.

We are now in a position to expand and complete the suggestions offered above in connection with the Hamlet problem. Here, as through-out, I closely follow Freud's interpretation given in a footnote to his *The Interpretation of Dreams*. He there points out the inadequacy of the earlier explanations, deals with Hamlet's feelings towards his mother, father, and uncle, and mentions two other matters, the significance of Hamlet's reaction against Ophelia and of the probability that the play was written immediately after the death of Shakespeare's own father. The story thus interpreted would run somewhat as follows. As a child Hamlet had experienced the warmest affection for his mother, and this, as is always so, had contained elements of a disguised erotic quality. The pre-sence of two traits in the Queen's character go to corroborate this assump-tion, namely her markedly sensual nature and her passionate fondness for her son. The former is indicated in too many places in the play to need specific reference, and is generally recognised. The latter is also manifest; Claudius says, for instance (Act IV, Sc. 7), 'The Queen his mother lives almost by his looks'. Nevertheless Hamlet seems to have with more or less success weaned himself from her and to have fallen in love with Ophelia. The precise nature of his original feeling for Ophelia is a little obscure. We may assume that at least in part it was composed of a normal love for a prospective bride, though the extravagance of the language used (the passionate need for absolute certainty, etc.) suggests a somewhat morbid frame of mind. There are indications that even here the influence of the old attraction for the mother is still exerting itself. Although some writers, following Goethe, see in Ophelia many traits of resemblance to the Queen, surely more striking are the traits contrasting with those of the Queen. Whatever truth there may be in the many German conceptions of Ophelia as a sensual wanton—misconceptions that have been confuted by Loening and others—still the very fact that it needed what Goethe happily called the 'innocence of insanity' to reveal the presence of any such libidinous thoughts demonstrates in itself the modesty and chasteness of her habitual demeanour. Her naive piety, her obedient resignation and her unreflecting simplicity, sharply contrast with the Queen's character, and seem to indicate that Hamlet by a characteristic reaction towards the opposite extreme had unknowingly been impelled to choose a woman who should least remind him of his mother. A case might even be made out for the view that part of his courtship originated not so much in direct attraction for Ophelia as in an unconscious desire to play her off against his mother, just as a disappointed and piqued lover so often has resort to the arms of a more willing rival. It would be hard otherwise to understand the readiness with which he later throws himself into this part. When, for instance, in the play scene he replies to his mother's request to sit by her with the words 'No, good mother, here's metal more attractive' and proceeds to lie at Ophelia's feet, we seem to have a direct indication of this attitude; and his coarse familiarity and bandying of ambiguous jests with the woman he has recently so ruthlessly jilted are hardly intelligible unless we bear in mind that they were carried out under the heedful gaze of the Queen. It is as though his unconscious were trying to convey to her the following thought: 'You give yourself to other men whom you prefer to me. Let me assure you that I can dispense with your favours and even prefer those of a woman whom I no longer love.' His extraordinary outburst of bawdiness on this occasion, so unexpected in a man of obviously fine feeling, points unequivocally to the sexual nature of the underlying turmoil.

Now comes the father's death and the mother's second marriage. The association of the idea of sexuality with his mother, buried since infancy, can no longer be concealed from his consciousness. As Bradley well says: 'Her son was forced to see in her action not only an astounding shallowness of feeling, but an eruption of coarse sensuality, "rank and gross," speeding post-haste to its horrible delight'. Feelings which once, in the infancy of long ago, were pleasurable desires can now, because of his repressions, only fill him with repulsion. The long repressed desire to take his father's place in his mother's affection is stimulated to unconscious activity by the sight of someone usurping this place exactly as he himself had once longed to do. More, this someone was a member of the same family, so that the actual usurpation further resembled the imaginary one in being incestuous. Without his being in the least aware of it these ancient desires are ringing in his mind, are once more struggling to find conscious expression, and need such an expenditure of energy again to re-press them that he is reduced to the deplorable mental state he himself so vividly depicts.

There follows the Ghost's announcement that the father's death was a willed one, was due to murder. Hamlet, having at the moment his mind filled with natural indignation at the news, answers normally enough with the cry (Act I, Sc. 5):

> *Haste me to know't, that I, with wings as swift*
> *As meditation or the thoughts of love,*
> *May sweep to my revenge.*

The momentous words follow revealing who was the guilty person, namely a relative who had committed the deed at the bidding of lust. It is not maintained that this was by any means Claudius' whole motive, but it was evidently a powerful one and the one that most impressed Hamlet. Hamlet's second guilty wish had thus also been realised by his uncle, namely to procure the fulfilment of the first—the possession of the mother —by a personal deed, in fact by murder of the father. The two recent events, the father's death and the mother's second marriage, seemed to the world to have no inner causal relation to each other, but they represented ideas which in Hamlet's unconscious fantasy had for many years been closely associated. These ideas now in a moment forced their way to con-scious recognition in spite of all repressing forces, and found immediate expression in his almost reflex cry: 'O my prophetic soul! My uncle?'. The frightful truth his unconscious had already intuitively divined his consciousness had now to assimilate, as best it could. For the rest of the interview Hamlet is stunned by the effect of the internal conflict thus re-awakened, which from now on never ceases, and into the essential nature of which he never penetrates.

One of the first manifestations of the awakening of the old conflict in Hamlet's mind is his reaction against Ophelia. This is doubly con-ditioned, by the two opposing attitudes in his own mind. In the first place, there is a complex reaction in regard to his mother. As was explained above, the being forced to connect the thought of his mother with sensuality leads to an intense sexual revulsion, one that is only temporarily broken down by the coarse outburst discussed above. Combined with this is a fierce jealousy, unconscious because of its forbidden origin, at the sight of her giving herself to another man, a man whom he had no reason whatever either to love or to respect. Consciously this is allowed to express itself, for instance after the prayer scene, only in the form of extreme resentment and bitter reproaches against her. His resentment against women is still further inflamed by the hypocritical prudishness with which Ophelia follows her father and brother in seeing evil in his natural affection, an attitude which poisons his love in exactly the same way that the love of his childhood, like that of all children, must have been poisoned. He can forgive a woman neither her rejection of his sexual advances nor, still less, her alliance with another man. Most intolerable of all to him, as Bradley well remarks, is the sight of sensuality in a quarter from which he had trained himself ever since infancy rigorously to exclude it. The total reaction culminates in the bitter misogyny of his outburst against Ophelia, who is devastated at having to bear a reaction so wholly out of proportion to her own offence and has no idea that in reviling her Hamlet is really expressing his bitter resentment against his mother. The identification is further demonstrated in the course of the play by Hamlet's killing the men who stand between him and his mother and Ophelia (Claudius and Polonius). On only one occasion does he for a moment escape from the sordid implication with which his love has been impregnated and achieve a healthier attitude toward Ophelia, namely at the open grave when in remorse he breaks out at Laertes for presuming to pretend that his feeling for her could ever equal that of her lover.

The intensity of Hamlet's repulsion against woman in general, and Ophelia in particular, is a measure of the powerful repression to which his sexual feelings are being subjected. The outlet for those feelings in the direction of his mother has always been firmly dammed, and now that the narrower channel in Ophelia's direction has also been closed the increase in the original direction consequent on the awakening of early memories tasks all his energy to maintain the repression. His pent up feelings find a partial vent in other directions. The petulant irascibility and explosive outbursts called forth by his vexation at the hands of Guildenstern and Rosencrantz, and especially of Polonius, are evidently to be interpreted in this way, as also is in part the burning nature of his reproaches to his mother. Indeed towards the end of his interview with his mother the thought of her misconduct expresses itself in that almost physical disgust which is so characteristic a manifestation of intensely repressed sexual feeling.

> *Let the bloat king tempt you again to bed;*
> *Pinch wanton on your cheek; call you his mouse;*
> *And let him, for a pair of reechy kisses,*
> *Or paddling in your neck with his damn'd fingers,*
> *Make you to ravel all this matter out,*   (Act III, Sc. 4)

Hamlet's attitude towards Polonius is highly instructive. Here the absence of family tie and of other similar influences enables him to indulge to a relatively unrestrained extent his hostility towards the prating and sententious dotard. The analogy he effects between Polonius and Jephthah is in this connection especially pointed. It is here that we see his fundamental attitude towards moralising elders who use their power to thwart the happiness of the young, and not in the over-drawn and melodramatic portrait in which he delineates his father: 'A combination and a form indeed, where every god did seem to set his seal to give the world assurance of a man.'

It will be seen from the foregoing that Hamlet's attitude towards his uncle-father is far more complex than is generally supposed. He of course detests him, but it is the jealous detestation of one evil-doer towards his successful fellow. Much as he hates him, he can never denounce him with the ardent indignation that boils straight from his blood when he reproaches his mother, for the more vigorously he denounces his uncle the more powerfully does he stimulate to activity his own unconscious and repressed complexes. He is therefore in a dilemma between on the one hand allowing his natural detestation of his uncle to have free play, a consummation which would stir still further his own horrible wishes, and on the other hand ignoring the imperative call for the vengeance that his obvious duty demands. His own evil prevents him from completely denouncing his uncle's, and in continuing to repress the former he must strive to ignore, to condone, and if possible even to forget the latter; *his moral fate is bound up with his uncle's for good or ill.* In reality his uncle incorporates the deepest and most buried part of his own personality, so that he cannot kill him without also killing himself. This solution, one closely akin to what Freud has shewn to be the motive of suicide in melancholia, is actually the one that Hamlet finally adopts. The course of alternate action and inaction that he embarks on, and the provocations he gives to his suspicious uncle, can lead to no other end than to his own ruin and, incidentally, to that of his uncle. Only when he has made the final sacrifice and brought himself to the door of death is he free to fulfil his duty, to avenge his father, and to slay his other self—his uncle.

Having identified himself with his uncle's erotic life he must, as a consequence of his incestuous sexual guilt, turn the death wish against his uncle (the father-imago) against himself according to the law with which all neurotics ultimately direct against themselves death wishes relating to others. In the last analysis Hamlet deals himself the punishment of death because death represents the most absolute form of castration.

There is a second reason why the call of duty to kill his step-father cannot be obeyed, and that is because it links itself with the unconscious call of his nature to kill his mother's husband, whether this is the first or the second; the absolute repression of the former impulse involves the inner prohibition of the latter also. It is no chance that Hamlet says of himself that he is prompted to his revenge 'by heaven and hell'.

In this discussion of the motives that move or restrain Hamlet we have purposely depreciated the subsidiary ones, which also play a part, so as to bring out in greater relief the deeper and effective ones that are of preponderating importance. These, as we have seen, spring from sources of which he is quite unaware, and we might summarise the internal conflict of which he is the victim as consisting in a struggle of the repressed mental processes to become conscious. The call of duty, which automatically arouses to activity these unconscious processes, conflicts with the necessity of repressing them still more strongly; for the more urgent is the need for external action the greater is the effort demanded of the repressing forces. Action is paralysed at its very inception, and there is thus produced the picture of apparently causeless inhibition which is so inexplicable both to Hamlet and to readers of the play. This paralysis arises, however, not from physical or moral cowardice, but from that intellectual cowardice, that reluctance to dare the exploration of his inner soul, which Hamlet shares with the rest of the human race. 'Thus conscience does make cowards of us all.'

Finally, in order to amplify the psychological interpretation given above, we shall examine certain aspects of the original Hamlet saga. Dealing with earlier versions of the play Storfer writes: 'When we compare the earlier versions of the Hamlet theme with Shakespeare's tragedy, Shakespeare's great psychological intuition becomes evident. The earlier versions turned on a political action relating to the state: the heir to the throne wreaks vengeance on the usurper for the murder of the king. In Shakespeare the family tragedy is placed in the foreground. The origin of all revolutions is the revolution in the family. Shakespeare's Hamlet is too

philosophical a man, too much given to introspection, not to feel the
personal and family motive behind the general political undertaking.
Laertes, on the other hand, is blind and deaf to this etymology of feeling,
to the unconscious mind; his response to his father Polonius' murder is a
political revolt. The behaviour of the two men whose fathers had been
murdered well characterises the conscious and the unconscious mind in the
psychology of the revolutionary and of the political criminal.'

Here may be mentioned a matter which on account of its general
psychological interest has provoked endless discussion, namely Hamlet's
so-called 'simulation of madness'. There is of course no question of insanity in the proper sense of the word; Hamlet's behaviour is that of a
psychoneurotic and as such naturally aroused the thought on the part of
those surrounding him that he was suffering from some inner affliction.
The traits in Hamlet's behaviour that are commonly called 'feigning madness' are brought to expression by Shakespeare in such a refined and subtle manner as to be not very transpicuous unless one compares them with
the corresponding part of the original saga. The fine irony exhibited by
Hamlet in the play, which enables him to express contempt and hostility
in an indirect and disguised form—beautifully illustrated, for instance,
in his conversations with Polonius—is a transmutation of the still more
concealed mode of expression adopted in the saga, where the hero's audience commonly fails to apprehend his meaning. He here combines a veiled
form of speech, full of obvious equivocations and intent to deceive, with
a curiously punctilious insistence on verbal truthfulness. Saxo gives many
examples of this and adds: 'He was loth to be thought prone to lying
about any matter, and wished to be held a stranger to falsehood; and
accordingly he mingled craft and candour in such wise that, though his
words did not lack truth, yet there was nothing to betoken the truth and
betray how far his keenness went'. Even in the saga, however, we read
that 'some people, therefore, declared that his mind was quick enough, and
fancied that he only played the simpleton in order to hide his understanding, and veiled some deep purpose under a cunning feint'. The king and
his friends applied all sorts of tests to him to determine this truth, tests
which of course the hero successfully withstands. It is made plain that
Amleth deliberately adopts this curious behaviour in order to further his
scheme of revenge, to which—thus differing from Hamlet—he had whole-
heartedly devoted himself. The actual mode of operation of his simulation
here is very instructive to observe, since it gives us the clue to a deeper
psychological interpretation of the process. His conduct in this respect has
three characteristics, first the obscure and disguised manner of speech just

referred to, secondly a demeanour of indolent inertia and general purpose-lessness, and thirdly conduct the childish and at times quite imbecilic fool-ishness (*Dummstellen*) ; the third of these is well exemplified by the way in which he rides into the palace seated backwards on a donkey, imitates a cock crowing and flapping its wings, rolling on the floor, and similar asininities. His motive in so acting was, by playing the part of a harmless fool, to deceive the king and court concerning his projects of revenge, and unobserved to get to know their plans and intentions; in this he admirably succeeded. Belleforest adds the interesting touch that Amleth, being a Latin scholar, had adopted this device in imitation of the younger Brutus: both names signify 'doltish', 'stupid'; the derived Norwegian word 'amlod' is still a colloquialism for 'fool'. Belleforest evidently did not know how usual it was for famous young heroes to exhibit this trait; similar stories of 'simulated foolishness' are narrated of David, Moses, Cyros, Kaikhosrav, William Tell, Parsifal, and many others besides Ham-let and Brutus.

The behaviour assumed by Amleth in the saga is not that of any form of insanity. It is a form of syndrome well-known to occur in hysteria. The complete syndrome comprises the following features: foolish, witless be-haviour, an inane, inept kind of funniness and silliness, and childishness. Now, in reading the numerous examples of Amleth's 'foolish' behaviour as narrated by Saxo one cannot help being impressed by the *childish* characteristics manifested throughout in them. His peculiar riddling say-ings, obviously aping the innocence of childhood, his predilection for dirt and for smearing himself with filth, his general shiftlessness, and above all the highly characteristic combination of fondness for deception as a thing in itself (apart from the cases where there is a definite motive) with a punctilious regard for verbal truth, are unmistakably childish traits. The whole syndrome is an exaggeration of a certain type of demeanour displayed at one time or another by most children, and psycho-analysis of it has demonstrated beyond any doubt that their motive in behaving so is to simulate innocence and often extreme childishness, even 'foolishness', in order to delude their elders into regarding them as being 'too young to understand' or even into altogether disregarding their presence. The pur-pose of the artifice is that by these means children can view and overhear various private things which they are not supposed to. It need hardly be said that the curiosity thus indulged in is in most cases concerned with matters of a directly sexual nature; even marital embraces are in this way investigated by quite young children far oftener than is generally sus-pected or thought possible. The core of Amleth's attitude is secrecy and spying: secrecy concerning his own thoughts, knowledge, and plans; spying as regards those of his enemy, his step-father. These two character traits are certainly derived from forbidden curiosity about secret, i.e. sexual matters in early childhood. So is the love of deception for its own sake, a trait which sometimes amounts to what is called pathological lying; it is a defiant reaction to the lies almost always told to the child, and always detected by him. In so behaving the child is really caricaturing the adult's behaviour to himself, as also in the punctiliousness about verbal truth that is sometimes combined with the tendency to deceive; he is pretending to tell the truth as the parent pretended to tell it to him, deceiving going on all the while in both cases. That the theme of the Amleth *motif* is derived from an infantile and sexual source can easily be shewn from the material provided in the saga itself. The main test applied to him by Feng in order to discover whether he was really stupid or only pretending to be so was to get a young girl (the prototype of Ophelia) to seduce him away to a lonely part of the woods and then send retainers to spy on them and find out whether he knew how to perform the sexual act or not. Then follows a long story of how Amleth is warned of the plot and manages to outwit the spies and also to attain his sexual goal. This passage, so obviously inappropriate if taken literally as applying to a man of Amleth's age and previous intelligence, can only be understood by correlating it with the unconscious source of the theme, and this always emanates from the impulses of childhood. 'Knowledge' is often felt to be synonymous with 'sexual knowledge', the two terms being in many contexts interchangeable: for instance, the legal expression 'to have knowledge of a girl', the Biblical one 'and Adam knew Eve his wife' (after eating of the tree of knowledge), and so on. If a child has mastered the great secret he feels that he knows what matters in life; if he hasn't he is in the dark. And, as in the Amleth saga, to prove that someone is ignorant of this fundamental matter is the supreme test of his stupidity and 'innocence'.

Spying and overhearing play such a constant part in the Amleth saga as to exclude the possibility of their being unconnected with the central theme of the story. After the plot just mentioned had failed Feng's counsellor, the prototype of Polonius, devises another in which Amleth is to be spied on when talking to his mother in her bedroom. During the voyage to England the king's retainers enter Amleth's bedroom to listen to his conversation. Before this Amleth had spied on his companions and replaced their letter by one of his own. In the later part of the saga, not utilised by Shakespeare, two other instances of spying occur. In 'Hamlet'

Shakespeare has retained those scenes and added one other. The first time is when the interview between Hamlet and Ophelia, doubtless taken from the test described above, is overlooked by the king and Polonius; the second when Hamlet's interview with his mother is spied on by Polonius, who thereby loses his life; and the third when the same interview is watched by the Ghost. It is appropriate to the underlying theme of sexual curiosity that two out of these should take place in the mother's bed-chamber, the original scene of such curiosity; on both occasions the father-substitute comes *between* Hamlet and his mother, as though to separate them, the reversal of a theme common in primitive cosmogonies. The most striking example in 'Hamlet' of a spying scene is the famous 'play within a play', for in a very neat analysis Rank has shewn that this play scene is a disguised representation of the infantile curiosity theme discussed above.

From this point of view we can specify more nearly the precise aspect of the father that is represented by the 'decomposed' figure Polonius. It is clearly the spying, watching, 'all-knowing' father, who is appropriately outwitted by the cunning youth.

Amleth's feigned stupidity in the saga is very crudely depicted and its meaning is quite evident. The use Shakespeare made of this unpromising material, and the way in which he made it serve his aim of completely transforming the old story, is one of the master-strokes of the drama. Amleth's gross acting, for a quite deliberate purpose, is converted into a delicately drawn character trait. Merciless satire, caustic irony, ruthless penetration together with the old habit of speaking in riddles: all these betray not simply the caution of a man who has to keep his secret from those around him, as with Amleth, but the poignant sufferings of a man who is being torn and tortured within his own mind, who is struggling to escape from knowing the horrors of his own heart. With Amleth the feigned stupidity was the weapon used by a single-hearted man in his fight against external difficulties and deliberate foes; with Hamlet it—or rather what corresponds to it, his peculiar behaviour—was the agent by which the secret of a man torn by suffering was betrayed to a previously unsuspecting foe and increasing difficulties were created in his path where none before existed. In the issue Amleth triumphed; Hamlet was destroyed. The different use made of this feature in the story symbolises more finely than anything else the transformation effected by Shakespeare. An inertia pretended for reasons of expediency becomes an inertia unavoidably forced on the hero from the depths of his nature. In this he shews that the tragedy of man is within himself, that, as the ancient saying goes: Character is Fate. It is the essential difference between pre-historic and civilised man with his highly developed sense of guilt arising out of the ceaseless conflict between ego and the personal and social super-ego; the difficulties with which the former had to contend came from without, those with which the latter have to contend really come from within. This inner conflict modern psychologists know as neurosis, and it is only by study of neurosis that one can learn the fundamental motives and instincts that move men. Here, as in so many other respects, Shakespeare was the first modern.

It is highly instructive now to review the respects in which the plot of 'Hamlet' deviates from that of the original saga. We are here, of course, not concerned with the poetic and literary representation, which not merely revivified an old story, but created an entirely new work of genius. The changes effected were mainly two and it can be said that Shakespeare was only very slightly indebted to others for them. The first is as follows: In the saga Feng (Claudius) had murdered his brother in public, so that the deed was generally known, and further had with lies and false witnesses sought to justify the deed by pretending it was done to save the Queen from the cruel threats of her husband. Those acquainted with psycho-analytic work will have no difficulty in discerning the infantile sadistic origin of this pretext. Young children commonly interpret an overheard coitus as an act of violence imposed on the mother and they are in any case apt to come to this conclusion whichever way they are enlightened on the facts of sex. The view in question is certainly an aggravating cause of the unconscious hostility against the father. This point again confirms our conclusion that Claudius partly incorporates Hamlet's repressed wishes, for we see in the saga that he not only kills the father-king but also gives as an excuse for it just the reason that the typical son feels. This view of the matter he successfully imposed on the nation, so that, as Belleforest has it, 'son péché trouva excuse à l'endroit du peuple et fut reputé comme justice envers la noblesse—et qu'au reste, en lieu de le poursuyvre comme parricide et incestueux, chacun des courtisans luy applaudissoit et le flattoit en sa fortune prospere'. Now was the change from this to a secret murder effected by Shakespeare or by Kyd? It is of course to be correlated with the introduction of the Ghost, of whom there is no trace in either Saxo or Belleforest. This must have been done early in the history of the Elizabethan 'Hamlet', for it is referred to by Lodge in 1596 and is also found in 'Der bestrafte Brudermord', though neither of these reasons is decisive for excluding Shakespeare's hand. But purely literary considerations make it likely enough, as Robertson has pointed out, that the change was introduced by Kyd, who seems to have had a partiality for Ghost scenes. In the saga there was delayed action due to the external difficulties of penetrating through the king's watchful guard. Kyd seems to have retained these external difficulties as an explanation for the delay, though his introduction of the Ghost episode for reasons of his own—probably first in the form of a prologue—somewhat weakened them as a justification, since to have the Ghost episode the murder had to be a secret one—otherwise there would be nothing for the Ghost to reveal and no reason for his appearance. But his Hamlet, as in the saga, had a quite single-hearted attitude towards the matter of revenge; he at once confided in Horatio, secured his help, and devoted himself entirely to his aim. There was no self-reproaching, no doubting, and no psychological problem. Shakespeare, however, saw the obvious advantages of the change in the plot—if he did not introduce it himself—for his intention of transforming the play from an external struggle into an internal tragedy. The change minimises the external difficulties of Hamlet's task, for plainly it is harder to rouse a nation to condemn a crime and assist the avenger when it has been openly explained and universally forgiven than when it has been guiltily concealed. If the original plot had been retained there would be more excuse for the Klein-Werder hypothesis, though it is to be observed that even in the saga Hamlet successfully executed his task, herculean as it was. The present rendering makes still more conspicuous Hamlet's recalcitrancy, for it disposes of the only justifiable plea for delay. That Shakespeare saw the value of the change thus unwittingly and ununderstandingly introduced by Kyd is proved by the fact that later on he took steps to remove the last traces of even a relative publicity concerning the murder. In the first Quarto Hamlet secures his mother's promise to help him in his plans of revenge, and later Horatio in an interview with the Queen speaks with knowledge of Hamlet's plans of revenge and learns from the Queen that she sympathises with them. Both these passages were omitted in the second Quarto. The omission unmistakably indicates Shakespeare's intention to depict Hamlet not as a man dismayed by external difficulties and naturally securing the cooperation of those he could trust, but as a man who could not bring himself to speak to his best friend about his quite legitimate desire for revenge, simply because his own mind was in dire conflict on the matter.

The second and all-important respect in which Shakespeare, and he alone, changed the story and thus revolutionised the tragedy is the vacillation and hesitancy he introduced into Hamlet's attitude towards his task, with the consequent paralysis of his action. In all the previous versions Hamlet was throughout a man of rapid decision and action wherever possible, not—as with Shakespeare's version—in everything except in the one task of vengeance. He had, as Shakespeare's Hamlet felt he should have, swept to his revenge unimpeded by any doubts or scruples and had never flinched from the straightforward path of duty. With him duty and natural inclination went hand in hand; from his heart he wanted to do that which he believed he ought to do, and thus was harmoniously impelled by both the summons of his conscience and the cry of his blood. There was none of the deep-reaching conflict that was so disastrous to Shakespeare's Hamlet. It is as if Shakespeare, on reading the story, had realised that had *he* been placed in a similar situation he would not have found the path of action so obvious as was supposed, but would on the contrary have been torn in a conflict which was all the more intense for the fact that he could not explain its nature. Bradley might well say that this was the only tragic situation to which Shakespeare himself would not have been equal, and we now know the reason must have been that his penetration had unconsciously revealed to his feeling, though not to his conscious intelligence, the fundamental meaning of the story. His own Oedipus-complex was too strong for him to be able to repudiate it as readily as Amleth and Laertes had done, and he could only create a hero who was unable to escape from its toils.

In this transformation Shakespeare exactly reversed the plot of the tragedy. Whereas in the saga this consisted in the overcoming of external difficulties and dangers by a single-hearted hero, in the play these are removed and the plot lies in the fateful unrolling of the consequences that result from an internal conflict in the hero's soul. From the struggles of the hero issue dangers which at first did not exist, but which, as the effect of his untoward essays, loom increasingly portentous until at the end they close and involve him in final destruction. More than this, every action he so reluctantly engages in for the fulfilment of his obvious task seems half-wittingly to be disposed in such a way as to provoke destiny, in that, by arousing the suspicion and hostility of his enemy, it defeats its own purpose and helps to encompass his own ruin. The conflict in his soul is to him insoluble and the only steps he can make are those which inexorably draw him nearer and nearer to his doom. In him, as in every victim of a powerful unconscious conflict, the Will to Death is fundamentally stronger than the Will to Life, and his struggle is at heart one long despairing fight against suicide, the least intolerable solution of the problem. Being unable to free himself from the ascendency of his past he is necessarily impelled by Fate along the only path he can travel—to Death. In thus vividly exhibiting the desperate but unavailing struggle of a strong man against Fate Shakespeare achieved the very essence of the Greek conception of tragedy, but he went beyond this and shewed that the real nature of man's Fate is inherent in his own soul.

There is thus reason to believe that the new life which Shakespeare poured into the old story was the outcome of inspirations that took their origin in the deepest and darkest regions of his mind. He responded to the peculiar appeal of the story by projecting into it his profoundest thoughts and emotions in a way that has ever since wrung wonder from all who have heard or read the tragedy. It is only fitting that the greatest work of the world-poet should have had to do with the deepest problem and the intensest conflict that have occupied the mind of man since the beginning of time—the revolt of youth and of the impulse to love against the restraint imposed by the jealous eld.

BIBLIOGRAPHY ENTRY FOR RESEARCH PAPERS:

> Jones, Ernest. "The Problem of Hamlet and the Oedipus-Complex." Introduction in *Hamlet, Prince of Denmark, by William Shakespeare, with a psycho-analytical study by Ernest Jones, M.D.*, London, 1947. In *Interpreting Hamlet*, ed. Russell E. Leavenworth. San Francisco, 1960

FIRST FOOTNOTE:

> * Ernest Jones, "The Problem of Hamlet and the Oedipus-Complex," introduction in *Hamlet, Prince of Denmark, by William Shakespeare, with a psycho-analytical study by Ernest Jones, M.D.* (London, 1947), in *Interpreting Hamlet,* ed. Russell E. Leavenworth (San Francisco, 1960), pp. 173-196.

SUBSEQUENT FOOTNOTES:

> * Jones, *op. cit., IH,* p. ■■.
> * Jones, "Problem of Hamlet," *IH,* p. ■■.
> * Jones, *IH,* p. ■■.

In place of *"IH,"* "ed. Leavenworth" may be used in these subsequent-footnote forms.

PAUL S. CONKLIN

ON

the Hamlet Stage Tradition

Paul Conklin (b. 1900) is Professor of English at New Mexico A & M College. We reprint Chapter 2 of his A History of Hamlet Criticism, 1601–1821 *(New York, 1947; copyright 1957 by Humanities Press, Inc.), by permission of the author and Humanities Press, Inc.*

HISTRIONIC TRADITION TO THE RETIREMENT OF GARRICK

THE EIGHTEENTH CENTURY, as has been said before, saw the growth to considerable proportions of a formal body of critical dogmas on Shakespeare.[1] The first impetus came from Dryden, but genuine headway came only in the next century. As time passed, the volume of this critical current increased, and into it flowed the foreign streams of French and German criticism, to make up in the Nineteenth Century an ocean of print touching every conceivable phase of Shakespeare's art. In this general body of criticism, *Hamlet* at times played a modest part, but finally almost a predominant role.

---

[1] See Nichol Smith, *Shakespeare in the 18th Century* (Oxford, 1928); T. S. Eliot, "Shakespearian Criticism from Dryden to Coleridge," in H. Granville-Barker and G. B. Harrison, *A Companion to Shakespeare Studies,* 1934. For critical excerpts, see Nichol Smith, *18th Century Essays on Shakespeare* (Glasgow, 1903); and A. Ralli, *A History of Shakespearian Criticism* (2 v., Oxford, 1932).

As a background for the growth of Shakespearian criticism, and at times serving to color its texture and determine the direction of its growth, were certain social and cultural changes. One may speak of the enormous extension of the reading habit in England. This is the period when periodicals multiplied, when the novel was born, and when the reading public which these new literary vehicles encouraged, increased by leaps and bounds. Many new editions of Shakespeare appeared; the literature of his plays and the literature about them grew constantly. The radius of Shakespearian criticism was extending into France and Germany, and (of more immediate moment to our purpose) into Scotland. Furthermore, certain changes were working out in the English habit of thought and taste. The tide of sentimentalism and romanticism was mounting. All of these things had their influence on Shakespearian criticism. The effect on *Hamlet* might be set forth thus:

1. *Hamlet* criticism takes on a professional character

2. After 1770, the emphasis changes most noticeably from the spectator to the reader, and often not the English, but the Scotch or German reader. In other words, watching the play becomes an increasingly less important thing

3. *Hamlet* criticism, therefore, from the 1770's on, becomes largely the story of a departure from the direct perspective; and the task of this study a description and criticism of the new attitudes that arise[2]

The materials at hand for a study of the eighteenth-century Hamlet are plentiful, and in their variety confusing. It will be helpful to start with the more specific theatrical tradition. Although, as I have indicated in my last paragraph, *Hamlet* criticism underwent important modifications in the century, it started as a simple continuation of seventeenth-century tendencies. And the center of vitality in *Hamlet* tradition at the beginning of the century, and through Garrick, was a most vigorous dramatic—a theatrical—tradition. This cannot be denied. The evidence for such a statement comes from both theatrical records and from a fairly voluminous gen-

---

[2] For my focal idea here, the point of view around which I have built my descriptive account, I am indebted mainly to Mr. E. E. Stoll, particularly to his *Hamlet: An Historical and Comparative Study* (*Research Publications of the University of Minn., Stud. in Lang. and Lit.*, No. 7, Mpls., 1919); and his chapter on Hamlet in *Art and Artifice in Shakespeare* (Cambridge, 1933). [See page 104 in this collection.]

eral literature. *Hamlet* as a play kept the boards in fairly consistent fashion from the Restoration to Garrick's retirement.[3]

The point of departure, then, for my study here is this theatrical tradition. If it is possible to speak of a "real" eighteenth-century Hamlet, this Danish prince of the theatre might well claim the honor. For is it' not sound criticism to insist that a dramatic entity can appear only in its fullest reality when the written words and the situation, including the character himself, are "given flesh" and being on the stage? Any number in the Eighteenth Century, high and low, educated and vulgar, give their testimony to the fact that they knew *this* Hamlet. The list, among others, includes Addison and Steele, Tony Aston, Cibber, Fielding, Mrs. Montagu, Francis Gentleman, Aaron Hill, and such foreigners as Abbé Prévost, Voltaire and Lichtenberg—not to mention the recorded comments of any number of others who belong to the multitude itself,—forgotten actor, schoolboy and stage-struck apprentice.

Hamlet as a play was the common possession of all classes of the English public. The records give impressive testimony to this fact. As nowadays a youngster wishes to break into Hollywood, so, in the Eighteenth Century, most young fellows with stage ambitions wanted to play Hamlet! In his *Memoirs,* Tate Wilkinson speaks of acting Hamlet at Portsmouth in 1759.[4] There are also several accounts of the performance of the role by young Charles Holland at his first benefit: "He was a clerk . . . when the night came, his friends attended, and his native village was left almost literally empty."[5] Two accounts of Holland's début in the

---

[3] For the last 40 years of the 17th Century, and the first ten of the next, no exact record of performances is available. Pepys, however, records them in 1661, 1663 and 1668. John Genest adds two more years in his *Some Account of the English Stage* (Bath, 1832): 1662 and 1673. An indication of how incomplete Genest is can be seen by the fact that he fails to record at all performances for the years Pepys gives. Some weight can be paid to what Downes says in his *Roscius Anglicanus* concerning the popularity of Betterton's Hamlet: *supra,* p. 24. [Not included in this selection.]

For the 18th Century, G. C. D. Odell in his *Shakespeare from Betterton to Irving* (New York, 1920), I, 224 and 227, speaks of the play's vitality on the stage. From 1710 to 1742, it was acted in London every year but two; from 1742 to 1776 it was acted every year at Drury Lane, and every year but two at Covent Garden. Shaftesbury in 1711 speaks of the play as "That Piece of his, which appears to have most affected *English* Hearts, and has perhaps been oftenest acted of any which have come upon our Stage, ..." (*Characteristics,* London, 1732 edit., I, 275-6).

[4] (New York, 1790), II, 100-1.

[5] John Jackson, *The History of the Scottish Stage* (Edinburgh, 1793), pp. 338-40.

part seem to have been given mainly in order to describe the humorous incident that occurred when the young actor's hat blew off. John Bernard gives a delightful account of the first time he played the role at school.[6] Later he gives an amusing incident—of how an Irish churchyard was robbed of a skull for use as property in the play.[7] Another amusing account of Bernard's tells of how the actor Crawford, in a performance in which he found himself deserted by the musicians so dear to an Irishman's heart, came before the audience in his "Hamlet clothes," and played "Paddy O'Rafferty" to them on his fiddle.[8] Or one may mention the now-forgotten actor, "Mr. Frodsham," spoken of so contemptuously by Tate Wilkinson, whose extreme egotism led him to believe that his Hamlet was better than Garrick's![9] Yes, they all wanted to play Hamlet! Jackson tells of a provincial troupe in which there was a small rebellion because each of the actors wished the leading role: "one and all, with one voice, cry out, 'Hamlet or nothing!' " Thus, one winter, the troupe had six Hamlets but no one willing to take lesser roles. Finally the play had to be abandoned for the winter.[10]

The catholicity of appeal in Shakespeare's leading roles, including Hamlet, is given satirical treatment by Arthur Murphy in his *Apprentice,* a short play which treats flippantly, also, another contemporary fashion, the rage for Shakespeare allusions. One prologue used with the play, says in part:

> Our hero is a youth . . . whose stage struck mind
> Nor *fate* could rule, nor his *indentures* bind.
> A Place there is where such young *Quixotes* meet,
> 'Tis call'd the SPOUTING CLUB;—a glorious treat!
> Where prentic'd kings—alarm the gaping street!
> There *Brutus* starts and stares by midnight taper,
> Who all the *day* enacts—a *woollen-draper.*
> There *Hamlet's* Ghost stalks forth with doubl'd fist;

---

[6] *Retrospections of the Stage* (London, 1830), I, 4-8. The incident is dated about 1772.

[7] *Ibid.,* I, 260-1.

[8] *Ibid.,* pp. 297-8.

[9] *Op. cit.,* IV, 36, ff.

[10] *Op. cit.,* pp. 159, ff. It must not be supposed that the lesser roles in *Hamlet* were always despised. Wm. Cooke gives the Ghost as one of Barton Booth's leading roles (*Memoirs of Charles Macklin,* London, 1804, pp. 360 and 376). Wilks, too, was famous for the same part (*Ibid.,* p. 356). One performer has gone down in the records because he boasted that he had played with Garrick as the cock in *Hamlet!* (Cooke, *Memoirs of Samuel Foote,* London, 1805, III, 100.)

Cries out with hollow voice—*List, list, O list,*
And frightens *Denmark's* prince—a *young Tobacconist.*
The Spirit too, clear'd from his deadly white,
Rises—a *Haberdasher* to the fight!
But hark! I'm call'd,—be warn'd by what you see,
Oh! spout no more: *Farewell, remember me.*[11]

As a corollary fact that goes with the widespread appeal of *Hamlet* and its central figure, there is the assumption that this stage tradition must have involved a fairly settled interpretation of the focal dramatic situation and of the title role.[12] No other single characteristic is more typical of popular art. A conception such as this becomes the common possession of the age; it belongs to high and low. It becomes almost legendary, as, in another literary medium, does the figure of King Arthur or Robin Hood; or, in American fictional and dramatic history, the figure of "Uncle Tom." One is well justified, then, in looking for such a settled tradition concerning *Hamlet;* and to take absence of contradictory evidence as a basis for assuming that the play follows this general rule. It is common knowledge what happened when Garrick tried to change, not his interpretation of the leading role, but the grave-diggers scene and the fencing-match between Hamlet and Laertes in the fifth act. In deference to pseudo-classical prejudice, he omitted them both. The result that might be expected followed. Tom Davies says: "The people soon called for Hamlet as it had been acted from time immemorial."[13] Another revealing comment on Garrick's changes is: "No bribe but his own inimitable performance could

---

[11] *Theatrical Bouquet* (London, 1780), pp. 172-3.

[12] Thos. Wilkes in *A General View of the Stage* (London, 1759), speaks of the fact that certain well known dramatic situations had settled interpretations; they "have obtained all the perfection they are capable of, or at least [he thinks] that custom has so far authenticated them as not now to be conveniently departed from. Of this kind is that of Hamlet at the appearance of the ghost, and of Romeo in the Tomb-scene, etc." (*Ibid.,* pp. 152-3.) Wilkes goes on a little later to illustrate this point further by telling of the experience of a "young gentleman of genteel figure" who tried to play Hamlet with certain innovations. The rash young gentleman's friends turned out in large numbers to witness his performance, only to be much disappointed; while the others in the audience accepted the entertainment as burlesque. (*Ibid.,* pp. 167-8.)

Tony Aston, a minor figure in the dramatic world of the early century, gives testimony to the power of such a dramatic tradition when he remarks that in his opinion a younger Hamlet than Betterton would have been more appropriate, but "no one else could have pleas'd the Town, he was so rooted in their Opinion." (Hazelton Spencer, *Shakespeare Improved,* Cambridge, Mass., 1927, p. 68)

[13] *Dramatic Miscellanies* (2nd edit., London, 1785), III, 153.

have prevailed on an English audience to sit patiently and behold the martyrdom of their favorite author."[14]

We have examined the scattered but widespread testimony concerning the now-forgotten smaller figures in the eighteenth-century dramatic world of England, Scotland, and Ireland. There exist in addition rather ample records describing the performances of the Hamlets who led in the role. These include Betterton, who lived through most of the first decade; the minor Hamlets of Barton Booth, Wilks and Quinn; the great interpretation of Garrick; the less important one of Henderson; and finally, the late-century portrayal of Kemble. It is safe to conclude that the interpretations through Garrick's time should provide a descriptive account of the traditional role. It was about the time of the death of Garrick that new forces somewhat altering the main lines of *Hamlet* criticism must be taken into account.

Coming from the late Seventeenth into the early Eighteenth Century is, for this study, like changing from a place of shadows into a lighted room. Where before it has been necessary to pick up a fragment here or there, with no detailed account to guide us, now it is possible to get in comfortable detail reactions to the performances of Betterton, Wilks, Garrick, Kemble, and the other Hamlets of the period. One link, however, there is between the centuries, and that is Betterton. Over a span of years that was almost half a century, he acted Hamlet for the English people. It will be well, then, to remember that his Hamlet as seen by eighteenth-century men, must, with due allowance for any changes in interpretation over the years, and for the eighteenth-century vocabulary and point of view with which he is described, be also a portrayal that Pepys or Evelyn saw.

This, then—the eighteenth-century Hamlet—is the first one that can take on full outlines for us. His contours change somewhat, from actor to actor. In the changes can be found a register of the varying abilities of each, his emotional capacity and ability to read his "score"; and also the register of a changing zeitgeist. Eventually, after the seventies, come the changes in interpretation that were motivated by perusal of *Hamlet* in the study. One logical terminal point for such a critical tendency comes early in the Nineteenth Century with Lamb, who was willing to banish Hamlet from the actual stage completely. Lamb would make him an actor on the stage which a reader may set up in his imagination. He wished no other Hamlet!

---

[14] *Biographia Dramatica* (London, 1812), II, 144. Another discussion of this point is to be found in Tate Wilkinson's *Memoirs*, IV, 260.

Betterton's Hamlet, however, was of quite a different aesthetic species. He walked the boards as a creature of flesh and blood. His was not an interpretation overloaded with subtleties, but it was moving. Hardly a "glass of fashion" or a "mould of form" himself, he nevertheless offered a "sweet prince" who pleased many an audience. It is recorded of him that at first he played the role in the dress of a courtier of Charles II, and later with streaming shoulder-knots, cocked hat, and powdered wig.[15] As has been observed already, but on not too authentic evidence, his interpretation is said to have been the one approved by Shakespeare himself.[16]

In 1709, Steele in the *Tatler* says apropos of Betterton's last recorded performance in the role at the Haymarket:

> Had you been to-night at the play-house, you had seen the force of action in perfection: your admired Mr. Betterton behaved himself so well, that, though now about seventy, he acted youth; and by the prevalent power of proper manner, gesture, and voice, appeared through the whole drama a young man of great expectation, vivacity, and enterprise.[17]

The closing words of this description offer an illuminating contrast with some of the impressions of later periods. This is a Hamlet who conforms quite adequately to what the man in the street expects of a "hero."

In addition to his ability to portray a prince who possessed the proper qualifications for popular success, Betterton had genuine capacity to move even his more critical fellow actors. Barton Booth, who played the ghost opposite him, said: "When I acted the Ghost with Betterton, instead of my awing him, he terrified me. But divinity hung round that man!"[18] The most impressive account of Betterton's Hamlet, however, comes from the pen of another actor, Colley Cibber. What is more, he includes descriptive details not given by the others:

> You have seen a Hamlet, perhaps, who, on the first appearance of his father's spirit, has thrown himself into all the straining vociferation requisite to express rage and fury, and the house has thundered with applause; though the misguided actor was all the

---

[15] H. P. Phelps, *Hamlet from the Actor's Standpoint* (New York, 1890), pp. 5-6.

[16] Downes, *op. cit.,* p. 21.

[17] *Tatler* 71 (ed. Chalmers, London, 1822), II, 177-8. Steele speaks here in the person of "Mr. Greenhat."

[18] Quoted from Hazelton Spencer, *Shakespeare Improved,* p. 10.

while, as Shakespeare terms it, *tearing a passion into rags.* I am the more bold to offer you this particular instance, because the late Mr. Addison, while I sat by him, to see this scene acted, made the same observation, asking me, with some surprise, if I thought *Hamlet* should be in so violent a passion with the *Ghost,* which, though it might have astonished, had not provoked him? For you may observe that in this beautiful speech, the passion never rises beyond an almost breathless astonishment, or an impatience, limited by filial reverence, to inquire into the suspected wrongs that may have raised him from his peaceful tomb, and a desire to know what a spirit so seemingly distressed might wish or enjoin a sorrowful son to execute, towards his future quiet in the grave. This was the light into which Betterton threw this scene, which he opened with a pause of mute amazement; then rising slowly to a solemn, trembling voice, he made the *Ghost* equally terrible to the spectator as to himself, and in the descriptive part of the natural emotions which the ghastly vision gave him, the boldness of his expostulation was still governed by decency, and manly but not braving; his voice never rising into that seeming outrage or wild defiance of what he naturally revered. But, alas! to preserve this medium, between mouthing and meaning too little,—to keep the attention more pleasingly awake by a tempered spirit, than by mere vehemence of voice,—is, of all the master-strokes of an actor the most difficult to reach. In this none yet have equalled Betterton.[19]

Cibber's description contains a good portion of what may be termed the "orthodox interpretation" of Hamlet in this period. Other more subtle touches were to be added later in the century, to modify Betterton's rather simple portrayal. However its essential outlines persisted: a mortal man visited by the supernatural, which enjoined revenge upon him as a sacred duty; the terror, coupled with a determination to get at the truth; the "sorrowful son," filled with "filial reverence." These are notes in the interpretation that persisted through the time of Garrick. Some of Betterton's straightforward manliness was tempered, and new notes were added. The rest persisted.

During the years between the passing of Betterton and the rise of Garrick, many actors took the role. Of these, only Robert Wilks and Barton Booth deserve any detailed mention. Wilks was evidently the more successful of the two. Although not a worthy successor to Betterton, he

19 *An Apology for the Life of Mr. Colley Cibber* (London, 1822), pp. 89-90.

received at least a critical attention not bestowed upon Booth, or upon his now forgotten competitors in the part.[20]

Two facts concerning the role as played in this period stand out from contemporary histrionic criticism. Hamlet is a part that consistently demands, from an actor, extreme versatility: he must be both thoughtful and carefree, tender and brutal, delicate and bawdy—with a change from mood to mood that is lightning-like in rapidity. When a lesser artist tries the part, the inevitable result is that he can capture some of the moods, but not all. In attempting the others, he is apt to fail lamentably. So it is that Aaron Hill, a critic of the period we are now in, speaks of the fact that contemporary theater-goers had seen only "Half a Prince Hamlet." Wilks could play the "gay half" and Booth the "solemn."[21] Together, they would make an effective Hamlet:

> IN *This,* then, the Double Capacity, of *Mr.* WILKS, and *Mr.* BOOTH, shou'd *unite,* in ONE Actor.—The First cou'd be *wanton;* but, He was *wanton* without *Weight:*—The Second cou'd be *Weighty:* but, He was *Weighty,* without *Easiness.*—*Mr. Wilks* had a Spirit, that ran away with his Body: *Mr. Booth* had a Body, that dragg'd too heavy, on his Spirit.—When the One was *most* delightful, He seem'd animated, without *Purpose:* When the Other was most strong, He gave IMPRESSION, without *Briskness.*[22]

Of Wilks we have another interesting comment that brings to light a different type of blemish that the interpretation of a less gifted actor may possess. Wilks could not capture completely the imagination of the listener. He gave a performance in which one noticed the externalities, the speeches, the gestures. The eloquence which is always a part of every Hamlet became less a matter of the perfect expression of an inner vitality of spirit than with Betterton; it took on the character of stage business. This is the impression one gathers from a contemporary account.[23] The

---

[20] A list of these minor actors would include: John Thurmond, George Powell, Thomas Elrington, Lacy Ryan, Henri Giffard, John Mills, Milward, Dennis Delane, and William Havard (W. Widmann, *Hamlets Bühnenlaufbahn,* 1601-1877, Leipzig, 1931, p. 39).

[21] From his words, one judges that Hill had never seen Booth in the role.

[22] *The Prompter,* No. 100 (October 24, 1735).

[23] I have not been able to trace the ultimate source of this account. My source is a note by Edmund Bellchambers at the end of his edition of Cibber's *Apology,* 1822, pp. 513-14. It is possible that my analysis of Wilks' performance may be too harsh, for Bellchambers adds, "Wilks, indeed, was so successful in his representation of this part, that 'Hamlet' was frequently chosen, as a favourite play, to open the season with."

quality of externality seen in such an actor as Wilks, however, emphasizes anew the very presence of the eloquence that is always implicit in
Hamlet's character. Unless an actor has an adequate imagination and
emotional power, the eloquence becomes an outer thing, a matter of
elocution and gesture, not the full voice of something within. Betterton
could carry the part. Wilks couldn't.

It is Aaron Hill who sets forth a critical specification of what his age
should demand from an actor in the role. He does it in the same essay in
which he comments upon the failure of both Wilks and Booth. This is
the Hamlet whom he would wish to see:

> THE characteristic Distinction, that *marks* the Temper of
> *Hamlet,* is a *pensive,* yet *genteel,* HUMANITY.—He is, by *Nature,*
> of a *melancholy Cast:* but, His polite Education has illuminated
> the *Sable;* and, like the Sun, through a *wet* MAY *Morning,* mix'd
> a *Gleam,* with his *Sadness.*—When he *grieves,* he is never
> *Sullen:* When He *trifles,* he is never *light.*—When, *alone,* He is
> *seriously solid:* When in Company, *designedly flexible.*—He
> *assumes,* what he pleases: but he *is,* what He ought to be;—the
> Lamenter of his murder'd *Father:*—the Discerner of his
> *Mother's* Levity: and the Suspecter of his *Uncle's* Baseness.
>
> How *weigh'd,* then, and *significant,* should he be found in his
> *Looks,* and his *Actions!*—When He counterfeits Distraction with
> *Ophelia,* and perceives that she is *observing* him, All his Air is
> as light, and as empty of Purpose, as if *really* as mad, as He de-
> signs She should *think* him.—But, no sooner has he declin'd
> himself from the Glances of HER Eye—than His OWN gives us
> Marks, of his *Pity,* and his *Prudence.*—The WILDNESS He but
> *affects,* quits his Air in a Moment, and a touching Sensation of
> SORROW *paints* his *Soul,* in his *Gesture:* which again, the next
> Moment, He transforms into *Wantonness,* in the very instant of
> Time, while He *returns* toward the Lady.[24]

There are several new notes here: the "humanity," the "melancholy
cast," the intense mobility of spirit, with its roving quickness and intel-
lectuality, its sensitivity. This is a Hamlet who retains all of the old
cleverness of the malcontent, without his acid maliciousness or cynicism.
This is an eighteenth-century Hamlet. Hill shows himself here a critic
who can get almost a complete reading from the score offered by Shakespeare. As we have seen, however, there was no actor in 1735 who could
interpret fully Hill's reading. Indeed, one feels that Betterton himself
could not have satisfied Hill completely; Betterton was not so subtle as

---

[24] *Op. cit.*

this. No wonder a Wilks or a Booth could not succeed. One wonders what Hill thought of Garrick.

With the exception of Quinn, whom Garrick supplanted, there was no other important portrayer of the role before him. Quinn need not be discussed, as his performance of the part hardly merits attention.[25]

Much may of course be said concerning the Garrick Hamlet. From any one of a number of sources it is possible to gather detailed information on the man, his art, and his particular importance in this study.[26] I shall restrict myself here to the characteristic features of his portrayal of the role. He seems to have taken the more robust Hamlet of Betterton and subtilized it, made it more "feeling," more sentimental, more "delicate." The melancholy asked for by Aaron Hill was more in evidence. This melancholy was a meditative thing, with little bitterness in it. It was gentle and "philosophical"—in the full eighteenth-century tradition as it is seen in graveyard poetry, having as one of its ingredients a rationalistic playing with one's own emotions—half thought and half feeling—a psychological inversion whereby the contemplator gains pleasure out of pain. This is the type of musing on death and the after life that one sees, for example, in Young's *Night Thoughts*.[27] Garrick's interpretation of the

---

[25] One critic says of Quinn's Hamlet: "As to Quinn, he was in such a rage at his father's ghost, that he was more than half afraid he would have killed it, instead of filial reverence, terror at beholding the awful and beloved shade, compassion for its mortal and then wretched fate—he stamped and then raved at it." From *Reformer* No. 9, March 24-1747-48. (Quoted in *Early Life and Correspondence of Edmund Burke*, ed. Samuels, Cambridge, 1923, p. 174.)

[26] Practically every set of "memoirs" written by an eighteenth-century actor or about actors, dwells voluminously on Garrick. The incidental literature of the times is fairly crowded with references to Garrick and his acting. For more formal accounts, there is the contemporary biography of Thomas Davies, first edition, 1780. Other valuable records are Arthur Murphy's *The Life of David Garrick, Esq.* (2 V.), 1801; and Percy Fitzgerald's *The Life of David Garrick*, 1868.

[27] It would make a fascinating side study to record the many cases in which motifs from *Hamlet* are echoed in Eighteenth Century poetry of a melancholy or graveyard cast. For example, William Broome in 1729, echoes Hamlet's expression, "ponderous and marble jaws" in his *Melancholy: An Ode*:

> Open thy marble jaws, O tomb
> Thou earth, conceal me in thy womb!
> And you, ye worms, this frame confound;
> Ye brother reptiles of the ground!
>
> (quoted by Reed, *Op. cit.*, p. 104)
> [Amy Reed, *The Background of Gray's Elegy*, 1924]

Grainger's *Solitude* contains a distinct echo of Hamlet's words to his father (Act I, v, lines 58-63):

> Save me! what's yon shrouded shade,
> That wanders in the dark-brown glade?

famous "to be" soliloquy seems to have owed its popularity to the fact that it fitted in so well with eighteenth-century predilections for melancholy and gentle scepticism.[28] Garrick knew how to fit the temper of his age.

> It beckons me!—vain fears adieu,
> Mysterious ghost, I follow you.
> Ah me! too well that gait I know,
> My youth's first friend, my manhood's woe!
> (Dodsley's *Collection,* London, 1770, IV, 234)

Other examples, less definite, are Thomas Warton's *Pleasures of Melancholy,* line 47, ff; Blair's *The Grave,* which Miss Reed (*Op. cit.,* p. 191) says is reminiscent of the grave-diggers scene; and Mallet's *William and Margaret,* also mentioned by Miss Reed.

[28] That such an interest in the "to be" soliloquy was very real in the century is attested in various places. Both Mrs. Elizabeth Montagu and James Boswell discuss it. Mrs. Montagu's analysis puts the interpretation in a most typical eighteenth-century manner:

> Every possible sentiment is caught by this great genius; every shade of passion, every gradation of thought is marked. In the famous soliloquy, "To be or not to be?" how naturally do all the questions arise! and how finely are those circumstances set forth which are most grievous to the discontented mind. The insolence of office, the rich man's contumely, the law's delay, the thousand scorns that patient merit from the unworthy takes, these are the grievances a splenetic mind complains of; it is not the anguish or the fear of bodily diseases that prompts the desperate hand of self-murder, it is gloomy pride and discontent at the offences offered by fellow creatures that drives the soul to sullen desperation. (From a letter to Lord Lyttleton: *The Letters of Mrs. Elizabeth Montagu,* London, 1813, IV, 299 ff.)

Boswell gives expression to a more specific angle of eighteenth-century interest in the "to be" soliloquy; he takes up the subject of suicide. In his *Hypochondriak* 51 (Dec. 1781) he calls the soliloquy "a capital piece of philosophical reasoning" which "everybody recollects, and which cannot be answered unless one had an undoubted intimation from the world of spirits. . . ." (Quoted from 1928 edition, arranged by Margery Bailey, Stanford, Calif., 1928, II, 139.)

Possibly the piece which exhibits most characteristically what an eighteenth-century approach to the "to be" soliloquy could be, is a poem of William Hamilton's: *A Soliloquy—In Imitation of Hamlet.* I shall quote the concluding lines only, where Hamlet is given some delightfully pious advice:

> Then Hamlet, cease; thy rash resolves forego
> God, nature, reason, all will have it so;
> Learn by this sacred horror, well suppress,
> Each fatal purpose in the traitor's breast.
> This damps revenge with salutary fear,
> And stops ambition in its wild career,
> Till virtue for itself begin to move,
> And servile fear exalt to filial love.
> Then in thy breast let calmer passions rise,

Enough has been said to indicate that Garrick made himself a splendidly adequate mouthpiece for Hamlet's eloquence. He had the inner energy to carry it completely. The inner force seeks expression in words. Shakespeare furnishes the words for any actor who can take them as his own. Garrick could accomplish this miracle.

Finally, it should be said that with the greater delicacy that Hamlet put on in Garrick's interpretation, there was, paradoxically, no sense of a prince who could not act, or who was unmanly. "The progress of his impassioned sensation" became the "action"! There is, to be sure, a touch of sentimentalism in the picture, but it remains a mere ingredient in the whole. It doesn't dominate. Melancholy is there, as Aaron Hill would have it; but, though it may be a malady like the malcontentism of earlier days, it does not paralyse initiative or dissolve resolution.

It will be profitable to get the testimony of one who really witnessed Garrick's acting. Tom Davies says:

> When Mr. Garrick first saw the Ghost, the terror he seemed to be impressed with, was instantaneously communicated to the audience; his expostulations with the vision though warm and importunate, were restrained by filial awe. The progress of his impassioned sensation, till the Ghost beckoned him to retire with him, was accompanied with terror and respect. His determination to obey the repeated invitation of the Ghost, by action, to withdraw, was vehemently resolute; his following him, awful and tremendous. . . . The soliloquies of Hamlet are distinguished by peculiar and pathetic feelings of the mind; all the varieties of sentiment, impressed with passion, were delivered by Garrick with singular exertion.[29]

This illuminating account, combined with hints from Fitzgerald, who gathered his material from many contemporary sources, allows one to see the central details of Garrick's portrayal. He seems to have made the character his own through a progressively effective interpretation. The main secret of his dramatic effectiveness here lies in the fact that he saw the whole play in terms of action! Hamlet's every thought was registered

---

Pleas'd with thy lot on earth, absolve the skies.
The ills of life see friendship can divide;
See angels warring on the good man's side.
Alone to virtue happiness is given,
On earth self-satisfy'd, and crown'd in heaven.
    (Quoted from *A Complete Edition of the Poets of Great Britain*, Edinburgh, 1794, IX, 431.)

[29] *Memoirs of the Life of David Garrick* (London, 1808), I, 64-5.

on Garrick's wonderfully mobile face; every gesture and movement were vital action.[30] Hamlet's following the ghost had as great a dramatic value for the spectators as they could find, for example, in the meeting of Hotspur and Prince Hal on the battlefield at Shrewsbury. What is more, this portrayal had other qualities not possible in a play where the "action" is carried out on an orthodox level. The "progress of impassioned sensation" wore as its characteristic garment melancholy, expressed at this period in terms of a delicate eighteenth-century meditativeness. There was no hint of a madness akin to Bedlam, or reminiscent of the cruder exhibitions that Elizabethans might have applauded.

It remains for me to call attention to one comment that contains at least a small hint of another type of Danish prince. This is found in Thomas Wilkes' *A General View of the Stage* of 1759. Wilkes is discussing Garrick's Hamlet:

> The author has drawn this prince of a reserved cautious turn, arising from a melancholy stamped on him by his father's untimely death, and some consequent misfortunes. The passions whereby he is actuated do not, except in a few places, rise to any height; and to distinguish his feigned madness from his real provocation, is a master-piece which he hits off admirably. His manner of receiving his father's ghost on its first entrance has a fine mixture of astonishment, deference, and resolution; . . .[31]

In the hands of future closet critics, this "reserved, cautious turn" of Hamlet's was to become a devastating thing. Before the century is over, it will bear all of the aspects of a genuine "tragic flaw."[32] With Wilkes,

---

[30] There is eloquent testimony to the extent of Garrick's achievement in making Hamlet's total *experience* a dramatic thing. The ghost scene illustrates this well. Such a scene would in any event be "dramatic"; but Garrick succeeded in giving a histrionic value to every shred of Hamlet's experience in the scene. In connection with it one remembers Partridge as described by Fielding in *Tom Jones* (Mod. Lib. edit., pp. 737-40); or the vivid account given by Lichtenberg, who saw the play on a visit to England. [See page 38 in this collection.] The latter is quoted by Fitzgerald (*op. cit.,* 258). For original, see *Vermischte Schriften* (1844), III, 209-10.

[31] Pp. 249-50.

[32] Possibly a close reading of Cibber's words on Betterton [herein quoted; credited in footnote 19] or Aaron Hill [herein quoted; credited in footnote 24] might cause some careful critics to see in these earlier interpretations a hint of what becomes later a "tragic flaw." Both critics imply that Hamlet has a thorough control over the extent to which he will allow himself to feel. Hill calls this characteristic "prudence." Later century critics were not so charitable. However, before these earlier simple suggestions can take on an uglier note, a number of complexities of interpretation that could develop only with time and a changing zeitgeist, must be taken into account.

however, there is a mere suggestion of such a thing, a suggestion that received its full negation in the last sentence of the paragraph I have just quoted.

One other minor note of dissent is recorded by Fitzgerald. It seems that some spectators thought Garrick too rough and violent in his treatment of Ophelia.[33] This would offer a clue that Garrick was not blind to the biting "malcontent" quality of many of Hamlet's words to Ophelia. However, the prevailing impression seems to have been in agreement with the opinion of Wilkes, that Garrick showed Hamlet's "real tenderness for Ophelia" and his "ineffectual endeavors to hide it."[34]

The full outlines of the eighteenth-century Hamlet of the stage are now before us. Garrick it surely was who fixed the century's orthodox picture of the Danish prince.[35] This picture held until the last quarter of the century, at least.[36] In this period he wore a characteristic mental and emotional garb in which "humanity" and "melancholy" were the chief ingredients. His madness, here, never put on a comic tinge—it would have taken a primitive sense of humor not possessed by the Eighteenth Century to have allowed such a thing as that—his madness was made artistic and intellectual. His "filial reverence" and "awe" were emphasized. Under Garrick, his every sensation took its place as part of the action. He was meditative with an eighteenth-century rationalistic touch. For a century that produced deism and Hume's scepticism, he talked most appropriately of life after death, and suicide. In spite of his "caution," he was still a fairly heroic prince. And notwithstanding a few doubts to the contrary, he was "tender" to Ophelia.

I have said enough already to indicate the immense importance of

---

[33] It is true that the general charge of Hamlet's "cruelty" had been voiced before 1759. We hear it first, however, in a form that precludes its discussion here as part of the "dramatic" picture. As set forth by Hanmer in 1736, it is distinctly closet criticism. I cannot find evidence that would lead me to believe that Hamlet's "cruelty" was in this period (or possibly in any later period!) a theatrical problem. As described by the closet critics, I shall treat it later.

[34] *Op. cit.,* pp. 249-50.

[35] Of the many minor actors who played the role of Hamlet during the Garrick period, one may mention the following: Thomas Sheridan, Cashell, Furnival, Banbury, Goodfellow, Lee, Barry, Murphy, Holland, Mossop, Fleetwood, Ross, William Powel, Lewis, Cautherley, and Smith (Widmann, *op. cit.,* p. 45).

[36] It is interesting that Murphy in *The Life of David Garrick, Esq.* (London, 1801, I, 45 ff.), interprets Garrick's portrayal of Hamlet in terms of a new point of view. Garrick for him made Hamlet a prince of "irresolute temper." Would Murphy have seen Garrick's prince in this light in 1759, or in 1770? It is notable that in the earlier periods no dramatic critic with a fully theatrical point of view, did so!

Garrick in fixing the interpretation of Hamlet in eighteenth-century histri-onic tradition. This importance can hardly be overemphasized. Besides the widespread notice taken of his Hamlet in other forms of the literature in the period, he was even made the prototype of a fictional hero, appear-ing as "Mr. Ranger," in Edward Kimber's novel.[37] What is more, it is surely true that he had a most potent secondary influence in shaping the tone and even the content of formal criticism during his long and distin-guished career. One discerning present-day critic speaks of that change in the Eighteenth Century which

> abandoned the neo-classical standards one and all and built up a
> new dramatic criticism which centered about the pole of character
> delineation rather than of plot structure, which treated Shake-
> speare's characters as living beings with lives of their own, and
> which found that the dramatist not only chronicled the stages of
> all life, but was also the profoundest of moral philosophers.[38]

Of this change in critical point of view toward Shakespeare so far as it effects *Hamlet*, I shall speak in some detail later. Suffice it to say here that Mr. Stone feels that Garrick was a definite influence in the move-ment. He

> presented a new type of acting,—a natural realistic type which
> showed a psychological understanding of character,—that made
> a great impression upon his audiences and which was diametri-
> cally opposed to the declamatory style which possessed the stage
> in 1740.[39]

If this is true of Garrick's service to the Shakespearian stage in general, it is surely doubly true of his service to the histrionic tradition of *Hamlet*, for here he gave his finest and most famous character delineation.

But Garrick, according to the same critic, did even more:

> Without Garrick, or some actor of equal intelligence, enthusi-
> asm, ability, and Shakespearian interests, Shakespeare would have
> been the plaything of the closet and of the academician in the
> Eighteenth Century.[40]

---

[37] For comment and quotation, see R. G. Noyes, "Shakespeare in the Eight-eenth Century Novel," [*Journal of English Literary History*], 11, 225.

[38] Geo. W. Stone, Jr., *Garrick's Handling of Shakespeare's Plays and his Influence upon the Changed Attitude of Shakespearian Criticism during the Eight-eenth Century* (Harvard doctoral dissertation, 1937), p. 489.

[39] *Ibid.*, p. 490.

[40] *Ibid.*, p. 494.

I feel that this generous evaluation of Garrick is not exaggerated, and that again, it has an added relevance as applied to *Hamlet*. In fact, it was Hamlet, as we shall see later, who was the foremost victim of closet criticism, and it is surely significant that the ravages of that movement set in with an accelerated tempo in the very decade that saw Garrick's retirement from the stage.

In spite of any changes in the outline of his character as interpreted over a century and three-quarters, a histrionic Hamlet was the common possession of the English public. Through all of his evolutions, including interpretations by a series of fine actors, he was an active prince with a task on his hands, a task which in due time he carried out successfully.

It is sound criticism, I believe, not to regard overseriously the rather distinct difference in outline between the Hamlet of 1610, and the prince of the time of Garrick. In spite of the fact that the lusty avenger with comic possibilities, or the malcontent in memento-mori background may seem sharply distinguished from the gentle prince of Garrick's day, the difference may well be more apparent than real. For the earlier period our data are at best fragmentary; for the later years, abundant. Such a fact alone must keep us from too dogmatic generalization.

It is safe to insist that the *Hamlet* stage tradition which we have seen in broken glimpses, would form a unity if our evidence were more complete. Seventeenth and Eighteenth Centuries would blend into each other. It cannot be otherwise, for such is the nature of the historical development of art. Unity is to be found in the midst of diversity. Seventeenth-century habits of thought are a correlative of the more simple, harsher interpretation which Shakespeare's lines justify. Eighteenth-century rationalism and sentimentalism must be seen as the correlative of a different, more "human" Hamlet. But the later conception grew from the earlier one; and underneath the difference there was a common denominator, a dramatic substratum that did not change. True it is that eighteenth-century men in increasing numbers read *Hamlet* in their studies, but their impressions gained there were always subject to modification and correction. A more potent Hamlet than any who could be met with in the study, still held the stage at Drury Lane and Covent Garden, and was seen not infrequently at a dozen and one provincial theatres in England, Scotland, and Ireland.

BIBLIOGRAPHY ENTRY FOR RESEARCH PAPERS:

Conklin, Paul S. "Histrionic Tradition to the Retirement of Garrick." Ch. 2 from his *A History of* Hamlet *Criticism, 1601-1821.* New York, 1947, 1957. In *Interpreting Hamlet,* ed. Russell E. Leavenworth. San Francisco, 1960.

FIRST FOOTNOTE:

    * Paul S. Conklin, "Histrionic Tradition to the Retirement of Garrick," ch. 2 from his *A History of* Hamlet *Criticism, 1601-1821* (New York, 1947, 1957), in *Interpreting Hamlet,* ed. Russell E. Leavenworth (San Francisco, 1960), pp. 197-213.

SUBSEQUENT FOOTNOTES:

    * Conklin, *op. cit., IH,* p. ■■.
    * Conklin, "Histrionic Tradition," *IH,* p. ■■.
    * Conklin, *IH,* p. ■■.

In place of *"IH,"* "ed. Leavenworth" may be used in these subsequent-footnote forms.

FRANCIS FERGUSSON

ON

the Meaning of Hamlet

Francis Fergusson (b. 1904) is professor of English at Rutgers University and a drama and literary critic of growing importance. The following are the first four sections of the fourth chapter from his The Idea of a Theater *(copyright 1949 by the Princeton University Press). By permission of the author and Princeton University Press.*

HAMLET, PRINCE OF DENMARK:
THE ANALOGY OF ACTION

THOUGH *Hamlet* was written long before *Bérénice*, or *Tristan*, modern readers are more at ease with it than with either of the others. We may admire the masterpiece of Racine, or be genuinely "sunk" by *Tristan*, but compared with *Hamlet* they are artificial, limited, and arbitrary. Shakespeare's mysterious play has, even in our day, a directness and an intimacy which the others lack.

That is because *Hamlet* was formed in a Theater which was close to the root of drama itself—that art which is both more primitive and more subtle than Philosophy. Since the destruction of the great "mirror" of the Elizabethan theater, it has been necessary to restore or invent the theater; and modern drama has been a succession of more limited *genres*, based upon more limited postulates about human life, like Racine's "action as rational," or Wagner's "action as passion." These sharp perspectives may seem to their own times to reveal the essence of life but to the next generation they may appear partial or even depraved. But *Hamlet,* like *Oedipus* and the *Purgatorio,* can take myth and ritual as still alive. Its imitation of human action "undercuts" or precedes all theory. If it is "the" modern play, it is also very ancient, the heir of the great tradition in its completeness. Thus it is necessary to examine *Hamlet* (mysterious though it is) in order to complete the study of the idea of a theater in our tradition.

This view of *Hamlet* has been emerging slowly since the end of the eighteenth century. Every generation has regarded it in the light of its own taste which was formed by the then regnant form of drama. The critics have been fascinated with it, but they have made it over in their own image: as Hamlet himself tells Ophelia, "the power of beauty will sooner transform honesty from what it is to a bawd than the force of honesty can translate beauty into his likeness: this was sometime a paradox, but now the time gives it proof." The beauty of *Hamlet,* its endless suggestiveness, the iridescent play of the analogical relationships within it, will no doubt continue to seduce, and then show up its well-intentioned lovers. But this process, as I say, has been going on for a hundred and fifty years at least; the efforts of Hamlet's critics to some extent correct each other; and in our time, with modern drama almost dead, it may be possible to get a little closer to the play itself.

For this purpose, the first step is to become aware of certain preconceptions, certain instinctive demands which the modern theater has taught us to make of all drama. The most common complaint made of *Hamlet* is that in spite of its vitality it is not intelligible; it is fascinating but an artistic failure. Is this criticism based upon an understanding of Shakespeare's dramaturgy or does it judge him on the basis of alien standards?

HAMLET *AS AN ARTISTIC FAILURE*

Robertson's essay on *Hamlet** together with Mr. Eliot's essay,† which was apparently inspired by a reading of Robertson, may be taken as typical of the objections which many critics make to the play: they cannot find that it has any unity, or intellectual consistency, as a whole. Thus Robertson, while he admits that it makes superb entertainment and that it is full of brilliant characterization and passages of wonderful poetry, reports that it leaves the critical intellect unsatisfied. He suggests that Shakespeare may

---

* "Hamlet," by J. M. Robertson.

† "Hamlet and His Problems," by T. S. Eliot. [See p. 86 of this book.]

have intended nothing more than an entertainment and never bothered about the deeper unity or wider meaning of the whole: "If Shakespeare could be re-created and asked why he managed here and there so oddly he might with an unanswerable effect open eyes of wonder and ask what should make us thus put his mechanism to the rack. 'Do you want an absolute,' he might ask, 'as a stage entertainment?' . . . But the critical intellect too has its right: its concern is simply conceptual truth."

Robertson, and after him Mr. Eliot, seek in *Hamlet* conceptual truth, and do not find it. They wish to be able to reduce *Hamlet* to terms which the reason can accept; and, in the attempt to satisfy this demand, they make an interpretation of the play which certainly makes it appear confused, formless, and, in short, a failure. "Mr. Robertson is undoubtedly correct," Mr. Eliot writes, "in concluding that the essential emotion of the play is the feeling of a son toward a guilty mother." He then shows that there are many elements and several entire scenes in the play which have nothing to do with the feeling of a son toward a guilty mother. He shows that on this interpretation, Hamlet himself is incomprehensible; and he concludes that Shakespeare failed to find "objective equivalents" for Hamlet's feeling: "Hamlet (the man) is dominated by an emotion which is inexpressible, because it is in excess of the facts as they appear. And the supposed identity of Hamlet with his author is genuine to this point: that Hamlet's bafflement at the absence of objective equivalent to his feelings is a prolongation of the bafflement of his creator in the face of his artistic problem."

I am not sure that I understand Mr. Eliot's famous formula of the objective equivalent of a feeling, at least in its application to this play. Does Mr. Eliot mean that the many objects, facts, and chains of events which Shakespeare presents to make us share and understand Hamlet's feeling, do not work for us? In other words, that as we read or see the play we cannot sympathize with Hamlet's feeling? Or does he mean that we cannot understand Hamlet's psychology? Hamlet is full of feeling— much more so than Polonius, for example; but is this feeling "in excess"? One may hazard the guess that what troubles Mr. Eliot here is not that the character fails to live dramatically—his stage vitality, his fascination for many and varied audiences proves the contrary—but rather that neither he nor his author explains his situation in the clear and univocal terms of reason. Hamlet is presented directly, in his concrete and many-sided setting, in his complex situation as prince, son, and lover. If we are to understand him, we must take him thus directly, and not try to simplify and reduce the picture Shakespeare offers.

The view that "the essential emotion of the play is the feeling of a son toward a guilty mother" is a drastic reduction of the play as Shakespeare wrote it. Hamlet's feeling toward his guilty mother is certainly essential, but not more essential than his dismay at the loss of a father. Stephen Daedalus in *Ulysses* builds up an interpretation of the play on this basis, which reveals at least as much as the Eliot-Robertson interpretation. And Mr. Dover Wilson offers an explanation of Hamlet's feeling which is perhaps still more fruitful: Hamlet has lost a throne, and he has lost thereby a social, publicly acceptable *persona*: a local habitation and a name. It is for this reason that he haunts the stage like the dispossessed of classical drama: like an Electra, who has lost the traditional life which was her due as daughter, wife, and mother—or even like the ghost of Polyneikes, who cannot rest because the ritual order of society which might have provided such a place has been destroyed. And Mr. Wilson assures us that an Elizabethan audience (more or less aware of such implications as these) would have accepted the loss of the throne as sufficient explanation for Hamlet's dismay.

It is not necessary to rule out the Eliot-Robertson, or the Joycean interpretation, merely because one accepts Mr. Dover Wilson's: on the contrary, the various critics should be taken as Jamesian "reflectors," each lighting a facet of the whole from his own peculiar angle. Mr. Dover Wilson's "angle," however, has a special value, for it enables one to see beyond the plight of Hamlet as an individual to certain traditional values of society which underlie the play as a whole. And one of the chief objections to the type of criticism which Mr. Eliot brings to bear, is that it does not distinguish clearly between the story of Hamlet the individual and the story of the play as a whole. He objects to the criticism of Hamlet abstracted from the work in which he appears; but his own essay deals with "Hamlet without the Prince of Denmark"—i.e., the character without reference to the society in which he endeavors to realize himself. Hence he cannot understand the relevance of the minor characters, nor the significance of certain scenes which do not bear directly upon Hamlet's individual fate.

"There are unexplained scenes," he writes, "the Polonius-Laertes and the Polonius-Reynaldo scene—for which there is little excuse." There is no explanation and no excuse for them if Shakespeare was merely trying to convey the feeling of a son toward a guilty mother. If he was also picturing the relation of a son to his father, then the whole Polonius-Laertes-Reynaldo sequence makes sense as a comic-pathetic sub-plot, with many ironic parallels to the story of Hamlet and his father's Ghost. If to this we add Mr. Dover Wilson's suggestions, we see that the welfare of Denmark—the traditional order of society, with its father-king upon whom depend "the lives of many"—is the matter of the play as a whole, rather than Hamlet's individual plight. In the welfare of Denmark, Polonius, Laertes and Reynaldo have a stake also. The postulate upon which the entire action is based (from the first scene on the parapet, with the soldiers peering through the darkness to discern what danger may threaten the body politic) is that "the times are out of joint." It is Hamlet's misfortune that, as Prince, and as a man of profound insight, he especially should have been "born to set them right."

The Eliot-Robertson reading of *Hamlet* makes it clear that none of the characters, and none of the plots or narrative sequences, is intended to convey the meaning of the play as a whole. Nor does the play offer, even in the meditations of Hamlet, the finality of conceptual truth wherein the reason could find its satisfaction and its rest. This reading has the value of showing what *Hamlet* is not, rather than throwing light upon its actual complexity. It has also the value of summing up a sense of the theater and of drama which has largely prevailed since the Elizabethan theater ceased to exist. The demands and the criticism which Robertson and Eliot make would have been approved by the critics of the age of reason from Corneille to Voltaire. They are, in principle, very much like those that William Archer made in his book on Elizabethan drama, *The Old Drama and the New*. Archer demanded naturalistic psychology like that of Ibsen and his structural principles were the rationalistic ones of the well-made play. Therefore he too found the drama of Shakespeare's theater unsatisfying. It is our habit to insist on literal unity and conceptual truth; the value of the Eliot-Robertson reading is that it does so with such clarity as to show what we are doing. Once we understand that, the way is clear, and we may inquire whether Shakespeare was not composing on a different principle altogether.

For such an inquiry there is plenty of material available. There are studies of that characteristic device of the Elizabethans, the double plot. And there are the many recent works which show the Elizabethan theater not from our contemporary standpoint but as the heir of the Middle Ages and, behind that, even of classical antiquity. In their light one can see, if not the unity of *Hamlet,* as least the kind of "oneness by analogy" which Shakespeare's dramaturgy aimed at.

HAMLET *AS MULTIPLE PLOT*

It has been well established by now that the Elizabethan "double plot," at its best, is more than a device for resting the audience. The comic sequences which are woven through the tragedies are not to be dismissed as mere "comic relief," or as punctuation for the main story, like the music that Corneille used between the acts. In Shakespeare, and in the best of his contemporaries, the minor plots are essential parts of the whole composition. This much is, I think, generally recognized. But there is little agreement about the nature of these relationships: we lack a generally accepted critical vocabulary for describing them.

Thus Moulton, in his *Shakespeare the Dramatic Artist,* studied the plots themselves as intelligible chains of events, and showed (for *Lear* and *The Merchant of Venice,* for example) that the various narrative strands depend causally upon each other; that their climaxes, coming together, reinforce each other; and that their denouements are interdependent. Moulton was thinking of the objections of rationalistic critics like Robertson, and answering them in their own terms. But Mr. William Empson, in his extremely illuminating study, *Some Versions of Pastoral,* is interested, not in the logical concatenation of the stories, but in the ironic parallels between them: the tragi-comic parallel between the motivations of love and war, as in *Troilus and Cressida;* between the lives of "clowns" and the lives of "heroes" in the whole tradition of British drama to the middle of the eighteenth century.

Henry James's technical concept of the "reflector" is akin to the notion of the double plot as Mr. Empson explains it. The "occasions," or the more or less peripheral intelligences which James used to mirror his action, serve to reveal it from various (ironically different) angles. Neither the author nor the protagonist is to be allowed to break down and "tell all": that would not be truly dramatic; it would not be "objective" in the realist sense. The situation, the moral and metaphysical "scene" of the drama, is presented only as one character after another sees and reflects it; and the action of the drama as a whole is presented only as each character in turn actualizes it in his story and according to his lights. This is as much as to say that the various stories with their diverse casts of characters are analogous, and that the drama as a whole is therefore "one by analogy" only. It does not have the literal and rational unity of the single logically and causally connected chain of events or story. And if we are to grasp a novel of Henry James or a play by Shakespeare we must be prepared to follow these shifting perspectives, as we move from character to character and from story to story, trying, as we go, to divine the supreme analogue, the underlying theme, to which they all point in their various ways.

This "supreme analogue" or "underlying theme" is the main action of the play, as Aristotle explains in a neglected passage of the *Poetics.*

Aristotle knew plays with a double plot-thread, one of which issues "happily," the other tragically; and he did not like them—they are "less perfect," he says, than pure tragedy; a concession to popular taste. But in his few remarks on the *Odyssey* he comes closer to describing a multiple plot as Shakespeare employed it. The *Odyssey* has neither the literal unity of the one cast of characters, nor the rational unity of the single plot-line. There is the story of Telemachus's search for his father, the *Telemacheia*. There is the intrigue between Penelope and the suitors. There are the many smaller stories of Odysseus' adventures on the islands and the sea; and at last his conflict with the suitors. The stories are many but they are analogous: they are all "actualizations" of the one general action, which is the attempt "to return home." The Odyssey (*hoi nostoi*) sets forth, in many figures, this basic action, this quest for home.

In considering the structure of *Hamlet,* all of these studies of the properties of the double plot are useful. The stories of the play—the struggle between Hamlet and Claudius; between Hamlet, Polonius and Laertes; between Fortinbras and Claudius' regime—are tightly woven together, causally and logically interdependent, in the manner Moulton demonstrates for *The Merchant of Venice*. At the same time the various stories are presented as ironically parallel in the ways Mr. Empson describes. Polonius, for instance, plays the "clown" to Hamlet's "hero," to use Mr. Empson's words; at the same time Hamlet frequently feels himself in the role of clown in relation to Fortinbras and even Laertes. Or, taking Henry James's phrase, you may put it that we are continually shifting from reflector to reflector throughout the play: from the simple soldiers of Scene 1 to the smoothly hypocritical Claudius of Scene 2; from the myopic shrewdness of Polonius, to the troubled but profound intuitions of Ophelia. The action is illumined from so many angles that we have an embarrassment of riches; the problem is not to demonstrate that the play moves in ironic parallels but rather to show that they add up to something—are intended to convey (with however rich a profusion) an underlying unity of theme. For this purpose Aristotle's notion of analogous actions is the most useful.

The main action of Hamlet may be described as the attempt to find and destroy the hidden "imposthume" which is poisoning the life of Claudius' Denmark. All of the characters—from Polonius with his "windlasses" and "assays of bias," to Hamlet with his parables and symbolic shows—realize this action, in comic, or evil, or inspired ways. And the organic parts of the plot—the movement of the play as a whole—show forth the beginning, middle, and end of this action according to the traditional scheme.

The Prologue includes approximately the first three scenes of Act I. Scene 1, Act I (the parapet) makes the simplest and most general statement of the main theme or action of the play. The soldiers, in the cold and darkness of the night, are watching for the hidden danger (the physical or metaphysical malady) which may threaten the present Danish regime. Is it war—and thus connected with young Fortinbras in neighboring Norway? Or something less natural, and thus connected with Hamlet's father's ghost, who appears but will not speak? The soldiers' peering-through-the-dark constitutes a sort of overture, in sensuous terms, to their speculations about the Ghost and his meanings.

Act I, scene 2 (Claudius' Court) restates the main theme, this time from the point of view of Claudius and his regime. What possible ill is threatening his rule? His marriage to Gertrude on the heels of the death of Hamlet's father has been accepted by all, so that cannot be the danger. But three young men, unaccountable quantities, all with the restlessness of youth, are potential sources of trouble. Fortinbras, who wishes to avenge his father for the loss of lands to Denmark, is threatening war in nearby Norway. Laertes is asking his father, Polonius, for permission to travel; and Hamlet, in black, moody, seems not to have accepted Claudius' regime with good grace—perhaps because of the loss of *his* father. Claudius deals with Fortinbras through his uncle, the present king of Norway; satisfies Laertes by giving permission for the traditional fling in Paris; but fails to appease Hamlet, who thus begins to appear to him as the most dangerous center of infection. When Claudius departs, with his glittering court, and Hamlet, in his solemn black, is left alone on-stage, we get his sharply different version of Denmark's trouble: "Things rank and gross in nature possess it merely." And then, when Horatio and the soldiers come to report the Ghost, we are led to connect this apparition with Hamlet's sense that the body politic is sick.

Act I, scene 3 (Polonius' house) is a comic variation on the main theme. Laertes is warning his sister Ophelia about the dangers of youth, particularly Hamlet's youth—for Laertes, with his simple-minded conventionality, instinctively thinks of Hamlet as the source of infection, much as Claudius does, though for less specific reasons. When Polonius appears, he gives Laertes the same advice that Laertes had given Ophelia. We see that Laertes is a chip off the old block; and that for this family there is no hidden malady which ordinary prudence and the experience of the aged cannot find and cure. But Ophelia, with her love for Hamlet, throws doubt on Polonius' simple diagnosis. (Ophelia, like Gertrude, has great symbolic value in the economy of the play as a whole. Both women base their very

beings upon their men; and both of them are attached at once to Hamlet
and to Claudius' regime. Thus they are at once touching reminders of what
might have been—the unity and health of the whole state—and victims
of its actual illness and disunity.)

The Agons, or conflicts of the play, are developed in scenes 4 and 5
of Act I, in Act II, and in the first scene of Act III. It is established that all
of the characters are seeking to identify and to destroy the actual or potential malady of Claudius' Denmark; but they interpret it differently, and
hence conflicts and contrasts develop between their various lines of action.
Because the "malady" is so mysterious, and because it would be perilous to
trouble the smooth surface of Claudius' regime, the characters all act
secretly, indirectly, and in mutual mistrust. Hamlet does not even trust the
Ghost; he cannot tell whether it is a "spirit of health or goblin damned";
and thus there is contrast and conflict even in this relationship. Polonius is
endeavoring to serve Claudius' regime; but Claudius does not trust Polonius' diagnosis of the trouble; he summons Rosencrantz and Guildenstern
as a check. Thus the struggles which develop in this part of the play are all
struggles in the dark, as though the antagonists, waiting and listening,
could not find each other, and fought only briefly and desperately when
they happened to bump together.

But by the first scenes of Act III the main lines of the many-sided conflict which the Prologue prepared, are visible. Claudius, having satisfied
Laertes with his trip to Paris, and having diverted the dutiful Fortinbras
from Denmark to Poland, has decided that Hamlet is the source of his
dis-ease, and must be rendered harmless. Polonius agrees with him, and is
now beginning to feel a little out of his depth: he is no longer sure that
Hamlet's malady is merely thwarted love for Ophelia. As for Hamlet, he
sees Claudius as the chief plague-spot, and his main antagonist though, at
the same time, the spreading disease has vitiated his every relationship.

I have said that the agon shows conflicts *and contrasts.* The contrasts
between the visions and the lines of action of the various characters are
more important than their overt struggles, and reveal far more about the
real malady of Denmark and the attempt to find and destroy it. These *contrasts* are brought out by the order of the scenes, as we shift from comic
to tragic versions of the main action. This may be illustrated by considering
the alternation of the Polonius story and the Hamlet story in Acts I and II
—the scenes for which Mr. Eliot says there is no explanation or excuse.

The last scene of the Prologue, Polonius' house (Act I, scene 3) is at
once a comic version of the opening statement of the main action, and the
prologue to the story of Polonius and Laertes which is closely analogous in

many respects to the story of Hamlet's "father" (the Ghost *and* Claudius) and Hamlet. The clownish and comic father-son relationship of Polonius and Laertes throws ironic lights upon the tragic relationship of Hamlet to his anomalous parent. Thus as soon as we have seen Polonius attempting to guide and advise Laertes in preparation for his trip to Paris, we are shifted to the dark parapet with Hamlet awaiting word from his Ghost-father and hearing, below, the roaring and the booming which Claudius, his other "father," is making at his drunken celebration. The Ghost appears, and speaks to Hamlet; but, from the other side of the grave, he can convey little to his son—and that only in hints and metaphors. He is definite enough about the fact that Claudius killed him; but Hamlet does not know what to make even of that:

> *O all you host of heaven! O earth! What else?*
> *And shall I couple hell? O fie!*

After this we return to Polonius who is sending Reynaldo to Paris to watch over Laertes. It is another father trying to reach and guide his son—who is not on the other side of the grave, this time, but on the other side of the sea; yet as absurdly remote as Hamlet from the Ghost. We can be sure that when Reynaldo gets to Paris, and tries to apply to Laertes the "bait of false-hood," the "indirections" and "windlasses and assays of bias" which father Polonius devised to reach him, Laertes will also reply "O fie!"

Thus these three scenes are closely parallel, yet sharply contrasted: the divided world of Polonius-Laertes is incommensurable with the divided world of the Ghost-Hamlet; and this incommensurability is deeper than any overt conflict, and shows more about Hamlet's problem and the true malady of Denmark than any fact, or any explicit issue, could do. And when Ophelia appears on Reynaldo's exit, torn and frightened by her sight of Hamlet, we have before us the most pathetic victim of this division within the sick society; and with this vision, the Hamlet-Ghost, Laertes-Polonius sequence ends.

The Climax, Peripety and Recognition are presented in Act III, scenes 2, 3, and 4—the players' scene, and the two scenes following. In the first of these scenes which follow the players' scene (scene 3) Claudius, convicted of the crime, attempts to pray, and Hamlet rejects his chance to kill him. In the next (scene 4) Hamlet faces his mother with her guilt, and inadvertently kills Polonius.

Hamlet's presentation of his play to the Danish Court is both a direct attack on Claudius, as his chief antagonist, and an attempt to resolve the deeper "contrasts," the divided counsels, the incommensurable visions, which constitute the malady of Denmark—or at least its chief symptom. By hinting broadly at Claudius' crime Hamlet, of course, shakes Claudius' whole position, for that depends upon concealment. At the same time he convicts all of the supporters of the regime, even including Ophelia and Gertrude, of a share in the guilt.

The further meanings of Hamlet's play are considered at more length below. At this point I merely wish to point out that the presentation of the play is the peripety: it puts the King and his regime on the defensive, and justifies the most hidden intuitions of Hamlet and the most secret messages of the Ghost. The two scenes following the players' scene merely drive home its effects: Claudius becomes in his own eyes an outlaw; Gertrude's heart is "cleft in twain" and, as a sort of absurd and pathetic parenthesis, Polonius is destroyed. The "hidden imposthume," in all its ramifications, is opened; and from this point the action, beyond anyone's control, runs down to its fated end.

The Pathos and/or Sparagmos coincides with Act IV. Both the state and the individuals that compose it "suffer" the results of Hamlet's opening the "hidden imposthume." Laertes, hearing of his father's death, comes back to avenge him, and starts a rebellion; and the scenes which show this overt social disorder alternate with Ophelia's mad scenes: "Schism in the State and Schism in the soul," in Toynbee's phrase. Meanwhile Hamlet, on his trip to England and his return, and Fortinbras, at the head of his troops, approach for the kill. The King (who conceals Hamlet's murder of Polonius, minimizes Ophelia's tragedy, and corrupts Laertes' demand for justice) is trying to "skin and film the ulcerous place." But his efforts do not re-establish his regime; they make at most a horrible simulacrum of a healthy state; smooth on the surface but dead within.

The Epiphany or Collective Revelation is shown in Act V. It is Shakespeare's habit to wind up his complicated plots at the very end; and the big killings do not occur until the last scene. But these sensational events tell us little that is new; they seem to be only minor corollaries of the great peripety in Act III. The substance of Act V is chiefly what Hamlet, the "chief reflector," sees, when he returns, spent, nervously exhausted, but clear-eyed, from England. He sees the fatal illness of Denmark: the literal bones in the graveyard; the many details of social disorder (the Prince, for instance, on a level with the grave-digging clowns); the "maimèd rite" of Ophelia's funeral, and the death-trap of Claudius' last court assembled for his duel with Laertes. The widespread malady of Denmark is clear at last; and with the end of Claudius and his regime it is gone like a bad dream. Fortinbras appears at last in Denmark: a new hope for a new, purged state.

The purpose of this sketch, of course, is not to exhaust the analogical relationships among the narrative strands in *Hamlet,* but only to suggest, by means of a few illustrations, that they are there, and that they are an all-important element in the structure of the play. They point, I think, to the main action, and to the concern for the welfare of Denmark which all the characters share.

Ernest Jones* has an interpretation of the play also based upon analogies between its stories and characters, but reducing them all to the machinery of the Oedipus complex: "The main theme of this story," Dr. Jones writes, "is a highly elaborated and disguised account of a boy's love for his mother, and consequent jealousy of and hatred toward his father." Dr. Jones's study is very suggestive and, while confirming what might be called the analogical texture of the play, it raises important questions about the essential nature of these analogical relationships and the underlying theme to which they all point. I have no doubt that the father-son relationships are there: I have suggested it in my remarks on the Polonius-Laertes, Ghost-Hamlet sequence. Shakespeare seems to have missed none of the tensions, none of the ambivalence, in this crucial relationship. But can it be regarded as the fundamental theme of the play?

My objection to Jones's interpretation is that it reduces the motivation of the play to the emotional drives of the Oedipus complex. This overworks that complex, and takes us too far from the play itself. Thus part of the point of the Polonius-Laertes, Ghost-Hamlet analogy is the comic similarity and the tragic difference between the insights of Hamlet and Polonius; and this tension cannot be reduced to the Oedipus complex. The Oedipus complex does not account for the fact that Hamlet, besides being a son, is also a dispossessed prince; nor that Claudius, besides being a father symbol, is also the actual ruler of the state. But the actual movement of the play—to say nothing of its ultimate meaning—depends upon such objective facts and values as these.

Jones has studied the changes and elaborations which Shakespeare made in the Hamlet story, with its very ancient mythic roots, transforming it from what was perhaps a simple revenge motif into something much deeper. Jones thinks that the "deeper" theme which Shakespeare unconsciously felt was the son's desire to kill his father and possess his mother; and that the elaborations and variations he made were disguises of the theme which really held him. But the elaborations Shakespeare made could

---

* *Hamlet.* By William Shakespeare. With a psycho-analytical study by Ernest Jones M.D. New York: Funk and Wagnalls, 1948. [London, 1947. See page 173 in this collection.]

equally well be understood as due to his extremely critical and skeptical bent; his need to criticize one version of his theme by means of another analogous one.

In short, the analogous stories, situations, and relationships in *Hamlet* point, not to the Oedipus complex, but to the main action or underlying theme of the play. And in that the emotional tensions of the Oedipus complex are only one element. The disease which is killing Denmark does not have a purely psychological explanation and cure, and the attempt to understand and destroy it has a moral as well as an emotional content. The religious, cultural, moral values of the tradition are at stake in this action; and the play as a whole has dimensions which cannot be completely understood if one thinks of it in these psychological terms, in abstraction from the theater in which it was formed.

A study of the interwoven plots of *Hamlet* points to the underlying theme, the main action of the play as a whole. But it does not quite enable us to understand Hamlet's shifting motives; and it does not throw much light upon the rhythms, the spectacular effects, and the rise and fall of tension, in the play considered as a performance before an audience. If we are to come a little closer to the play as play, it is necessary to consider the whole idea of the theater which Shakespeare used and assumed in his audience; for this theater offered means of "imitating the action" which cannot be subsumed under the art of plot-making as it is generally understood.

HAMLET *AS RITUAL AND IMPROVISATION*

If one could see a performance of *Hamlet,* uncut, unbroken by intermissions, and employing the kind of simple make-believe which Shakespeare, with his bare stage, must have intended, we should find much to enthrall us besides the stories themselves. The stories, of course, start at once, and are felt continuously as working themselves out: fate, behind the scenes, makes, from time to time, its sudden pronouncements. But on-stage, the music and the drums and the marching of royal and military pageantry, are directly absorbing, and they assure us that something of great and general significance is going on. From time to time the stage is emptied; the pageantry is gone; the stories seem to be marking time—and Hamlet emerges, alone, or with one or two interlocutors. Sometimes he suffers his visions before us; sometimes he makes jokes and topical allusions; sometimes he spars with his interlocutors like the gag-man in a minstrel show, or the master of ceremonies in a modern musical.

The scenes of pageantry are all civic or military or religious rituals;

THE PARTS OF THE PLOT	RITUAL SCENES	IMPROVISA-TIONAL ENTERTAIN-MENT
The Prologue	Act I, sc. 1 The changing of the Guard Act I, sc. 2 Claudius' First Court	
The Agons — development of conflicting purposes of various characters; contrasts of their stories; "purposes mistook"; indecision and fighting in the dark		Act I, sc. 4 Hamlet' sermon on drunkennes (in Denmark and/o England) Act II, sc. 2 Hamlet ex changes wisecracks with Polonius, Rosencrantz Guildenstern, and th players. Act III, sc. 2 Hamlet' charge to the players— his opinions on the ar of acting.
The Climax, Peripety, and Recognitions; all narrative strands brought together	RITUAL AND ENTERTAIN-MENT Act III, sc. 2 The performance of Hamlet's play is both rite and entertainment, and shows the Prince as at once clown and ritual head of the state.	
The Pathos or "sparagmos," both of the state and the individuals, leading to the epiphany or "collective revelation" of the general disease. (Cf. Toynbee's "schism in the state and schism in the soul")	Act IV, sc. 5 Ophelia's Madness is a mock ritual, a mixture of false and lewd marriage, and false and savage funeral; refers also the the. funeral of Hamlet's father and Gertrude's false marriage. Alternates with rebellion in the state.	

THE PARTS OF THE PLOT	RITUAL SCENES	IMPROVISA-TIONAL ENTERTAIN-MENT
The Epiphany, or Final Vision of the under-lying truth of the action	Act v, sc. 1 Ophelia's funeral. A "maimed rite" but a real death. Act v, sc. 2 The duel between Hamlet and Laertes. This duel is sur-rounded with all the ceremonies of Claudius' Court, like the players' scene, and Claudius' other loud and drunken celebrations; but every element in it is false or mistaken: a mockery of invocation; and it even-tuates in death, and "resurrection" in the shape of Fortinbras, who, now that Clau-dius' regime is gone, can appear with his new faith and hope.	Act v Hamlet jokes and moralizes with the Gravedigger and Hora-tio. He feels like the gag-man and the royal victim in one. Grave-digger corresponds to Polonius.

the changing of the guard, the formal assembling of the court of Denmark; the funeral of Ophelia. Though they all have their relevance to the inter-woven stories of the play and to the discordant purposes of the various characters, their chief function is to show forth the main action or under-lying theme, at various stages in its development. At these ritual moments the plot-lines are, as it were, gathered together; the issues are held in sus-pension, and we are reminded of the traditional social values in which all have some sort of stake.

Hamlet's monologues, and his nimble exchanges with Polonius or Rosencrantz and Guildenstern, his "topical allusions" to drunkenness or to the state of the theater, make a very different kind of theatrical appeal. He steps out of the narrative course of the play, out of the "world of Denmark" which is the basic postulate of the make-believe, refers directly to the paral-lels between "Denmark" and the England of his audience. From one point of view Shakespeare seems to be counting on the inherent dramatic and theatrical interest which this character has apart from the story—permitting him, like the first violin in a concerto, a cadenza on his own, after which we are returned to the matter in hand. From another point of view, Hamlet's "improvized" moments are carried by our confidence in him as "chief reflector": we look to him, as to the ritual scenes, to show us the underlying theme of the whole.

Both the ritual and the improvisational elements in *Hamlet* are essential—as essential as the stories—in the structure of the whole. The Elizabethan theater, at once as frankly "theatrical" as vaudeville, and as central to the life of its time as an ancient rite, offered Shakespeare two resources, two theatrical "dimensions" which the modern naturalistic tradition of serious drama must try, or pretend, to do without. In the table [on the preceding pages] I have shown the chief ritual and the chief improvisational scenes in relation to the main parts of the plot.

If one thinks over the succession of ritual scenes as they appear in the play, it is clear that they serve to focus attention on the Danish body politic and its hidden malady: they are ceremonious invocations of the well-being of society, and secular or religious devices for securing it. As the play progresses, the rituals change in character, from the dim but honest changing of the guard, through Ophelia's mock rites, to the black mass of Claudius' last court. And it appears that the improvisational scenes bear a significant and developing relationship to the rituals. In general, they throw doubt upon the efficacy of the official magic, as when Hamlet refuses to take Claudius' first court at its face value; yet even the most cutting ironies of Hamlet do not disavow the mystery which the rituals celebrate, or reject the purposes that inform them.

The rituals, the stories, and the improvisations together make the peculiar rhythm of *Hamlet* as a performance. Denmark is shown as waiting, as it were, in the darkness of its ineffective ceremonies and hollow communal prayers while the infection, "mining all within," divides every man in secret from every other and bursts forth, from time to time, in savage but brief and ineffective fights.

But before examining the sequence of rituals, with its center in the players scene, it is necessary to endeavor to support the view that the Elizabethan theater had, in fact, this ritual aspect: that Shakespeare's audience, like that of Sophocles, was prepared to accept his play not only as an exciting story but as the "celebration of the mystery" of human life.

THE GLOBE THEATER AND THE
FESTIVAL OF DIONYSOS

The main evidence (apart from the play itself) for taking *Hamlet* as a species of ritual drama, is provided by recent studies which show that a great deal of the religious culture of the Middle Ages was still alive in Shakespeare's time. Tillyard's *The Elizabethan World Picture,* for example, makes this clear. Mr. Tillyard quotes Hamlet's famous speech on man: "What a piece of work is a man: how noble in reason; how infinite in faculty; in form and moving how express and admirable; in action how like an angel; in apprehension how like a god; the beauty of the world, the paragon of animals."—"This has been taken," Mr. Tillyard explains, "as one of the great English versions of Renaissance humanism, an assertion of the dignity of man against the asceticisms of medieval misanthropy. Actually it is in the purest medieval tradition: Shakespeare's version of the orthodox encomia of what man, created in God's image, was like in his prelapsarian state and of what ideally he is still capable of being. It also shows Shakespeare placing man in the traditional cosmic setting between the angels and the beasts. It is what the theologians had been saying for centuries." And Mr. Tillyard proceeds to show that most of the "world picture which the Middle Ages inherited" was still tacitly assumed by the Elizabethans: "an ordered universe arranged in a fixed system of hierarchies but modified by man's sin and the hope of his redemption."

The Elizabethan stage itself, that central mirror of the life of its times, was a symbolic representation of this traditional cosmos: it was thus taken both as the physical and as the metaphysical "scene" of man's life. Mr. Kernodle has shown this in detail in his illuminating study, *From Art to Theater.* He traces the genealogy of the symbolic façade of the Elizabethan stage house back through street pageantry to painting and to the architecture of tombs and altars; and thence to the arcade screen of the Greek tragic theater itself. "More than an arrangement of side doors and inner and upper stages, that façade was itself a symbol of castle, throne, triumphal arch, altar, tomb"—in short, an all-purpose, eminently practicable setting, implying the constant elements in the Elizabethan world picture, yet flexible enough to serve the shifting make-believe of the actors. Over the whole was a permanent canopy, painted to represent the heavens, a vault literally "fretted with golden fire."

The symbolic character of this stage seems to imply a conception of the theater akin to that of ritual: the celebration of the mystery of human life. This stage and its drama did not, it is true, develop directly from the Mass; it developed from the secular theater of the Middle Ages and, as Mr. Kernodle shows, from royal and civic pageantry. But in the Renaissance the monarchy and its rites was taking over some of the religious significance of the church and its rites. The pope tended to be superseded by the prince as vicar, or "type" of Christ, the pageantry and ceremony of the church by the pageantry and ceremony of the national state. The Tudor monarch was the symbol, and the visible center of the traditional world order, so that Donne could write, on the death of Prince Henry:

> *Of Weight one Centre, one of Greatness is,*
> *And Both my Centres feel this Period.*

The role of the monarch in Shakespeare's time (and in his plays) was thus very close to that of Sophocles' Oedipus or Creon: he was at once ruler, high priest, and father of the community. And the ceremonies which Shakespeare and Hamlet's Danes engaged in—whether obviously religious, like the funeral, or more secular, like the Court—were taken as celebrating and securing the welfare of the whole, of the monarchy, and of the "lives of many" that depended on it.

The Elizabethan theater may thus be regarded as the heir of the Greek tragic theater with its ritual basis. The Elizabethan cosmos is still that of the great tradition*, which the Middle Ages inherited from the city state. The physical stage itself is symbolic in the same way as the tragic stage of the Greeks; and the ritual component in its drama has similar deep and general meanings.

This does not mean, of course, that Shakespeare's audience, or even Shakespeare himself, could have expounded this genealogy and these parallels. If the tradition was alive in Shakespeare's time, it was as a "habit of thought and feeling" rather than as an explicit and integrated philosophy. But Shakespeare seems to have felt the essential elements of this great "theater" as alive still; to have assumed that his audience would respond to them, and to have based his dramaturgy upon them.

If Shakespeare's theater is thus akin to the theater of Sophocles, their drama should be composed on similar principles: appealing in both cases to ancient and publicly accepted values and modes of understanding, rather than preaching, inventing, and arguing in the manner of modern drama. And the comparison should throw some light on both.

The themes of *Oedipus* are, from many points of view, strikingly similar to those of *Hamlet.* Oedipus gave his name to that "complex" to which, as we saw, Ernest Jones reduces *Hamlet.* Whatever one may think of this reduction, it is clear that in both plays a royal sufferer is associated with pollution, in its very sources, of an entire social order. Both plays open with an invocation of the well-being of the endangered body politic.

---

* *The Great Chain of Being,* by Arthur Lovejoy, is a chief source of this view of what the Renaissance inherited.

In both, the destiny of the individual and of society are closely intertwined; and in both the suffering of the royal victim seems to be necessary before purgation and renewal can be achieved.

But my purpose here is not to attempt an extended comparison of the two plays; it is, rather, to contrast the structural principles of these two ritual dramas, one from the beginnings of the tradition, the other from the end, at the very brink of the modern world.

The extraordinary unity and clarity of *Oedipus,* in comparison with *Hamlet,* is perhaps due of the fact that it is closer to the form, purpose, and occasion (the Festival of Dionysos) of its ritual source than *Hamlet,* in the Globe Theater, is to its ritual sources. Oedipus is the one and obvious protagonist, his story the literal subject of the play. He is the diagrammatic royal scapegoat, a marked man, from the first. And the parts of the play, which show the stages of his destruction, correspond very closely to the stages of the ancient ritual sacrifice.

In *Hamlet* it is as though every one of these elements had been elaborated by a process of critical analysis. Hamlet himself, though a prince, is without a throne; though a sufferer for the truth, he can appear in public as a mere infatuated or whimsical youth. We have seen how many ironic parallels Shakespeare provides to his story—and to this I may add that it takes both Hamlet and Claudius to represent the royal victim of the tradition. Though the play has the general shape of the tragic rhythm, and the traditional parts of the plot, each part is presented in several ironically analogous versions. The prologue is in three scenes of contrasting moods. The agon is so complicated that the very purposes of the antagonists are critically seen as false, hidden, or "mistook." It takes all of Act v to represent the epiphany, the final vision of death, from all the angles that Shakespeare knows.

Even the ritual process itself is, in *Hamlet,* directly dramatized: i.e., presented in a tragic, ironic light. There are no rituals in *Oedipus:* Oedipus is a ritual. But Hamlet has an extremely modern and skeptical, a Pirandellesque, theatricality as well; Shakespeare plays with the basis of his own make-believe. Sophocles uses the tragic theater with its ritual basis to mirror human life directly. Shakespeare uses the Elizabethan theater in the same way; but at the same time he has another mirror—his own and Hamlet's supermodern awareness—in which the making of the ritual is itself ironically reflected.

Oedipus moves, as it were, straight to its end, in clear figures of the tragic rhythm. But in *Hamlet* there is also a movement of ironic analysis, represented by the analogous versions of the main theme which the interwoven plots embody, and by Hamlet's monologues and wry jokes: improvisations which are beside the story of the play, in closer relationship to the audience. But though Shakespeare thus sees the ritual order of Claudius' Denmark as it were from without, he does not, like Euripides, simply satirize the values and the order of the traditional religion: the movement of analysis is corrected from time to time by a synthesis (a funeral or a Court scene) in which the main theme of the play, and the interdependence of all the dramatis personae, is reaffirmed. These rituals in *Hamlet* are not simply absurd, as a Euripidean *deus ex machina* is absurd; they are rather tragic failures, like Claudius' private attempt to pray: "Words without thoughts never to heaven go." In spite of the ironic device of the double plot, and the deeper irony of the Pirandellesque improvisation (Is all the world a stage or the stage life itself?) Shakespeare also clings to the conception of the theater as ritual.

BIBLIOGRAPHY ENTRY FOR RESEARCH PAPERS:

Fergusson, Francis. *"Hamlet, Prince of Denmark:* The Analogy of Action." Ch. 4 from his *The Idea of a Theater.* Princeton, 1949. In part in *Interpreting Hamlet,* ed. Russell E. Leavenworth. San Francisco, 1960.

FIRST FOOTNOTE:

* Francis Fergusson, *"Hamlet, Prince of Denmark:* The Analogy of Action," from his *The Idea of a Theater* (Princeton, 1949), in part in *Interpreting Hamlet,* ed. Russell E. Leavenworth (San Francisco, 1960), pp. 215-234.

SUBSEQUENT FOOTNOTES:

* Fergusson, *op. cit., IH,* p. ■■.
* Fergusson, *"Hamlet," IH,* p. ■■.
* Fergusson, *IH,* p. ■■.

In place of *"IH,"* "ed. Leavenworth" may be used in these subsequent-footnote forms.

GEORGE REYNOLDS

ON

the Hamlet Stage Tradition

George Fulmer Reynolds (b. 1877), Professor Emeritus at the University of Colorado, is the author of many studies of Elizabethan stagecraft. The following essay was first printed in Shakespeare Survey, IX (1956). *By permission of the author and Cambridge University Press.*

HAMLET AT THE GLOBE

How HAMLET was given at the Globe is a somewhat troublesome in-quiry, not because it makes any particularly difficult demands, but because there are in the original texts so few specific demands of any kind. Its direc-tions authorize no discoveries by a curtain or any scene in the balcony. One textual allusion, it is true, has been held to hint at use of the latter. *Hamlet* (IV,iii,39) says of Polonius's body, "you shall nose him as you go up the stairs into the Lobby." But to argue that the lobby thus referred to is the one in which II,ii and III,i were played, or that such a reference means the balcony, seems to confuse a 'dramatic' with a 'theatrical' allusion. The fact is that *Hamlet* could if necessary be given almost anywhere, even on an arena stage, with less distortion than most Elizabethan plays. Differences of opinion on the way it was presented come mostly from our own different assumptions and inferences.

These have changed considerably in recent years. Formerly students assumed that all scenes in rooms were played in the inner stage, since it was a room; that no properties of any size were admitted to the front stage (two or three stools were assumed enough to require the use of the inner stage); and that no pauses were permitted to allow the resetting of the inner stage. These assumptions were natural enough, but have been disproved by modern performances in the more or less Elizabethan manner. Thus at Stratford-upon-Avon, even on its proscenium stage, but with no lowering of the front curtain, the settings have been changed before the eyes of the audience, and properties—like the throne in *Henry VIII*—left on the stage throughout the play. The conventions of the Elizabethan platform stage were in many respects unlike those of a proscenium stage. The latter, as it is usually employed, attempts to create unified and consistent stage pictures. The platform stage was by its very structure only a stage as the medieval stage had been before it; it might be set with some of the necessary properties, to be used in the performance as they were required, but otherwise disregarded by the audience.

Perhaps the greatest change of opinion concerns the importance of the curtained space. Formerly emphasized and used on the slightest pretext, it seems today more and more avoided. The most emphatic statement I have seen in print about it is that of Bernard Miles and Miss Josephine Wilson, founded on their experience in the Mermaid Theater and at the Royal Exchange, 1951-3: "We have learned that it is impossible to play scenes on the so-called 'inner stage', or even far upstage at all. When the expanse of platform is there to be used, you have to use it."[1] Some scenes were certainly played in the curtained space, and all directors will scarcely concur in so sweeping an opinion, but the position of it at the far end of the front stage makes action on it less easy to see, speech from it less easy to hear, and—a matter receiving increasing emphasis—rapport with the audience less easy to establish. We need to note also that the very existence of a permanent inner stage at the Globe at the time when *Hamlet* was produced is more and more in question. The Swan picture shows none in that theatre, and really few of the plays produced by Shakespeare's company before *Hamlet* precisely require such an arrangement of the stage. Discoveries in bed are specified, but beds had their own curtains and could be thrust out. Other properties such as the tent or shop or tomb could also disclose persons. The three caskets of the *Merchant of Venice* were behind a curtain, but they would require no large space. Most of the plays, though some of their scenes could advantageously be discovered and perhaps were, do not even hint at such a presentation, and have been supposed to have

---

[1] 'Three Festivals at the Memorial Theatre' (*Shakespeare Quarterly,* V [1954], 307-10).

been so staged mainly because of modern custom. It is possible, therefore, that up to the time of *Hamlet* and even later, discoveries were made not only in the special properties, but also by means of a curtain hung on a removable frame placed on the stage only for the plays which required it. Such a furnishing would have projected in front of the tiring-house wall instead of forming an alcove within it, and would presumably have been not very deep nor so wide that more supports would have been required than at the corners. To keep the possibility of such an arrangement in mind I refer to it here as the curtained space rather than as the rear stage, and never as the inner stage. In such circumstances many room scenes would have been played on the front stage, with the arras as their background. And this would have been especially true of the more intimate and quiet scenes, which to hold the attention of the spectators could often do so more easily if acted closer to them. Scenes with many characters or with much action, like those for instance before the gates of a city or castle, might well use the whole stage, the curtains being drawn back to an inconspicuous position, the framework serving as an architectural emphasis on the middle door.

Hamlet occasions another change of assumptions about the staging, necessary as soon as it is mentioned. Many modern productions have treated the play within the play as the centre of interest in that scene, but Allardyce Nicoll has rightly pointed out that our interest is really in the effect on Claudius of *The Mousetrap* and of Hamlet's comments. It is Claudius therefore who should be placed conspicuously, not the play within the play. But where on the Elizabethan stage is the most easily observed position? On this there are differences of opinion. Some have thought that it should be in the centre rear, that is in the curtained space, opened in this scene for the king's and queen's formal seats. Others, influenced by the opinions already expressed about the ineffectiveness of the curtained space, have put the royal seats at one side further to the front and slightly turned so that the king is so placed that he can at least seem to be watching the play, but also be easily observed by the audience. (This position for the throne is also likely in other plays.) Hamlet then sits across the stage by Ophelia where, without turning his back on the audience, he can watch the king continuously, and be himself a second centre of interest for the audience.

This scene, III,ii, is the most important in determining the staging schedule for the whole play. The two early quartos differ on what was done in it. If, as students seem generally to agree, the Second Quarto represents Shakespeare's manuscript, he expected the scene to be played with a bank of flowers on which the player king "dies," and from which, according to the explicit direction, he is removed at the end of the dumb-show by attendants of the treacherous "nephew." This removal may imply, but not necessarily, that the bank stood on the front stage. Claudius breaks off the performance of the play, and the "dead" king presumably went out in the resulting confusion along with the spectators. But in the First Quarto, the directions of which J. Dover Wilson accepts as what the piratical reporter saw at the Globe,[2] the player king enters to sit in an arbour, and at its end is left there "dead" with no one to remove him. This seems to call for a curtain, but perhaps, as acting only in a dumb-show and having to re-enter immediately in the play itself, he was expected to walk off by himself. I remember, however, no such loose end in any other dumb-show. Or perhaps the arbour was a free-standing structure with its own curtain, on the stage only with the royal seats, placed there before the play began, and left on till the end. If this was the way the play was given at the Globe, there would scarcely have been any other curtained space, speculation about other possibly discovered scenes becomes unnecessary, and the staging of the whole play was either simplicity itself, or, if more completely furnished with properties, unmistakably medieval. Is it not more likely that this arbour was a device to substitute for the theatre's curtained space when the company was in the provinces or playing in a private house?

The staging of this scene is also conditioned by the other scenes, more or less formal, in which the king and queen are seated: I,ii; II,ii; and V,ii. In modern productions these seats may differ to suit the scenes. In III,ii and V,ii chairs elaborate enough to be called thrones and placed on a dais have often been used.[3] Dover Wilson specifies thrones in I,ii; even if it is a council and not a court scene, a similar council scene in *Henry VIII* (I,ii) has a direction, "the king riseth from his state." As for II,ii, Granville-Barker,[4] pointing out its generally informal atmosphere, thinks a throne would not be suitable, but A. C. Sprague,[5] noting what probably provoked this remark, says "I have often seen Hamlet, as he cries 'O Vengeance,' lunge with his dagger at the empty throne." In I,ii the entrance and departure of the king and queen are announced by a flourish of trumpets, as is their entrance in II,ii and III,ii. So though these scenes do differ in formality and may be differently furnished in modern

[2] *Hamlet* (Cambridge, 1934), p. xxvi.

[3] See R. Mander and J. Mitchenson, *Hamlet through the Ages.*

[4] *Prefaces, Third Series, Hamlet* (1937), p. 66.

[5] *Shakespeare and the Actors* (Cambridge, Mass., 1944), p. 149.

productions, is it not likely that, on the Elizabethan stage, the same formal seats would be used for all these scenes? Sometimes for brevity I shall refer to them as thrones, more or less elaborate seats raised on a dais, but not necessarily provided with a canopy.

Other properties raise few questions.[6] The pictures of Hamlet's father and Claudius (III,iv) could most effectively have been miniatures worn by Hamlet and the Queen respectively. Large portraits could have been hung only on the rear wall, as in the Rowe picture of the scene, an awkward arrangement since the Queen would have had to turn her back on the audience to see them. It is another situation like that of the play within the play; what matters to the audience is the effect on the Queen of Hamlet's speeches, not the pictures themselves. The only other large property is the table brought in or discovered in V,ii. The grave (V,i) could have been the trapdoor in the curtained space, but would perhaps have been more effective as the front stage trap nearer the audience.

In accordance with these considerations of bringing the action forward and keeping it immediately clear, the following schedule may be tentatively suggested. It supposes a curtained space of only moderate size, its curtain the arras of the text. The royal seats are on the front stage throughout the play. The curtained space is used for the bank of flowers and for the table of V,ii. The two or more seats of I,i could have been either in the curtained space or, better, because closer to the audience, ready on the front stage. So with the scene in the Queen's closet. Her chair might be in the curtained space, but the scene would presumably be more immediately effective if played on the front stage; moreover, if she did sit in the curtained space, Polonius must have been concealed behind a second curtain, perhaps a wall-hanging concealing part or all of the middle door.

This is not a very good place for his concealment, but such a wall-hanging might be useful as an aid to clarity. I can see no advantage in the use of sceneboards, "Denmark" or "Elsinore," in this play, though such boards were still being used when *Hamlet* was produced. But care in the employment of the doors, for instance use of the one on the right for entrance from away or for departures in that direction, might help in keeping the action clear. And this wall-hanging, when displayed, would show that the curtained space was a room, but when the hanging was not visible, the scene would at once be indicated as an exterior scene, suitable for the platform of the castle, or the scene with Fortinbras. I do not

---

[6] A faldstool has been suggested for Ophelia to kneel at, but A. C. Sprague (*op. cit.*, pp. 151, 344) finds no record before 1847 of her kneeling.

urge this at all, but I mention it because I think the problem of clarity on the Elizabethan stage has not received the attention it should.

The act divisions are retained in the schedule not as significant, but for ease of reference. Brief phrases are given as reminders of the contents of each scene.

ACT I

Sc. 1. The platform; ghost appears: FULL STAGE.

The Ghost enters, perhaps by the trapdoor of the curtained space. Darkness is suggested by Bernardo's and Francisco's challenges, by allusions to the striking clock, "yond same star," and in the first eighty lines by ten mentions of "night."

Sc. 2. A court or council scene; embassy sent to Norway; FRONT STAGE; throne used.

Sc. 3. Laertes, Ophelia, Polonius; FRONT STAGE.

Sc. 4. The platform; second appearance of the Ghost; FULL STAGE. In contrast to *scene 1,* there are only two references to "night" in all the scene. The Ghost leads Hamlet off right, his friends following a few lines later.

Sc. 5. Then, illustrating the convention that exit by one door and immediate or almost immediate entrance at another means change to an adjacent location, the Ghost leads Hamlet in, perhaps at the left door. The Ghost goes out, perhaps through the trapdoor, and later speaks from under the stage. FULL STAGE.

ACT II

Sc. 1. Polonius, Reynaldo, Ophelia; FRONT STAGE.

Sc. 2. "Here in the lobby"; return of embassy from Norway; throne used; FULL STAGE, perhaps with wall-hangings.

ACT III

Sc. 1. Ophelia at her orisons; the King and Polonius from behind the arras, spying on Hamlet and Ophelia; FRONT STAGE.

Sc. 2. The play within the play; bank of flowers in the curtained space; throne used; FULL STAGE with wall-hangings. Torches as indications of a night scene.

Sc. 3. The curtains may have been closed during the last 109 lines of scene 2 and the first 35 lines of this one to allow the removal of the bank of flowers. Then FULL STAGE with wall-hangings, and the King at prayer, lines 72-96, in the curtained space, while Hamlet observes him from the front stage.

Sc. 4. Hamlet with the Queen. The Queen sits; Polonius killed behind the arras; Ghost appears, then goes out, according to a direction, "at the portall," thus not by the trapdoor; FRONT STAGE.

Suggestions for Assignments

MANY of the topics listed below need narrowing, and students should be encouraged to find more specific questions within the general area suggested. Several of the bibliographical problems should yield questions for papers; conversely, most of the other topics may be used for purely bibliographic investigations.

BIBLIOGRAPHY PROBLEMS

1. Recent scholarship on the Elizabethan stage.
2. The staging of the play scene. Or the fencing scene.
3. Recent scholarship on the text, date, or sources of *Hamlet*.
4. Problems in the First Quarto of *Hamlet*.
5. An actor's interpretation of the role of Hamlet.
6. Psychological criticism of *Hamlet*. Or Marxist criticism. Or other criticism.
7. Essex and *Hamlet*.
8. The Elizabethan audience.
9. Imagery, diction, or versification in *Hamlet*.
10. Using the *Year's Work in English Studies,* compile a list of books on *Hamlet* appearing in the last ten years which you believe ought to be acquired for your college library.

PROBLEMS FOR SHORT PAPERS

Research for these papers is intended to require only this book and the text of the play.

1. How would you produce the ghost scenes on the Elizabethan stage?
2. Purely on internal evidence, what could account for the peculiarities of the First Quarto "To be or not to be" speech?
3. What evidence in the text opposes a critic's interpretation of a scene in *Hamlet?*

4. Pick a paragraph from a critic and show to what degree he succeeds in keeping his discussion of the play clear from his discussion of the author.

5. What costuming would be appropriate for Ophelia?

6. What are Claudius's admirable qualities?

7. Trace one or two recurrent images or motifs in the play and relate them to the play's theme.

8. What is Hamlet's age?

9. Compare the play with the source in respect to the relations between Gertrude and Claudius.

10. Compare a scene or character in the play to its counterpart in the source.

11. Compare Goethe and Coleridge in their main interpretations of Hamlet's character.

12. What might Hazlitt have thought of Sir Henry Irving's performance?

13. What should the audience feel about Hamlet's former relations with Rosencranz and Guildenstern?

14. How important is Fortinbras to the play?

15. What does Bradley mean by "melancholy"? or Fergusson by "ritual"? or Eliot by "objective correlative"?

16. What is the time sequence in *Hamlet?*

17. What are the problems of staging the closet scene (III, iii)?

18. What can be inferred from Shaw's review of the Forbes-Robertson production about Irving's production?

19. What properties are desirable for a production of *Hamlet?*

20. Find a passage in one of the critical essays where you think the critic overstates his position. Restate the position in a way you think is more defensible.

PROBLEMS FOR LONGER PAPERS

Research for these papers is intended to require only this book and the text of the play.

1. Compare the closet scene (III, iii) to its counterpart in the source. How much did the source contribute to Hamlet's speeches? And what did Shakespeare add to it?

2. Edit the "To be, or not to be" soliloquy with notes justifying your method and decisions.

3. What problems of costuming and setting would be encountered by

a producer who adopts the interpretation of the play offered by one of the critics in this book—say Jones, Knight, Stoll, or Bradley.

4. Design a single-setting production of *Hamlet,* planning it scene by scene.

5. How the ghost (or any other secondary character) should be acted.

6. Resolve two contradictory or incompatible interpretations of *Hamlet* by appeal to the text of the play.

7. What should a drama critic, reviewing a production of *Hamlet,* look for?

8. Which of the critics represented in this volume most closely approximates Irving's interpretation of the role of Hamlet?

9. Examine the critics who speculate on Hamlet's life before the opening of the play. To what extent is this kind of speculation legitimate? Or to what extent are objections to it legitimate?

10. What dramatic advantages were gained by adapting the story to a Christian background?

PAPERS REQUIRING THE USE OF THE LIBRARY

1. What are the grounds for believing that *Hamlet,* as we know it, is a revision of an old play?

2. Does *Hamlet* reveal any relation to the political events in the closing years of Elizabeth's reign?

3. *Hamlet* and Elizabethan psychological theory.

4. The Folio text of *Hamlet.*

5. *Hamlet* and sixteenth-century philosophy.

6. *Hamlet* and the Senecan tradition.

7. Hamlet's bawdry.

8. Trace an important word, or a group of words, through Shakespeare's uses and those of his contemporaries. (The *Concordance* and the *Oxford English Dictionary* are minimum equipment for this project.)

9. Characterizing imagery in *Hamlet.*

10. The dramatic importance of the political motives in *Hamlet.*

11. The text of the Folio *Hamlet.*

12. "New readings" by famous actors in the role of Hamlet.

13. What features of *Hamlet* would have been regarded by an Elizabethan audience as perfectly conventional?

14. Take any great actor of *Hamlet* and show what his contribution was to the interpretation of the role.

15. What was the size and probable makeup of a typical audience at an early seventeenth-century production of *Hamlet?*

16. Explain what might have been gained and lost by the cutting of the play in a nineteenth- or twentieth-century production (for which records are available, of course).

17. Should Claudius see the dumb show? Consult John Dover Wilson's *What Happens in "Hamlet"* (Cambridge, 1935; 1937) and several subsequent discussions of the subject.

18. *Hamlet* and renaissance critical theory of tragedy.

19. Marxist interpretations of *Hamlet*.

20. When was *Hamlet* written?

DOCUMENTING YOUR RESEARCH PAPER

Footnotes and Bibliography*

THE READER of your research paper expects to find in it both your work and an accounting of the sources from which you have drawn your information. This accounting is your documentation. It is also your thanks, or at least your acknowledgment, to any people whose writings or other works have furnished you the information that you have organized into your paper.

Whether as thanks or as report of sources, your documentation must be explicit and specific. It must tell your reader where you found your information so that he can, if he wishes, appraise your sources, perhaps go to them himself and see whether you have conveyed their facts faithfully or reasoned soundly from them.

All of your sources are listed together in a bibliography at the end of your paper; this is *general* documentation. Any source you cite is named at the point where you cite it, usually in a footnote; this is *specific* documentation.

Most of your sources will be books or magazine articles, aside from the selections in this book.

DOCUMENTATION REFERRING TO A BOOK

A bibliography entry for a book will be organized thus:

May, Rollo. *Man's Search for Himself*. New York, 1953.

Period	Period	Comma Period
Name of the author, surname first for alphabetizing.	Title of book, in italic type or underscored to indicate that it is a publication.	City and year of publication. The name of the publisher may appear between the city and the date.

First line begins at margin; if there is a second line, indent it 5 spaces.

---

* Prepared for the series by the general editor of Howard Chandler, Publisher.

The footnote for a citation from this book would be organized thus:

¹ Rollo May, *Man's Search for Himself* (New York, 1953), pp. 223-224.

				Paren-thesis
		Paren-		thesis
	Comma	thesis	Comma	Comma
Index (number or asterisk).	Name of author, in normal order, as footnotes are not alphabetized.	Title of book, in italic type or underscored to indicate that it is a publication.	City and year of publication.	

Period

Numbers of pages that contain the
information documented. Some people prefer to omit the abbreviation "pp."
First line of footnote indented as paragraph; second line at margin.

The order of the items in this information, the use of the index mark (raised number or asterisk), the punctuation, the parentheses, and the use of italic or underscores are customs that spare a writer the labor of writing many words and his reader some quantity of reading. The footnote would otherwise have to be something like:

This information comes from pages 223-224 of a book by Rollo May, entitled *Man's Search for Himself,* published in New York in 1953.

If you name the publisher of a book, the forms for bibliography and footnote are:

May, Rollo. *Man's Search for Himself.* New York, W. W. Norton & Company, 1953.

¹ Rollo May, *Man's Search for Himself* (New York: W. W. Norton & Company, 1953), pp. 223-224.

DOCUMENTATION REFERRING TO A PLAY

Any citation of a play almost necessarily refers to it as published in a book. Accordingly you cite a play as you would a book. To specify the location of a passage, the page number may be sufficient. But it may be more useful to give act, scene, and if possible line numbers. Hence:

Shakespeare, William. *The Tragedy of Coriolanus,* ed. William Allan Neilson. New York, 1906.

¹ William Shakespeare. *The Tragedy of Coriolanus,* ed. William Allan Neilson (New York, 1906), Act IV, Sc. vii, lines 2-3.

DOCUMENTATION REFERRING TO A
MAGAZINE ARTICLE

If your source is a magazine article, your bibliography entry might read:

Kirstein, Lincoln. "The Future of American Opera," *Atlantic* 199:3 (March, 1957), pp. 50-55.

Comma	Period		Comma	
Name of author, surname first.	Title of article, in quotation marks to indicate that it is not a separate publication.		Name of magazine, in italic type or underscored to indicate that it is a publication.	Volume and number.

	Comma	Period
Issue, in parentheses.		Page numbers of the entire article.

First line begins at margin; second and subsequent lines indented 5 spaces.

Your footnote to this magazine article as your source might read:

¹ Lincoln Kirstein, "The Future of American Opera," *Atlantic* 199:3 (March, 1957), p. 54.

	Comma	Comma	Comma	
Index (number or asterisk).	Name of author, in normal order.	Title of article in quotation marks.	Name of magazine, italic or underscored.	Volume and number.

	Comma Period
Issue, in parentheses.	Page number to which the footnote refers.

First line of footnote indented as paragraph; second line at margin.

As is documentation from books, documentation from magazines is made briefer and less laborious by the customs of word order and punctuation.

DOCUMENTATION REFERRING TO A
NEWSPAPER ARTICLE

Citations from newspapers cannot be so precise as citations from books or magazines, since many newspapers have several editions in a day and the same article may appear on different pages in different editions; even more troublesome, it may be rewritten, reheaded, or dropped in later editions, and it may not appear in the early editions of a given date.

A bibliography entry concerning a newspaper might therefore appear thus:

"State to Up Vet Home Loan Rate," *San Francisco Chronicle,* Sept. 17, 1959. Dated Sacramento, Sept. 16.

The corresponding footnote might be:

[1] "State to Up Vet Home Loan Rate," *San Francisco Chronicle,* Sept. 17, 1959; dated Sacramento, Sept. 16.

If the writer of this newspaper article were named, his name would precede the title of the article in both the bibliography entry and the footnote. If the story were sent to the *Chronicle* by a news service, such as United Press International or Associated Press, this fact should appear in parentheses at the end of both bibliography and footnote, in full or abbreviated:

. . . Sept. 16 (United Press International).
. . . Sept. 16 (UPI).

THE ESSENTIAL IN DOCUMENTATION

Information comes to the writer from so many sources that specimen bibliography entries and footnotes for all possible needs would overflow any book. So it is necessary to keep in mind the basic reason for documenting: namely, to give the source of a statement so it can be appraised, and located, by the reader. These are basic, though some other details may be put into the documentation.

If your bibliography entries and footnotes answer the following questions, they will be satisfactory:

1. *Who?* Who is the author who made the statement? What individual, collaborating group, or institution is the author? Or is the statement published in a work that does not identify the author?
2. *In what publication?* What book, magazine article, newspaper story, speech, broadcast program, or other? At exactly what point in this work? (Can a reader find your citation, from what the documentation tells him?)
3. *When and whence?* In what city and in what year was the book published? On what date was the periodical published?

The next sections contain numerous models for footnotes and bibliography entries, but all are guided by these three principles. Since almost every research project will require documentation referring to some source not covered by a model, you need to perceive the principles as they are demonstrated in the models.

EXAMPLES OF BIBLIOGRAPHY ENTRIES

The entries in a bibliography are ordinarily arranged in alphabetical order, as these examples are. To help in comparing them with corresponding footnotes, the footnote examples (pages 253-256) are numbered in series and the explanatory remark that follows each bibliography entry gives the number of the footnote.

Baker, Charles T. "Patients' Perceptions of Psychologists." Unpublished master's thesis, Ohio State University, 1953. [An unpublished doctor's dissertation or other research paper would be treated in this same way. See footnote 18.]

Boddy, Francis M., *et al. Applied Economic Analysis*. New York, 1948. [This book has six authors. If only one author card is carried in a library catalogue for it, the card will be in the name of the senior author, here given. See footnote 3 and pages 262-263 of this book.]

Bowman, Isaiah. *The New World*. 4th ed., Yonkers and Chicago, 1928. [An often revised book in political geography; marked differences between editions make it important to specify the edition used, as here. See footnote 6.]

Brahms, Johannes. *Concerto No. 2 in B Flat Major for Piano*. Alexander Uninsky, piano; Willem van Oterloo conducting The Hague Philharmonic Orchestra. Epic LC-3303, 1958. [For some purposes it might be unnecessary to identify the musicians presented on a phonograph record, but the information usually is significant. The record number and the "publisher" appear on the record label. See footnote 23.]

Doe, John. "Indexing of Dissertations." Paper read at methodology seminar, —— University, October 19, 1962. In —— University Library. [If this paper were not in a library and you were citing from your notes, you would write instead, "Notes of reading," or something of the sort. See footnote 19.]

Dumas, Alexandre, fils. Letter to Joseph Méry, Oct. 18, 1844. Unpublished. Collection of Simone André-Maurois. [Letters of famous men often are microfilmed for study, even if not published. If you use a microfilm letter, mention it; as, "Microfilm in —— Library." See footnote 20.]

"The Good ex-President." *Time*, 74:14 (Oct. 5, 1959), p. 34. [A magazine article published without the author's name. It is therefore alphabetized according to its title, ignoring "The." See footnote 14.]

Gunther, John. "Inside Space." *John Gunther's High Road,* American Broadcasting Company (WABC-TV), Oct. 17, 1959. [A broadcast program in a series. The same form could be used for either radio or television. The station call letters and date might be enough in addition to the program name and the name of its "author." If no author, alphabetize on the program name. See footnote 26.]

Joyce, James. *Finnegan's Wake.* Folkways Records, FDF934, 1956. Tape. [It might be unnecessary to write "Tape," but may be useful. See footnote 25.]

Keats, John. *The Complete Poetical Works and Letters of John Keats,* [ed. Horace E. Scudder]. Cambridge, Mass., 1899. [Scudder's name does not appear in this book, but he is known to be the editor, hence the information is supplied but enclosed in brackets; if the fact appeared on the title page no brackets would be needed. Note that "Mass." is specified to avoid giving the impression that the book was published in Cambridge, England. See footnote 5.]

Kelly, Alfred H., and Winfred A. Harbison. *The American Constitution.* New York, 1948. [A book by two authors; observe that the second author's name is in normal order. Incidentally, this is the first edition of a book that was later published in a second edition; unless another edition is specified, the edition of a book is assumed to be the first. See footnote 2. See also the entry for Isaiah Bowman's book above.]

Kelly, George A. *The Psychology of Personal Constructs.* 2 vols. New York, 1955. [If your references were to only one of these volumes, you would write "2 vols., vol 1. New York, 1955." See footnote 7.]

Kirstein, Lincoln. "The Future of American Opera." *Atlantic* 199:3 (March, 1957), pp. 50-55. [Discussed earlier in detail. See footnote 13 and page 249 in this book.]

"Kite." *Encyclopedia Americana,* 1955 ed. [Encyclopedia article by an unnamed author. The names of editors and the like for a well-known reference book are not ordinarily needed. Neither is the page number in a book whose contents are alphabetically arranged. See footnote 12.]

Learned, Philip. Lecture given in English 346, Edwardian Criticism, —— University, May 17, 1962. Tape recording. [If there were no tape recording, an equivalent statement should appear: "Notes taken by John Doe, student," or the like. Observe that the course title is not italicized or enclosed in quotation marks. See footnote 21.]

Macaulay, Thomas Babington. "Bunyan, John." *Encyclopaedia Britannica,* 11th ed. [Macaulay signed this article simply "M"; the full name was gotten from the list at the end of the last volume. Observe the order of Bunyan's names; he is listed under Bunyan, not John. Observe that there are no page numbers or volume number, since neither is needed for locating an article in an alphabetically organized reference book. See also "Kite," above in this list. See footnote 11.]

May, Rollo. *Man's Search for Himself.* New York, 1953. [Discussed earlier in detail. See footnote 1 and page 247 of this book.]

Ohneschatten, Dermann, Director, —— State Hospital. Interview, May

27, 1964. Tape recorded. [The subject of the interview could be mentioned, if important. See footnote 22.]

Poore, Charles. Review of Henry B. Kranz, ed., *Abraham Lincoln: A New Portrait. New York Times,* Oct. 17, 1959. [See footnote 16, footnote 17, and "Review . . ." below.]

Quintanilla, Luis. "Basic Tenets of Latin American International Policy." In Philip W. Buck and Martin B. Travis, Jr., eds., *Control of Foreign Relations in Modern Nations.* New York, 1957. [See footnote 8.]

Review, unsigned, of Henry B. Kranz, ed., *Abraham Lincoln: A New Portrait. Reviews of the Quarter,* vol. 21, no. 4 (Nov., 1969), p. 37. [To alphabetize the entry for this review at K for Kranz would suggest that Kranz wrote the review or that the entry was for the book rather than for the review. There is much variety of opinion about how to handle this kind of entry. If your reader-instructor has a strong opinion, follow his preference. See footnote 17.]

Shakespeare, William. *The Tragedy of Coriolanus,* ed. William Allan Neilson. New York, 1906. [See page 248 of this book, and see footnote 9.]

"State to Up Vet Home Loan Rate." *San Francisco Chronicle,* Sept. 17, 1959. Dated Sacramento, Sept. 18. [Discussed on page 250 of this book. See footnote 15.]

Swedish Modern Jazz. Arne Domnerus and his group. RCA Camden, CAL-417, 1958. Record. ["Record" is unnecessary unless needed to distinguish the described item from a tape recording or other work of similar name. The record is a collection of works performed by one orchestra. If the name of one work or its composer were the important item, this information would be given first, followed by "In *Swedish Modern Jazz.* . . ." See footnote 24.]

Sypher, Wiley, ed. *Enlightened England.* New York, 1947. [An anthology. Any book identified by the name of its editor rather than an author would be presented similarly. See footnote 4.]

Two Thousand Years of Season's Greetings. New York: Photogravure and Color Company, 1951. [This is the kind of irregular publication sometimes called a "bulletin." Since it may be hard to locate, you help the reader by giving the name of the publisher. Since no author name is given, alphabetize it by the title. See footnote 10.]

We Discover the Dictionary. Coronet Films, 16V4906, 1949. Film. [The author's name, if one were given, would precede the title in this entry, and would govern the alphabetical position of the entry. "Film" may be unnecessary. See footnote 27.]

EXAMPLES OF FOOTNOTES

These specimen footnotes are numbered to help in referring to them for comparison with the corresponding specimen bibliography entries in the section preceding this.

[1] Rollo May, *Man's Search for Himself* (New York, 1953), pp. 223-224. [Book, single author. Discussed on page 248 of this book.]

[2] Alfred H. Kelly and Winfred A. Harbison, *The American Constitution* (New York, 1948), p. 64. [Book, two authors.]

[3] Francis H. Boddy *et al., Applied Economic Analysis* (New York, 1948), p. 346. [Book with many authors, in this instance six. Unless courtesy or other special reason calls for them, the names of the junior authors are replaced by *et al.* See pages 262-263 of this book.]

[4] Wiley Sypher, ed., *Enlightened England* (New York, 1947), p. 451. [Book, single editor. This is an anthology, containing works of numerous writers, who need not be named in this kind of entry. To cite the work of one author included in such a collection, follow the model of footnote 8 below.]

[5] John Keats, *The Complete Poetical Works and Letters of John Keats,* [ed. Horace E. Scudder] (Cambridge, Mass., 1899), p. 232. [Book by a single author in a version edited by another person. Observe the brackets enclosing the editor's name; these are present because Scudder is not named on the title page of the book but is known to be the editor; if the title page bore his name there would be no brackets; compare footnote 9, below. Note the "Mass." to prevent confusion with Cambridge, England, another publishing center.]

[6] Isaiah Bowman, *The New World,* 4th ed. (Yonkers and Chicago, 1928), p. 704. [Book, edition specified. Unless an edition is specified, it is assumed that the first edition is being cited.]

[7] George A. Kelly, *The Psychology of Personal Constructs* (New York, 1955), vol. 1, p. 133. [Book, more than one volume. The citation here is to a page in one volume, and the number of volumes need not be stated; that information is in the bibliography entry. If your paper were to have no bibliography, this kind of footnote should read: ". . . 1955), 2 vols., vol. 1, p. 133."]

[8] Luis Quintanilla, "Basic Tenets of Latin American International Policy," in Philip W. Buck and Martin B. Travis, Jr., eds., *Control of Foreign Relations in Modern Nations* (New York, 1957), p. 188. [Work of one author in an edited collection of works by several authors.]

[9] William Shakespeare, *The Tragedy of Coriolanus,* ed. William Allan Neilson (New York, 1906), Act IV, Sc. vii, lines 2-3. [Play, in book form. Unless the printed version has line numbers, a page number would be given rather than the line numbers. Discussed in the text of this book, page 248.]

[10] *Two Thousand Years of Season's Greetings* (New York: Photogravure and Color Company), p. 5. [Irregular publication, that is, something not published in the usual course of any publishing enterprise—the named publisher is an engraver-printer and this cited work is an advertising piece. The name of the publisher is therefore given even in a footnote plan which does not include names of publishers of standard books. If it had a named author, his name would be at the beginning, as usual.]

[11] Thomas Babington Macaulay in *Encylopaedia Britannica,* 11th ed., *s.v.* "Bunyan, John." [Signed article in a reference book alphabetically

organized. The abbreviation *"s.v."* means *"sub verbo"* or *"sub voce,"* English "under the word" or "under the heading." The word "Bunyan" is as accurate a guide as a page number could be, and may be better since encyclopedias are sometimes repaged to make room for new entries inserted late in the life of a numbered edition. Macaulay's article on Bunyan fills two pages; if it were a very long article, and the citation to a single sentence or other brief passage, the reader might be helped by being given a volume and page number: ". . . 'Bunyan, John,' vol. 4, p. 805." Observe the spelling *Encyclopaedia.*]

[12] "Kite," *Encyclopedia Americana,* 1955 ed. [Unsigned article in a reference book alphabetically organized. See footnote 11 concerning the omission of page number. Observe the spelling *Encyclopedia* in the title of this work.]

[13] Lincoln Kirstein, "The Future of American Opera," *Atlantic* 199:3 (March, 1957), p. 54. [Magazine article. Discussed at length in this book, page 249.]

[14] "The Good ex-President," *Time* 74:14 (Oct. 5, 1959), p. 34. [Magazine article, unsigned.]

[15] "State to Up Vet Home Loan Rate," *San Francisco Chronicle,* Sept. 17, 1959; dated Sacramento, Sept. 16. [News article in a newspaper. Discussed in this book, page 250.]

[16] Charles Poore, review of Henry B. Kranz, ed., *Abraham Lincoln: A New Portrait, New York Times,* Oct. 17, 1959. [Signed book review. Such reviews often have titles, either individual or departmental; it is usually unnecessary and confusing to give such titles.]

[17] Unsigned review of Henry B. Kranz, ed., *Abraham Lincoln: A New Portrait, Reviews of the Quarter* 21:4 (Nov. 1959), p. 37. [Unsigned review of a book, in a periodical—here an imaginary periodical. The bibliography entry corresponding to this footnote is alphabetized at Review.]

[18] Charles T. Baker, "Patients' Perceptions of Psychologists" (unpublished master's thesis, Ohio State University, 1953), p. 31. [Unpublished work, such as thesis or dissertation.]

[19] John Doe, "Indexing of Dissertations" (paper read at methodology seminar, —— University, October 16, 1962; in —— University Library). [Paper read but not published. See the specimen bibliography entry at Doe.]

[20] Alexandre Dumas fils, letter to Joseph Méry, Oct. 18, 1844, unpublished, in the collection of Simone André-Maurois. [Unpublished letter.]

[21] Philip Learned, lecture given in English 346, Edwardian Criticism, —— University, May 17, 1962, from a tape recording. [Unpublished lecture. If the lecture were cited from memory, or from the writer's notes, or from notes of another listener, that fact should be given instead of the reference to a tape recording.]

[22] Dermann Ohneschatten, Director, —— State Hospital, interview, May 27, 1964, from a tape recording. [Unpublished interview. No interviewer being named, the assumption is that the interview was with the writer. If the citation were not from a recording, that fact should be given instead.]

²³ Johannes Brahms, *Concerto No. 2 in B Flat Major for Piano,*
Alexander Uninsky, piano; Willem Oterloo conducting The Hague Philharmonic Orchestra (Epic LC-3303, 1958), record. [Phonograph record.
The word "record" may be unnecessary, or may distinguish between a
disk and a tape recording of the same work and performance.]

²⁴ *Swedish Modern Jazz,* Arne Domnerus and his group (RCA Camden CAL-417, 1958), record. [Phonograph record, title without composer's name. This record has several works by various composers and
is thus comparable to a book of the type cited in footnote 8 above.]

²⁵ James Joyce, *Finnegan's Wake* (Folkways Records, FDF 934,
1956), tape recording. [Recorded book. To locate a cited passage more
exactly, one might add "at 22 min." or the like. The tape does not contain
the entire book. When a recorded work has several tapes, the one concerned may be specified, as "tape 3 at 17 min."]

²⁶ John Gunther, "Inside Space," *John Gunther's High Road,* American Broadcasting Company (WABC-TV, New York), October 17, 1959.
[Television or radio broadcast; this footnote is for a television program.
The network being named, the station call letters and city are extra information; but the latter would suffice if there were no network or the network
were not known.]

²⁷ *We Discover the Dictionary* (Coronet Films, 16V4906, 1949), film.
[Film. If the text at the citation does not make it clear that a film is meant,
the word "film" is needed in the footnote, since many companies that
distribute films also distribute sound tapes, disk records, and books having
the same titles. Films usually are the work of writing-producing teams
and are published without any "author" name; if an author is named, his
name belongs first in the footnote.]

HOW TO FIND DOCUMENTATION DATA

Where do you get information for documentation?

Most books published in the United States and many published in
other countries carry this information in the preliminary pages of the
book itself. The title page normally has the name of the author (or
authors), the title of the book, the name of the editor instead of or in
addition to the name of the author, the name of the publisher, the volume
number and number of volumes if the book has more than one, the edition
number if later than the first, the city of publication, and sometimes the
date. But the date may appear only in the copyright notice on the back
of the title page, and there may be several copyright dates owing to re-
newals and revisions (if there are, use the latest). If the title-page date
is other than the copyright date, give both dates (as "New York, 1938;
title page dated 1949"). You and your reader, seeing this discrepancy,
may reasonably wonder whether the title-page date is an effort to suggest
that the book is more recent than it really is.

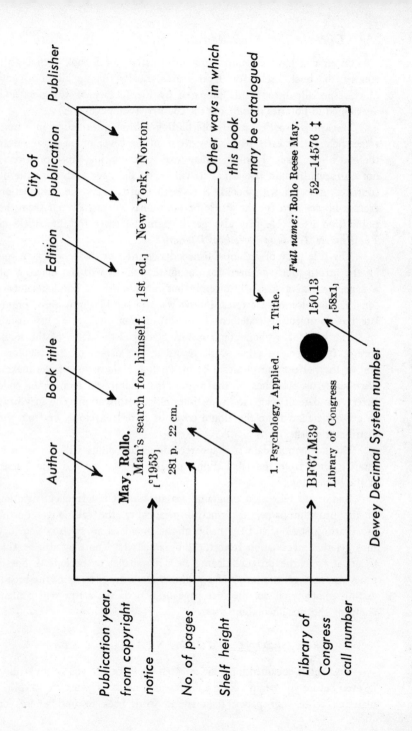

Publication year, from copyright notice

No. of pages

Shelf height

Library of Congress call number

Author

Book title

Edition

City of publication

Publisher

Other ways in which this book may be catalogued

Dewey Decimal System number

May, Rollo.
Man's search for himself. [1st ed.] New York, Norton
[ᶜ1953]
281 p. 22 cm.

1. Psychology, Applied.   ɪ. Title.

Full name: Rollo Reese May.

BF67.M39   150.13
                                          [58x1]
      Library of Congress   52—14576 ‡

Often you have documentation information on a book even before you see the book itself, for library cards usually contain all of it, and more, especially those cards prepared by the Library of Congress and distributed to libraries throughout the country. (See page 257.)

Magazines usually provide the bibliographical information in a note somewhere in the early pages, less often on the cover or on a page near the end of the issue. Finding it may take some hunting, since practice is not uniform. In most magazines it will be on the page with the table of contents. Also, as with books, a researcher often gets the information from a library card for the article before he has to search it out from the publication itself. He may also get it from the entry for the article in *The Readers' Guide to Periodical Literature.*

The title page of an unpublished dissertation or thesis will give you all the information you need for documentation, as will the file copy of a paper read at a scholarly meeting but not published. For letters, personal communications, lectures, interviews, and the like, you must formulate the documenting statement from information you get at first hand.

The label of a phonograph record gives you the name of the song, speech, collection, or other work recorded, the names of the composer and of the performing musician or his analogue, the name of the maker, distributor, or publisher of the record, his identifying number or code letters, the date of issue, and sometimes other information. You may have to get some facts from the album cover or record envelope, or from the distributor's list.

Documentation data for tape recordings and films will almost necessarily come from the label. Films usually carry it on the title frames at the beginning.

Radio and television programs contain almost too frequent mention of the program name, its principal personality, the call letters of the broadcasting station, and the name of the broadcasting system. You may thus get this information from the program itself. You may also be able to get it from the program listing in a newspaper or periodical. Sometimes you may get the script of a program from the sponsor or the broadcasting company; if so, the first page or two of the script will contain many of the documentation data.

RECORDING DOCUMENTATION DATA

You begin documenting your research paper before you begin writing it, even before you begin taking your research notes. If you were to collect material, write your paper, then try to work back to find where you got your material in order to document it, you would find the effort hopeless. When you decide to investigate a book or magazine article or other source, therefore, you should prepare a bibliography card immediately, recording all the documenting information you will need if you refer to the source—this before you take your first note! Then, when you write a note card, it should have a record of its source. The record need not be complete to identify it with your bibliography card—a short "slug" something like "May *Man's Search*" is enough. Thus your bibliography card would read:

> May *Man's Search*   M 150.13
>
> May, Rollo. *Man's Search for Himself*. New York, 1953.

Then a note card might look like this:

> May *Man's Search*   224
>
> "... Courage is the capacity to meet the anxiety which arises as one achieves freedom. ..."

With the note card and the bibliography card, you are prepared to put accurate documentation into your finished research paper.

CITATIONS AFTER THE FIRST—BOOKS

When a writer must cite numerous statements from the same source at intervals throughout his paper, repeating long footnotes would become tedious for him and for his reader. When the first footnote has given full information, later footnotes may be shortened in many ways, providing the shortening does not make them confusing.

A second citation from the May book might come immediately after the first one, with no other footnote intervening. For such immediately succeeding footnotes, scholars have long used this style of shortening:

² *Ibid.*, p. 231.

This means "From page 231 of the same source given in the immediately preceding footnote." The abbreviation *Ibid.* for *ibidem* (literally, "in the same") is typical of the many abbreviations and Latin expressions that we have inherited and continued to use since early scholars established them. Because they are in some sense part of an omnilingual scholarly vocabulary, many instructors require their students to learn them and use them. But some people think of them as Latin and, if they or their readers do not know Latin, feel that the use of Latin expressions is pretentious or even dishonest. Such people would prefer to use some equivalent English-language form like

² May, p. 231.

—or even, if May's name is mentioned in the text, nothing more than

² P. 231.

The writer of a research paper does well to learn what preference his instructor has in matters of this sort, and to follow it.

If some citation from other source material were to intervene between the first and second citations from the May work, then the *ibid.* would be wrong, for "in the same" would point to the most recently cited work. The old scholarly usage would be

³ May, *op. cit.*, p. 231.

This means, "From page 231 of the work by May which has already been cited." "*Opere citato*" is the unabbreviated Latin. Those who misgive Latin expressions might prefer to write any of four other forms:

³ May, p. 231.
³ May, *Man's Search*, p. 231.
³ *Man's Search*, p. 231.
³ P. 231.

The first-given form would serve if only one of May's books were being used as a source. If two or more were being used, it would be necessary to mention the title and to mention the author's name also, as in the second-given form, unless May's name were mentioned in the text. If the text mentioned May, but not the book title, the third-given form would be sufficient documentation. The last-given and briefest form would be correct and sufficient if the text language made clear what book and author were being considered.

When these English shortened forms are to be used, it is a frequent and helpful practice to tell the reader so in the first full footnote. Thus, after citing the source in full, you would add, perhaps: "This will here(in)-after be cited as May," or ". . . as May, *Man's Search*."

CITATIONS AFTER THE FIRST—
MAGAZINE ARTICLES

The short expression *op. cit.* is not used when the source cited is a magazine article or other work not independent and complete in itself, such as an article in a symposium, an encyclopedia entry, or a newspaper story. For such sources, instead of *op. cit.* the footnote Latin is *loc. cit.* for *locus citatus,* Englished as "the place cited" or "the passage cited." Thus several alternative entries for the later footnote to a magazine article:

[3] Kirstein, *loc. cit.*
[3] Kirstein, p. 55.
[3] Kirstein, "Future," p. 55.
[3] "Future," p. 55.
[3] P. 55.

These five forms of short documentation correspond in function to the similar five forms for books. But note that *loc. cit.* cannot be followed by a page number; such is the convention. The other forms may therefore be preferable as more specific.

CITING WORKS BY NUMEROUS AUTHORS

A Latin expression that often appears in documentation is the abbreviation combination *et al.* for *et alii,* which means "and others." Writers who are not alert in their Latin often punctuate this expression improperly; those who choose to use it need to remember that *et* is a word and that *al.* is an abbreviation.

The proper use of this expression is to save writing or repeating the names of two or more co-authors of a cited source. Thus a first and later footnote might be:

[1] Francis M. Boddy, Frank E. Childs, Wendell R. Smith, O. H. Brownlee, Alvin E. Coons, and Virgil Salera, *Applied Economic Analysis,* New York, 1948, p. 363.

[3] Boddy *et al., op. cit.,* p. 370.

Instead of *et al.,* those who object to Latin would use "and others":

[3] Boddy and others, p. 370.

If the names of the junior authors are not important for the citation, even the first footnote may have them packaged into *et al.* or "and others":

[1] Francis M. Boddy *et al., Applied Economic Analysis,* New York, 1948.

It is not courteous to use *et al.* in substitution for the name of a single author.

DOCUMENTATION WITHOUT FOOTNOTES

In some people's view the footnote is the most useful and explicit form of specific documenation, the least likely to be misconstrued, and the minimum civil acknowledgment that a writer can make to his source. With all these merits, footnotes are disliked by other people as obtrusive, overformal, distracting, and an extreme nuisance for the typist. Their preference is to put some or all of the specific documentation into the text itself.

In-text documentation for books, magazine articles, and other sources requires the same information that is given in footnotes. A writer citing a statement from a book might therefore write:

. . . A definition of Rollo May (*Man's Search for Himself,* New York, 1953, p. 224) describes courage as ". . . the capacity to meet the anxiety which arises as one achieves freedom." Seen as such, courage is demanded . . .

The parenthetical documentation would be worded to accord with the text language. If it were to follow the quoted passage rather than precede it:

"The capacity to meet the anxiety which arises as one achieves freedom" (Rollo May, *Man's Search for Himself,* New York, 1953, p. 224) is a definition of courage as it is demanded from all of us. . . .

A writer uses footnote or in-text documentation as he and his readers prefer. If his readers are instructors who grade his research papers, their preference may well overrule the writer's. The general documentation is needed, in the usual bibliography form, to support either style of specific documentation.

Some writers attempt to have the best features of both kinds of documentation by using a footnote for the first mention of a source, then using brief parenthetical notes for later references. This practice might give:

> . . . May found that "the greatest block to a person's development of courage is his having to take on a way of life which is not rooted in his own powers" (*Man's Search,* p. 231). . . .

Or it might give:

> . . . May (p. 231) found that . . .

Either of these two parenthetical documentations might be replaced by the more traditional *"op. cit.,* p. 231" or if proper by *"Ibid.,* p. 231."

BRIEF DOCUMENTATION

It is often unnecessary to give a complete footnote for every citation from a source, yet necessary to document the citation. It seems redundant, when a text has mentioned an author's name or his book's title, or both, to repeat them in a footnote. The footnote then need contain only those facts not given in the text; but all the documenting facts must be given in one place or the other. For examples:

> . . . Rollo May, in his *Man's Search for Himself,*[1] defines courage . . .
> [1] New York, 1953, p. 224.

> . . . Rollo May[1] defines courage as . . .
> [1] *Man's Search for Himself* (New York, 1953), p. 224.

Specific documentation can be kept brief by using the general documentation, the bibliography, after notifying the reader that footnotes or in-text references identify the names of sources given in full in the bibliography. Thus a writer might refer to Rollo May's book thus, even on first mention:

> . . . Courage is "the capacity to meet the anxiety which arises as one achieves freedom" (May, p. 224). Seen as such, . . .

The reader is then expected to understand that he will find the source given in full in the bibliography, thus:

> May, Rollo. *Man's Search for Himself.* New York, 1953.

If several books by May were in the bibliography, the brief documentation would have to be explicit enough to prevent confusion. To
this end, "May, *Man's Search*" would be used rather than "May" alone.

Sometimes the entries in the bibliography are numbered. If in such
a bibliography the May book were to be numbered 221, then the citing
note might read "221, p. 224."

DIVERSE PRACTICE IN DOCUMENTATION

Custom and agreement have not established uniform practice as to
correct documentation. Readers' needs differ; scholars in different fields
have different kinds of source material to identify and describe; and
editors, teachers, and research directors have strong preferences which they
can enforce on their contributors, students, and staff. The student writer
who goes beyond this discussion in exploring documentation can find
some additional and different recommendations in any of four books
especially:

ELINOR YAGGY, *How to Write Your Term Paper*. Howard Chandler,
Publisher, 660 Market Street, San Francisco 4, California. Contains
a thorough discussion of documentation forms, with numerous examples. Primarily for undergraduate writers.

BLANCHE ELLSWORTH, *English Simplified*. Howard Chandler, Publisher,
660 Market Street, San Francisco 4, California. An appendix on
Writing the Research Paper contains directions for preparing a bibliography and for using footnotes, with a chart of model footnotes
and corresponding bibliography entries in parallel columns. Primarily
for undergraduate writers.

KATE L. TURABIAN, *A Manual for Writers of Term Papers, Theses, and
Dissertations*. The University of Chicago Press, Chicago 37, Illinois.
Has chapters on footnotes and bibliography, with numerous examples.
Primarily for graduates and advanced undergraduate writers.

WILLIAM RILEY PARKER, compiler, *The MLA Style Sheet*. The Modern
Language Association of America, 6 Washington Square North, New
York 3, New York. Primarily for writers of material to be published
in Modern Language Association periodicals. This has a supplement
dealing with the preparation of masters' theses and doctors' dissertations. Widely accepted and authoritative, especially for papers on
literary subjects.

THE DOCUMENTATION OF MATERIAL IN
THIS COLLECTION

This collection, being a book of special character compiled for the convenience of students writing research papers, differs from general books and periodicals that might be found in a library. Footnotes and bibliographical entries describing sources in this collection must identify both the source and the collection. Acceptable forms for these are given at the end of each selection. These name the original source and its author (if known), giving facts of publication, and also name this collection and its editor.

There would be some question of propriety, or even of honesty, if a writer were to name an original source in a documentary citation without making it clear that he examined the material in a collection—whether this collection or another. A reader has the right to know whether a writer is working from original or secondary sources: whether for instance he has seen George Washington's actual diary or has seen only an edited version of the diary in print. For edited versions, even carefully and scrupulously edited versions, may depart from originals.